AF496510

The
CIGAR
Lexicon

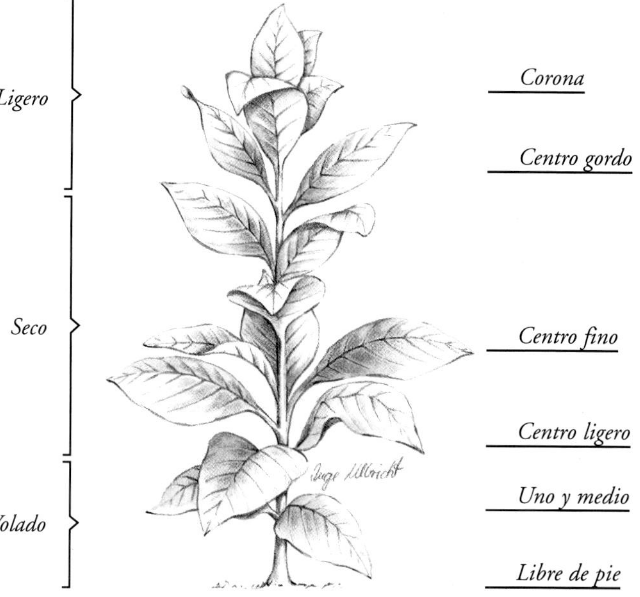

Ligero
Seco
Volado
Corona
Centro gordo
Centro fino
Centro ligero
Uno y medio
Libre de pie

The
CIGAR
Lexicon

**Terminology, Brands and Formats
Everything You Need to Know**

Dieter H. Wirtz

Picture Credits

The author's archive: 35, 125, 191, 264, 266, 272, 293, 303 b.
The author's archive, Inge Ulbricht Illustrations: 2, 53
Arnold André GmbH, Bünde: 36, 45, 47, 108, 130/131, 137, 142, 144 (2), 145 (2), 150, 176, 186, 188, 189, 204, 205, 206 l., 216, 234 t., 242, 243 (3), 244, 256, 257, 270, 273, 275, 276, 286 t.
August Schuster, Bünde: 65, 193, 202, 206 r., 281 t.
British American Tobacco (Germany) GmbH, Hamburg: 239
Chambrair GmbH, Hamburg: 8 t. r., 113, 129, 207 (2)
Dannemann Cigarrenfabrik GmbH, Berlin: 25, 26, 28, 34, 179, 180, 181, 182, 183, 220, 223, 320
Darier & Cleef GmbH, Marbach: 196, 197 (2)
dpa, Frankfurt/Main: 68, 76, 132, 133, 134, 135, 139, 141, 146, 147, 148 (2), 149, 152, 159, 161, 169, 233, 280, 293 t.
Golden Mile GmbH, Berlin: 200 r., 201 (2)
Habanos S.A., Havanna: 8 t. l., 8/9, 9 t., 11, 12, 13, 14, 15, 16 (2), 17, 19 t., 20, 21, 22, 23 (4), 24, 27, 29, 30, 32, 37, 38, 39, 40, 49, 51, 52, 53 t. (2), 54, 55 (3), 56, 57, 58 (2), 66, 67, 70/71, 72 (2), 73, 75, 77, 78, 79, 80, 86, 88, 90, 91, 94, 97, 98 (2), 99, 100 (2), 101 (3), 102, 105, 111, 112, 115, 116, 117, 119, 121, 122, 130 t. (2), 164, 165, 166, 184 l. t., 199, 200 l., 211, 212 (2), 213, 214 (2), 215 (2), 245 (2), 247 l. b., 247 r., 249 r. t., 249 r. b., 251 (2), 253 (2), 259, 260, 261, 263, 265 (2), 268 (2), 274 (3), 281 b., 282, 286 b., 287, 289, 294 (2), 296 b., 297 (2), 298 b., 299 (2), 303 t., 304 l. (2), 310, 311, 312 b., 313 (2)
Kohlhase, Kopp & Ct., Rellingen: 61, 93, 124, 126, 128, 153, 155, 156, 157, 158, 160, 162, 191 l., 195 (3), 217, 235 b., 246, 247 l. t., 248, 249 l. t., 250, 269, 288 (2), 302, 304 r., 307, 312 t., 315
Oettinger Davidoff Group, Basel: 10, 18, 19 b., 31 (3), 33, 42, 46, 83, 95, 107, 109, 131 t., 163, 170, 171, 172 (3), 174, 178, 184/185, 225, 227, 228, 229, 230, 231, 309, 318
P.G.C. Hajenius, Amsterdam: 62, 64, 136, 185, 254, 255
TLC Fotostudio: 50, 184 r. t., 198/199, 190, 192 (2), 208, 234 b., 235 t., 236, 252, 278, 284, 285, 291, 292, 296 t., 298 t., 300, 305, 306, 316

Author and publisher wish to thank all picture sources for their generous and friendly support, especially, however, the cigar manufacturer De Olifant from Kampen in the Netherlands.

© Naumann & Göbel Verlagsgesellschaft mbH, a subsidiary of
VEMAG Medien- und Aktiengesellschaft, Cologne

Tables from: Cigar Calendarium 2005. Printed by kind permission of
Elke Wirtz Verlag, Mönchengladbach

Complete production: Naumann & Göbel Verlagsgesellschaft mbH, Cologne

Printed in Germany
All rights reserved
ISBN 3-625-11252-3

www.cigarcalendarium.de
info@cigarcalendarium.de
www.apollo-intermedia.de

Introduction

Much has happened in the world of cigars over the last few years. The range of brands and series available has become so great that even the specialist retailer who tries to advise his business clientele can almost lose sight of it. A new cigar series is created almost daily, and – almost daily – an existing brand or certain format is withdrawn from the market, either taken out of a range or no longer produced. The reason for this may not be poor quality or lack of demand, but may lie in an insufficient amount of certain tobaccos being available.

This is a market subject to constant fluctuation and it can change dramatically from one day to the next. By contrast with a magazine, this kind of book has to accommodate this situation. Thus one is almost forced to limit the scope for practical – even essential – reasons. Therefore only very few cigars from the lower price sector are listed, and only one cigar that is not made 100 percent from tobacco.

As this is merely a lexicon rather than an encyclopaedia, it appeared sensible to concentrate mainly on the cigar brands of the higher price sector in addition to those that are designated premium cigars, as it is precisely these cigars that confer a certain distinction; and of course there are the ones that have become the stuff of legends as a result of their utterly fascinating qualities.

All Havana brands are presented, of course – even those only obtainable with difficulty. This would be requisite through pure respect for that Motherland of the Cigar – Cuba – were it not also essential for to the narrative of the history and origins of tobacco and the cigar.

All in all, the history of the cigar plays an important role in this book, for the cigar is an object of historic and cultural significance. As a ritual object, the cigar was integral to certain events in the cult and religious life of the pre-Columbian inhabitants of America centuries before that continent's discovery by the Europeans. The ceremony of drawing (literally) on the peace pipe was an act to which the North American Indians attached great significance. In practice, the shared smoking of tobacco signified the conclusion of a deal, it was the signing of the contract. It was, according to the situation, a sincere and important ritual, in which enjoyment played a secondary role.

Today, cigars are purely a source of pleasure – and yet, anyone who has lit up a cigar at the end of a day's toil anticipates the pleasure in store, but also recognises the attention a cigar demands during smoking. A cigar is not to be simply smoked on the side, like a cigarette. That is the major difference between these two tobacco products. Whereas cigarette smoking can easily lead to addiction, the smoking of one or two cigars a day has considerably more to do with pleasure than it does with addiction. And – here the wheel turns full circle – the stylish smoking of cigars still has something of the cult ritual about it.

And now a few words about the composition of this book. The first two sections are dedicated to key thematic points, to make the introduction to the world of cigars somewhat easier and to describe the correct handling of these pleasing stimulants. The last section picks up the actual idea of a lexicon by presenting the individual brands and companies.

Let us stay for a minute with the last section. Here, roughly 400 brands and series are listed in tabular form. The tables provide information as to the origins of each brand or series, its tobacco composition, and the range of strengths each range of cigar covers. In this way, many brands not discussed in the text can also be covered, thus somewhat reducing the gaps left by our limited scope.

Finally, nothing more remains for me to do than to wish all users of this cigar lexicon an entertaining and pleasurable read and, especially, that the use of this book is of personal benefit to them in their dealings with this "Brown Gold".

Dieter H. Wirtz

Contents

All About
Cigars

Production

Cultivation, Harvest, Fermentation, Production

The process from the sowing of the seeds to the production of the finished cigar is very similar – if not identical – in almost all countries where high quality cigars are produced. To understand how it all comes together, therefore, a single country will suffice to let us track the various stages involved in this complex process. Cuba, regarded as the "motherland of the cigar", will do very well.

A Havana must travel a long journey before it finds its way into a cigar box. As a plant in the fields it has been cared for by numerous *vegueros,* and has been at the mercy of wind and weather; after harvesting it has found itself in the drying sheds, has been subjected to several fermentation processes, has been twisted, turned and, together with other leaves, formed to a cigar by the *torcedor.* During all this, it has gone through many hands before being found worthy of taking its place as a Havana in the cigar box mentioned above.

To begin with, the ground must first be prepared before the seedling can be planted in the soil. The *veguero* is aided in the job of ploughing solely by

There are Other Worlds ...

It was during the years 1298 and 1299 that a Venetian traveller and adventurer, held prisoner by the Genoese, dictated the experiences and impressions he had gained during his journeys to Central Asia and Northern China (1271–75) and during his missions on behalf of the Mongol ruler Kublai (1275–92) to a fellow prisoner. With this, Marco Polo's descriptive account awoke the interest of the Old World in Asia and eventually led to the discovery of America (and tobacco).

draught animals, to ensure that the soil levels are treated with maximum care. A tractor would be much too destructive; therefore the *veguero* harnesses one or two oxen in front of his plough.

Now, a word about nutrients. A balanced nutrient base is enormously important for the quality of the later tobacco leaves and, therefore, for the cigars later to be made from them. Chlorine, potassium, calcium, magnesium, phosphorus and nitrogen are the most important nutrients for cultivating tobacco. If, for example, there is too much calcium present, the leaves become pale as well as brittle and wavy, which retards growth. If the resulting leaves reach the production process, the cigars will have an unsatisfactory burning quality.

The seeds are sown at the end of August to the beginning of September. Then, after almost exactly 45 days, when the seedlings have reached a height of between 15 and 20 centimetres, they are transplanted. The replanting takes place in stages, after which the tobacco plants require a further 45 days – some up to 50 days – before they reach their full maturity.

Intensive care and regular checks are the orders of the day for the *vegueros* during this time. For one thing, sprouts and side shoots must be continually removed from the plants in order to encourage growth. For another, weeds have to be pulled up and the carers have to be on their guard against pests. This battle against pests is essential; for once they have gained a foothold they can quickly cause extensive damage to the tobacco plants, which in turn results in a noticeable harvest and production shortfall.

A veguero at work. 1980 was a fateful year in Cuba, as almost all tobacco plants were afflicted by blue mould and only a small percentage of the expected amount could be saved for harvesting. It took the Cuban cigar industry several years to recover.

One of these pests is known by the harmless sounding name of the "Tobacco Beetle". The *Lasioderma*, to give it its Latin name, is aptly called the *Perforador del Tobaco* in Spanish. One can only say that it justly bears this name, for this disastrous pest diligently perforates every tobacco leaf it can find.

Laid as an egg on the tobacco leaf, the larva develops in a little over 20 days into a worm, whose sole purpose in life is to eat its unremitting way through the leaf, creating tiny holes and passages until, on reaching the appropriate size, it finally transforms itself into a beetle and then flies away. This may indeed be fascinating, but what remains is a tobacco plant that no longer merits the name.

But, to return to the care of the tobacco plants, the *vegueros* remove the flower heads as soon as the plants have reached their full size. In this way, the plants' growing strength is concentrated on the leaves, which thereby receive a final dynamic impulse to develop fully. This is so for all plants, but here we must turn the clock back somewhat in order to draw attention to two different "care programmes".

A Mayan Word becomes Fashionable

The term "Ciquar" is of Mayan origin. The word "Cigar" developed later from this term. And Europeans, in their turn, comprehensively and in graphic detail translated the word as: "something burnable that tastes and smells good".

First of all there is the *Corojo* plant, which is used for the extraordinarily important *capa* or wrapper leaves. To ensure that this plant produces a leaves with a regular, smooth and silky appearance, it must not be subjected to the direct rays of the sun. Therefore, just after the seedlings have been transplanted, the *vegueros* cover wide stretches of the tobacco fields with muslin covers to protect the plants against the sun. In contrast, the *Criollo* plants are intentionally subjected to direct sunlight. This enables the *vegueros* to achieve a wide band of flavours.

Up in the airy heights thanks to stilts – gauze cloths are stretched over the tobacco plants to protect them from excessive sunlight.

This range is simply essential for the various tobacco mixtures needed for the diverse Havana brands. Although there are many more species of tobacco plant than these two, they should nevertheless suffice

as examples to provide the reader with a better understanding.

Harvesting begins almost exactly 50 days after replanting, when each individual leaf is plucked by hand. As the *Corojo* plant possesses eight to nine pairs of leaves – each of which mature at different times – the leaves are plucked gradually, removing only the mature leaves. This occurs in intervals of six to seven days; it therefore takes 40 days for an individual *Corojo* plant to be fully harvested.

The *vegueros* differentiate the leaves of this plant as follows (from the bottom to the top): *libre de pie, uno*

y medio, centro ligero, centro fino, centro gordo and *corona.*

By contrast, *Criollo* plants bear six or seven pairs of leaves, which are separated into *ligero, seco, volado* and *capote.* The leaves found at the bottom of the plants have the least flavour, as they have grown mostly in the shade. By the same token, the top leaves, which have enjoyed the most sunlight, have a more pronounced aroma.

Following the harvest, the leaves of both the *Corojo* and the *Criollo* are brought to the *casas del tobacco,* the tobacco houses, to air-dry naturally.

This drying phase is a laborious process, for the leaves, fastened to long wooden poles *(cujes),* are subjected to continual checking, in which changing the hanging position of the poles – the poles are initially

After the harvest – on the way to the drying sheds.

In the drying sheds – the higher the tobacco leaves are hung, the darker their colour becomes.

hung near the floor, and are then rehung higher and higher up – ensures the uniform temperature and humidity of the leaves. This drying phase lasts for about 50 days. During this time the leaves which were originally green, first turn yellow and then, thanks to natural oxidation, take on that golden brown colour of many Havanas. The first fermentation may now begin.

Before that however, the leaves are packed into bundles *(gavillas)*. When they reach the fermentation house they are layered into piles *(pilones)* more than 60 centimetres tall.

The first fermentation phase takes up to 30 days. During this time the piles are continually checked. If the temperature of a bale exceeds 35 °C, it is opened up to allow the leaves to cool down before being layered together once again.

This phase is necessary to reduce the resin content of the leaves appreciably (this results in their becoming more supple, enabling them to be more easily worked later on). The leaves also take on a uniform colour during this process.

Before the second fermentation begins, the leaves are first dampened to prevent discolouration. Then the *Corojo* leaves, that is the wrapper leaves, are left to stand, while the *Criollo* leaves intended for the filler bunch and as binder leaves, are have their central veins removed. They are then sorted according to size, colour, composition and type of leaf.

For the second fermentation phase, the leaves are again packed into bundles and then again layered into piles *(burros),* however, this time they are much larger. An even stronger fermentation is caused by the humidity remaining in the leaves, supported by the size of the *burros*. This causes a chemical change

The tobacco is subject to constant temperature checks during fermentation.

in the tobacco, which assists the development of its aroma as well as the breakdown of the remaining foreign matter. During this phase, the temperature must not be allowed to exceed 42 °C.

Now the leaves must be left to rest. This is done by laying the leaves on airing racks. In this way they also lose the last of their excess humidity. On completion of the rest phase, the leaves are packed together once more, this time, however, in prepared bales, called *tercios*. Incidentally, these tercios are made from the bark of the Cuban royal palm, as tradition demands.

The *tercios* now remain in warehouses until they are required by a cigar factory. Although the length of this storage stage is usually several months, it can last for several years. The quality of the tobacco is not in the least impaired by this. Quite the opposite, in fact – experience shows that the leaves undergo an aging process during this time, which, in its turn, helps to develop their aroma.

After the *tercios* arrive at the cigar factory, the individual types of leaf are dealt with in different ways. First of all, the extremely sensitive composition of the wrapper leaves requires special attention. Now, at last, they will regain their supple smoothness and silky shine.

This happens through a special humidifying process that can only take place during the early morning, while it is cool. The resulting excess water is removed by both shaking the leaves and hanging them up overnight. The remaining humidity can then spread uniformly through the whole leaf.

The next morning belongs to the *despilladores,* the vein removers who remove the central veins by cut-

Tercios – the tobacco is allowed to rest in this manner before being further processed.

ting each leaf in half. Then the work of the *rezagadoras* begins. It is their job to sort the leaves according to colour, size and structure. The wrapper leaves are now ready for further processing.

The other four types of leaf are dealt with quite differently. In contrast to the wrapper leaves they

require no humidifying. The length of their time in storage is enormously important. While *capotes* and *volados* require roughly a year to mature, the *secos* need a little longer, and the full-flavoured *ligeros* take at least two years to attain their final full maturity.

This process is overseen by the mixture master. Only experienced *tabacaleros* can do this kind of work, for they ultimately have to decide when each individual leaf of each and every sort is authorised to proceed to the mixing department.

If an experienced mixture master is required to over-see the maturing process, then close-lipped reticence

is the qualification for mixing the filler. Each filler recipe for every Havana brand is subject to absolute secrecy. What is well known, however, is that if a filler contains more *seco* and *volado* leaves than *ligero* ones, then the end cigar will be mild in taste; while a higher *ligero* content in the filling ensures more strength of body. Finally, following this task, shrouded in secrecy as it is, the *torcedores* are given sufficient mixture to produce 50 cigars.

It is now that the cigar is to be given its shape – the work of the *torcedor* begins. All that he requires for his work is a table, a sharp blade (called a *chaveta*), a guillotine, a pot of vegetable glue and the *tabla,* a rectangular wooden board which serves as a worktop.

Firstly, the *torcedor* rolls the filler *(tripa)* in the binder leaf *(capote),* making the bunch *(bonche).* He then cuts the wrapper leaf to the right size using the *chaveta* and slowly rolls it over the wrap. Next, he takes a small piece of wrapper leaf, forming with it the cap at the end of the cigar. Finally, he uses the guillotine to help cut the burning end of the cigar to the intended size.

Before a Havana finds its way into the cigar box – and peace at last – it must undergo a few more production stages. These mainly serve the purpose of checking and (later) presentation.

Not all, but individual bundles manufactured by the *torcedor* land on the table of the *tasador,* the fore taster. He removes one or two cigars from a bundle and checks their quality – of course, he can only do so by smoking them. He then passes the bundle on to the *controllador,* whose job is to inspect the individual cigars of the bundle in respect of form, length, width and weight. If the former detects a shortcoming in quality, or the latter an excess of predetermined tolerance limits, then the respective cigars are not approved for release.

Now at last the finished cigar can find respite. The next stage is the humidor. In this room fitted with high cedar wood shelves, the cigars are stored for at least three weeks and up to several months under ideal conditions.

That is, temperature here lies between 16 °C and 18° C, with a relative air humidity of between 65% and 70%. This respite also serves a very useful

purpose – the cigars give up the humidity they have gained during the production process.

Following storage, the individual cigars are first sorted according to colour nuances; then each Havana receives its paper cigar band before taking its place in a colourful cigar box.

After the box has been furnished with an individual guarantee seal, the cigar can at last begin its journey to that distant land in which it will be acquired by an *aficionado* and finally smoked. If this person is someone who is not solely interested in superficial consumption, he – or she – will probably light his cigar with a degree of awe … for about 170 individual steps have been necessary to produce a cigar from a grain of seed.

The guarantee seal of the Cuban government, resembling a US dollar note, is one of the distinguishing features on boxes of genuine Cuban cigars.

Seed

Although newly developed strains of tobacco tend to
originate from Cuba, and sometimes from Connecticut, this development process can now also be
observed in the Dominican Republic, Ecuador, Honduras, Mexico, and Nicaragua among other countries.

The resulting tobacco is not very like its Cuban
counterpart – the seeds of which were used in its
propagation – but is usually rather stronger than the

Millions of tobacco seeds
will one day develop into
desirable plants.

second strain that was used in the creation of the new
hybrid. That is not necessarily a bad thing, for the
tabaquero does not want to develop an identical
plant, but rather something quite new – something
that has previously not existed, a newcomer that he
believes, or is certain, will enrich the Tobacco family
with respect to its aroma development and/or
strength.

In any case, the process is fascinating – and when the
result is satisfactory, cigar smokers will soon enjoy yet
another nuance in the already diverse variety of cigar
tobaccos available.

These budding tobacco plants are still in the cultivation phase.

Ara Fina

This Brazilian tobacco is mainly used as a binder leaf and a filler, but also as a wrapper. However, its quality and flavour does not quite match that of its counterpart, the *Mata Fina*.

Havana 2000

The Havana 2000 is a hybrid developed in Cuba with the aim of achieving a plant resistant to the dreaded blue mould. As far as the tobacco quality is concerned, *tabaquero* experience in various countries varies greatly.

Tabacalero

Irrespective of whether the word *tabacalero* or the word *tabaquero* is used, the meaning is the same — these general terms are used to denote all workers and employees of the tobacco industry in Spanish speaking countries.

Torcedor

On this person, the efforts of all who have cared for the tobacco in the fields and those who have treated and processed the harvested leaves (thereby preparing them for rolling into cigars) stand or fall. And this gives an indication of the occupation that lies behind the Spanish term *torcedor (torquedor)* – that is, cigar roller.

While the work of all other *tabacaleros* or *tabaqueros* cannot be deemed inferior, the *torcedor* – together with the *ligador* – forms the most important link in the long chain of all those who work in the fields, the tobacco houses and cigar factories. If the skill of the *torcedor* is poor, then the hard work of the *tabacaleros* has practically all been in vain.

This also explains why the cigar roller's training is the longest of all the *tabacaleros*. On average, it covers a period of over a year, although slight variations in the length of time may occur from factory to factory.

However, this is only the beginning of the actual process of becoming a *torcedor,* as it is only through years of experience that a cigar roller achieves that automaton-like ability to produce even the most difficult formats perfectly.

It is often asked how many cigars an experienced *torcedor* can produce a day. That of course depends on the size of the format, but even more so on the

An intermediate stage in the work of a torcedor – the bunch in a press.

format itself. A corona for example, is easier to roll than a pyramid, or even a torpedo.

Apart from that, it is of little use to produce a large quantity if the quality suffers thereby. But in general, it may be said that a good *torcedor* produces about 120 to 150 top quality Cigars in "Corona" format per day.

Incidentally, the room in which the *torcedores* roll their cigars is known as a *galera*. This term dates back to the first third of the 19th century, towards the end of which the demand for Cuban cigars rose steadily, leading rapidly to a real Havana boom. Because labour was scarce at the time, and the owners of the numerous factories refused to fall back on slaves, a large number of convicts were conscripted to carry out the work. Many a prison cellar was reminiscent of the below-decks of a ship, so the workroom of the *torcedores* is still named after that part of a ship where slaves would live out their wretched existence at the oars.

The work in today's Cuban *galera* is significantly pleasanter, not least because there is also entertainment for the workforce in the guise of the *lector,* who can only be found in such a context in Cuba. He acts according to the true meaning of the Latin word as a Reader or, more precisely, as a Fore-Reader. That is, he presents the working *torcedores* with world literature, as well as the work of contemporary authors, and reads aloud the latest news from the "Granma", the party newspaper of the "Partido Comunista de Cuba". He is only interrupted by the radio, which broadcasts Western hits and songs in addition.

Several decades ago, the first *fábrica* began to replace the *lector* completely or partly by loudspeakers, from

*Education and propaganda
– a lector reads out aloud
during the work.*

which tinny spoken and musical contributions from the radio forced (and still force) themselves into the ear.

Others followed this example. But it remains to be seen when, if ever, the time comes for the last *lector* to finish his last contribution. At any rate, the institution of *lector* still exists, now, as in the past.

In the past – it was 1850 when a *lector* entered the *galera* of the Partagás factory for the first time – the *lector* stepped up to the pulpit-like platform, drew a stool under himself and began to read out aloud. Soon there was a *lector* in every factory, and, day by day, the *torcedores* became widely read (to). The works of Honoré de Balzac, Charles Dickens, Alexandre Dumas, both the elder and the younger, and, in more recent times, the works of Ernest Hemmingway, have all contributed, and still contribute, considerably to expanding the listeners' education.

Although the Cuba of today is has one of the world's lowest illiteracy rates, and is a country where education and knowledge are conveyed to all members of society, the picture was frighteningly different before Castro took power. At that time, the *torcedores* of the cigar factories held a special position in the working population. They were considered the "intellectuals of the proletariat" thanks to the privilege of having a lector, who introduced them to aspects of the world's literature.

Veguero

The term used to describe all those tobacco farmers working in the tobacco fields, the *vegas,* who are responsible for sowing the tobacco seed, raising and nurturing the tobacco plants, and finally harvesting the tobacco leaves. Just how laborious the work of the *vegueros* can often be is described on pages 11 to 20.

Tobacco

It is well known that Columbus discovered the Americas during his expedition to find the sea route to India, and that he brought back to the Old World several things which had been unknown until then. Among these were two plants which continue to play a major role in Europe. The first is that well known tuber which today is one of the most important staple foods, the potato. The second is the plant which, processed in a variety of ways, is considered to be the stimulant most in demand in our society – tobacco.

Both the potato, *Salanum tuberosum,* and the tobacco plant, *Nicotiana,* belong to the nightshade family, which, as the name suggests, are active in the dark of the night, doing precisely what they are meant to do – growing.

In Pre-Columbian times, they generally did so relatively near to the equator, for here the days and nights are almost of equal length. This is of great importance to the nightshade family, for extremely short nights, as is the case with northern European summers, encourage neither growth nor the development of the plants.

Through appropriate cultivation and development of new strains it became possible to grow both types of plant in northern latitudes. Whatever is the case with the potato is also the case – although to a lesser degree – with the originally wild-growing tobacco plant, as well as the species of tobacco plant used for the production of cigars, despite the latter's preference for a more tropical or subtropical climate – that is, one characterised by high temperatures and pronounced rainfall. It is in such climatic regions that traditional cigar tobacco cultivation is to be found: in Brazil, Indonesia and the Caribbean.

As has already been mentioned, cultivation and development has made much possible. Thus, we can find cigar tobacco grown in North America, Italy, France and, yes, even Poland and Germany. The area of the Uckermark, stretching to the north of Berlin,

the Palatinate region around Speyer as well the Upper-Rhine plain between Heidelberg and Freiburg im Breisgau are the most important cigar tobacco growing areas of Germany. The best known tobacco grown here is the *Geudertheimer,* a mild tobacco, low in nicotine with a slightly nutty character, which can be used without problem as a filler component or as a binder.

The areas named are not only characterised by a climate that is favourable for growing tobacco, but they also possess the second important component which a nightshade family member cannot do without: a lightly loamy, but mainly sandy soil, which in addition enjoys a high level of nutrients.

A word about tobacco consumption. As with many stimulants – and foods for that matter – less usually brings more benefit than unbridled consumption. Such excess does not inevitably lead to health problems, but it can do so.

That is the case with unbalanced nutrition (e.g. fast food), with alcohol, and naturally also with tobacco. Anyone who eats mainly red meat (lamb, beef and pork) accepts the risk to health, as does anyone who drinks two or three bottles of wine a day; and anyone who smokes 30 to 40 cigarettes a day must no doubt accept that sooner or later his body will rebel.

As said above, it is not inevitable that excessive consumption leads to serious health problems, but, over time, it may do so.

Our body is designed to live with poisons, and also to cope when they are administered in small doses (inoculation and medication etc.). People must decide for themselves how much tobacco they wish to consume, but should also bear one thing in mind. Properly dosed pleasure – as is at least the case with smoking cigars – is definitely better than unbridled consumption.

Eight to ten, perhaps even more, cigars a week, smoked in peace, as a rule really do enhance a person's feeling of wellbeing; such consumption is a balm for the psyche, the balance of the mind, and in turn strengthens the immune system, which only serves to confirm that poison, when enjoyed in moderation, can be quite beneficial to health.

In the drying sheds or rancho – the air-drying of these tobacco leaves is already well advanced.

Content and Packaging

Cigar Boxes

Cigar boxes present themselves in all possible forms.
They may be large or small, rectangular, square, or
pyramid shaped; some have little drawers, some are
lacquered, others untreated; and some of them are
even equipped with an integrated humidifier.

Then there are very colourful containers. Most originate from Cuba, and it is mainly the romantically
drawn images that draw the eye's attention – mostly
lithographs representing cigar brands, dating from
the previous century.

The first to be seen is the *cubierta*, affixed to the
outer surface of the lid. The other two lithographs are
revealed to the observer once the box has been
opened. The *vista* is that lithograph fixed to the inner
surface of the lid, while the *bofetóns* are connected to
the base of the box and lie over the cigars, which can
first be surveyed when the printed paper is lifted and
folded forward.

These often quite colourful motifs sometimes made
use of as many as eight or ten colours. This was made
possible at the time by the invention of lithography
by the German, Alois Senefelder. The process
enabled colour printing by preparing a treated stone
plate for each respective colour. The principle of
lithography – as for today's offset printing – rests on
the use of greasy substances for the areas to be
printed, and water, which is known to be grease
resistant.

These colourful lithographs became the all the rage
around the middle of the 19th century, as further
development of lithography at this period enabled
their unlimited reproduction, and because many

*The vista of the brand Por
Larrañaga – one of the very
oldest Havana brands.*

printers had turned their backs on Germany as a result of Bismarck's Anti-Socialist laws, settling in the New World, including Cuba.

All this led the "Litográfica de Habana", the leading printer in Havana at that time, to enjoy bulging order books. Every cigar manufacturer simply had to have these *cubiertas, vistas* and *bofetóns* for each cigar brand – the more colourful the better.

It is easy to sneer at the frequently tacky appearance of the *vistas,* to dismiss them as pure bad taste or even to find them appealing because of their overdone unadulterated kitsch. Nonetheless, these lithographs bear witness to the predominant taste at that time, and this in turn lends them a cultural and historical importance.

Filler

The filler is the heart of a cigar. It is the prime determining factor in a cigar's flavour, as well as the development of the aroma set free during smoking.

Because great attention is always paid to the wrapper leaf (the "face" of a cigar that has to win the *aficionado's* favour at first glance), the filler is often not valued as highly as it should be.

It should be highly valued, however, for it is the filler that decisively shapes the character of a cigar, forming at least two thirds of its nature. In this light, it is also easy to understand why the composition of the filler mixture is protected like a state secret by many cigar manufacturers. It is true that the types of tobacco used in a filler and their provinces of origin are usually widely known, but the exact mixing ratio of the individual tobaccos is hardly ever betrayed.

The mixing of a filler can be compared to the composing of music. The notes available on the musical scales are just as well-known as the many tobaccos used for producing cigars. But it is the positioning of the notes that decides whether a piece of music sounds harmonious or discordant. A masterpiece is thus characterised by the relation of the individual notes to the whole.

The spread binder leaf and three filler leaves are about to be formed into a single unit.

The mixing of the filler for a top quality cigar is a similar affair. As every individual tobacco possesses a special note, it is the harmonious combination of the individual components that provides the unity experienced upon smoking, and which presents the *aficionado* with a perfect experience of flavour.

Whether the composition is undertaken for a short or a long filler is of secondary importance. Although mixing for a short-filler cigar provides more possibilities, in the end, the use of really good tobaccos in the right ratio is the decisive factor. Every great cigar manufacturer is familiar with this art – hence the special secrets guarded by each of them.

Binder Leaf

The binder leaf, the intermediary between the filler and the wrapper, has gained in significance recently. Longer ago, it primarily served to give the filler a certain amount of hold and thus completed the bunch – for which purpose a relatively neutral flavour was required. Today, however, it plays a stronger role in the composition of the filler and thereby the cigar as a whole. Quality is therefore required of the binder leaf – and quality leaves are now being delivered from almost all traditional tobacco growing areas.

Wrapper Leaf

As the name suggests, this leaf is used as a wrapper – or more precisely, it is the leaf wrapped around the

*Just before completion –
a bunch is rolled in the
wrapper leaf.*

filler and binder. It is wrapped around the bunch, the
name by which the incomplete product consisting of
filler and binder is known.

The wrapper, wound around the bunch from burning end to the head in a spiral fashion, has an influence on the flavour of a cigar which should not be
underestimated, that influence, however, is often
over estimated.

More important are the appearance, structure, consistence and quality of the fine veins (comparable to
the grain of wood) of the wrapper, or, to use the
Spanish term, *capa*.

For this is the covering leaf that is subject to the critical eye, first of the *escogedor,* the colour sorter, then
of the cigar dealer, and finally of the *aficionado* (to
name just a few of the people who are interested in
affording the finished product more than a fleeting
glance).

Content and Packaging

As the "face" of a cigar, the wrapper should possess a uniformity of structure and colour; for hardly any *aficionado* will take up with a cigar whose appearance does nothing to gain the smoker's trust, trust in all that lies hidden from view beneath the filler and binder. The hidden bunch must therefore keep the promise made by the wrapper.

The latter may well be outstanding, but if the filler, binder and wrapper do not form a unified whole or (to be more poetic) do not form a successful symbiosis, then no wrapper can save a cigar, no matter how excellent it may be. It would mean the death of a brand if its wrappers were to serve as nothing more than a bogus cover for a miserable content, i.e. a bad bunch. Such a wrapper would be not only deceptive, it would be a swindle.

Equally, even the best bunch is of no help if the wrapper is of inferior quality. It follows that a good bunch must be given an acceptable appearance through a good wrapper.

Tragacanth —that was the name of the odourless and tasteless vegetable glue previously used for working the cap and affixing the cigar ring. It leaves no residue whatsoever. Today, a different vegetable glue is used which also possesses these positive properties, but is also easier to use.

When the Gods Light-up …

There is no record of when the first cigar was formed and smoked. We only know for certain that the Mayans and Aztecs knew the "Ciquar", as the Mayans called the forerunner of our modern cigar, long before Columbus. We also know that the oldest form of inhaling tobacco smoke is the smoking of cigars. The smoking of the Ciquar was primarily reserved for the Pre-Columbian priesthood, and used by them to induce a trance in order to be closer to their gods and to contact the netherworld. The Mayans explained the origin of the Ciquar as follows: "The cigar was invented by the gods, in order to confer upon themselves the very special enjoyment of tobacco's flavour. Every time there is thunder and lightening, it is the gods striking fire in order to light a cigar."

A good wrapper must have more than an appealing appearance, it should above all be the primary bearer of flavour and aroma. A wrapper can be the carrier of more than half a cigar's total fragrance and flavour, and must also be capable of transporting and releasing the rest of the great abundance of aroma – the aroma of the binder and filler.

Moreover, a wrapper should be pliable and relatively thin in order to surround the bunch tightly, while, at the same time, its consistence should be strong enough to allow it to be processed without great difficulty. These properties – especially the thinness – have a positive effect on the burning quality when the cigar is later smoked.

There is no "best wrapper leaf", just as there is no "best cigar". However, excellent *capas* are grown in Cuba as well as in the Connecticut River Valley, but also in Honduras, Mexico, and Nicaragua, as well as in Brazil, Ecuador, Indonesia and Cameroon, and recently also in the Dominican Republic.

The colour of the wrapper leaf is a chapter in itself. Veritably eagle-eyed contemporaries are said to have discerned over 140 wrapper leaf colours, but this is probably a considerable exaggeration. It is roughly double the number of colour nuances that an escogedor – the factory tabacalero who, day in, day out, does nothing but sort the finished cigars of a particular format according to (slight) variations of colour – can tell apart. An experienced escogedor, who after many years of this work could lend his eyes to an eagle, might be able to distinguish about 80 capa colour variations.

As mentioned above, it is extremely important how well the *capa* (wrapper) harmonises with the *capote* (the binder) and *tripa* (filler). For example, in the Dominican Republic indigenous tobaccos very often form the bunch accompanied by either a *Connecticut Shade* wrapper or one grown in Ecuador. This is quite a good combination, and it is here on the west of the island of Hispaniola that many premium cigars bearing just this composition of leaves are produced. As with most things, it is a matter of achieving the right mixture – in this case the right *"ménage à trois"*.

Although the colour of the wrapper is not decisive for the flavour of a cigar, it does give an indication of this, as well as the cigar's strength and the richness of its aroma. While an experienced *escogedor* can discern about 80 nuances in colour, the seven-colour classification, explained in depth later, is usually sufficient for the *aficionado*.

However, we can only deal here with general rules based on empirical experience and must leave out the specifics. Flavour and quality are more strongly dependent on other factors. For example, questions arise such as whether the wrapper involved is a *semi-corona* or a *centro-fino* leaf, when the leaf was harvested (that is, how long the leaf was subjected to the sun), and finally about the fermentation.

The longer a leaf has enjoyed a "place in the sun", for example, the more oil and sugar it develops – and the sweeter the cigar will later taste, especially during the first third, when the flavour is mainly determined by the wrapper.

Leaving aside the exceptions to be found for every rule, it can be said that the darker a cigar's wrapper leaf, the more intense and sweet its flavour. The following overview therefore begins with the lightest colour category and ends with the darkest.

Claro Claro. Here we find all those wrapper leaves whose colour falls on the spectrum between yellow-green, through olive green – once known as "Clarissimo" and "Jade" – to a strong green-brown. These colour shades, also reminiscent of a dark blonde, are mainly the result of an early harvesting of the leaf, before full maturity is reached, followed by a short drying phase often accompanied by extra heat (where the leaves are usually suspended over charcoal embers). Further approved designations for *claro claro* are *doble claro* or *double claro,* and *candela* as well as *AMS,* the abbreviation for "American Market Selection" which is an indication of the past popularity of this colour in North America. Cigars with *claro claro* wrappers are usually very light in flavour and develop relatively little aroma.

Claro. The next light-coloured wrapper after *claro claro* can be compared to a pale brown, often also tinged with yellow. Many wrapper leaves grown in shade display this colour tone; for example, those grown in Connecticut and denoted with the designation *shade.* The *claros* are mostly harvested shortly before maturity and then air-dried. *Claro* wrappers – also known as *natural* – are often an indication of a mild cigar.

Colorado Claro. These wrapper leaves are light to golden brown and are from plants that may have been grown in the sun or the shade. The individual colour is not only determined by soil, climate and how long – if at all – they have been subjected to the sun, but also by the way they are further processed (mainly fermentation). However, in general, it can be said that these leaves have been subjected to more direct sunshine than leaves displaying the colour tones described above. Wrapper leaves grown in the sun in Cameroon, are often used as natural *colorado claros.* As a rule, the smoker of a cigar covered in this wrapper can expect a medium-full flavour with a balanced richness of aroma.

Colorado. This grouping is comprised of those wrapper leaves – on the whole quite numerous – that are coloured mid-brown, often with a reddish tone. *Colorados* usually have quite a pronounced flavour and aroma. As a sign of its past and present popularity in Great Britain, the abbreviation *EMS* (English Market Selection) is also applied to this wrapper leaf colour.

Colorado Maduro. The section of the spectrum containing the darker wrapper leaf colours begins with this designation. *Colorado maduro* – a luscious brown colour, usually denoting a cigar with a uncompromising rich aroma and fully pronounced flavour that is, to no small degree, the result of the timing of the harvest. The leaf is only plucked when it has fully matured.

Maduro. Oily and sweet – two characteristics of a mature *maduro* wrapper – and a dark, deep brown colour. A cigar with such a "fatty" wrapper leaf usually has a very intense flavour but does not always present the rich breadth of aroma characteristic of the *colorado maduro* (although this limitation applies only to the breadth). A *maduro* wrapper leaf is almost always from the upper part of the tobacco plant and has been subjected to the sun for quite a long period. This is the colour often seen on Havanas embodying the traditional style – rich in flavour and demanding respect for a manifest strength. The abbreviation for "Spanish Market Selection", *SMS*, is also used for the *maduro*, since such cigars are very popular in Spain.

Oscuro. The end of the spectrum begins with wrappers of a very deep brown and closes with black, thus giving rise to the term *negro* which is sometimes used for *oscuro* wrapper leaves.

A strong flavour without a fully pronounced breadth of aroma (and the emphasis here must be on fully) can almost always be expected from a cigar displaying this often very oily wrapper leaf. The leaves from which the *oscuros* are derived have almost without exception been grown in the sun, as indicated, for instance by the Connecticut wrapper designation *broadleaf* – although it may be more accurate to say that the *broadleaf* "can" indicate a leaf grown entirely in the sun, since *broadleaf* is also used for the previous two colour categories. Outside Connecticut, *oscuro* production is mainly concentrated in Brazil and Mexico.

Finally, it is important to emphasise the exceptions mentioned above. These relate to the strength of a cigar. A dark wrapper indicates a strong cigar, a light wrapper a mild one – this assumption does not always hold true, since a cigar with a dark wrapper leaf may very well be surprisingly mild, and one with a light wrapper quite strong. However, the cigar manufacturers are well aware of this widespread assumption, and often choose a wrapper leaf that corresponds with the content.

Colour (Mismatches)

Although it is primarily the palate that conveys the sensory experience of a taste in the human nervous system, another sensory organ also plays an important part – the eye.

This is primarily responsible for our expectation of pleasure and awakens that well-known foretaste that is fulfilled "in the blink of an eye". The eye plays a major role in our sensory experience of taste and flavour – and therefore also our experience of smoking.

The colour sorter, called the *escogedor* in Cuba, is found in all serious Caribbean and Central and South American cigar factories. When the completed rolled cigars leave the *torcedor's* station, they are next

An untrained eye can hardly differentiate between the many brown shades of wrapper leaves.

checked by four further testers before being subjected to the meticulous scrutiny of the *escogedor's* critical eye and sorted according to their colour nuances.

This sorter really does have to possess a highly refined sense of colour, since Havana wrapper leaves – as well as those of the rest of the Caribbean – display infinitely more colour shades than the seven categories described on pages 43 to 45 might suggest.

The work of the *escogedor* is of no little importance for the later sale of a box of premium cigars. The optical regularity of the cigars in a box presented to the observer depends heavily on the congruency of colour tone, which in turn prevents the slightest visual discord in a cigar row from becoming apparent.

This has to be so, for the eye plays a role in our smoking experience; and nothing quickens the heartbeat of an *aficionado* more than a box full of cigars that are almost identical in production, form and colour tone. When cigars in a box present themselves with a consistent colour shade, it not only provides the *connoisseur* with pleasure, but is also an elementary sales factor.

Another important sales factor can be described by the word "mismatch". A paradox? No, not at all. For, ultimately, various nuances of colour within a specific format are common – otherwise the job of *escogedor* would make no sense. But before this optical activity, the *tasador* must do his bit. He is responsible for "tasting" individual cigars from a produced batch to check the quality. Next comes the *controllador,* who satisfies himself that the cigars are properly rolled and conform to the established quality standards.

Cigars lying side by side in a box may display varying shades of colour, but this is no indication of their quality – which is the same as the ones whose colour tones all match. So the term "mismatch" is an important sales feature as it directly affects the cigar price. The sales patter runs like this: "granted, the colour tones don't match, but the quality is right – and so is the price!" That price can be quite favourable because, as we know, the eye is integral to the smoking experience (and in this case it is not quite so pampered).

Head

This is the end of a cigar that has to be cut off prior to smoking should it not already have been removed (which is hardly ever the case with long filler premium cigars). It is not known whether there is any connection between the term "head" and the action of "beheading".

"A woman is just a woman, but a good cigar is a smoke."

Rudyard Kipling

Burning End

This is the end of the cigar that is lit, and is also where the wrapper is most susceptible to damage. The Juan Clemente brand has, for example, taken this into account by its unusual use of the cigar band. This does not encircle the cigar on the upper third as usually is the case, i.e. toward the head or cap, but instead is attached to the burning end. Cigars of the Professor Sila brand are also protected in this way – in addition to carrying the normal cigar band.

Cigar Band

It was Gustav(o) Bock who first introduced the cigar band. That was in 1850. This resourceful cigar dealer, who made his fortune first through the import and export of Havana cigars and then later through the production of his own brand, was unconcerned with the elegant symmetry of the well-manicured finger – the protection of which had been a matter of constant worry for numerous titled and honourable cigar smokers – he was uninterested in shielding these fingers from every conceivable inconvenience but was thinking of something quite different.

The idea for the cigar band arose ostensibly from simple thoughts of filthy lucre. These paper bands – the first were in white – were designed distinguish Bock's cigars from those of his competitors. This they did – but not for long.

An argument that sometimes becomes an outright war of beliefs revolves around the question of whether a cigar should be smoked with or without its cigar ring. In response to this question many a distinguished connoisseur, lacking tolerance for the views of his opponent, has lost his composure and behaved liked a raging bull, and several have lamented the abolition of the once-popular duel. Nevertheless, whether a cigar is smoked with or without its cigar ring has no effect whatsoever on the flavour – unless, that is, someone should come up with the absurd idea of smoking the ring as well as the cigar!

Content and Packaging

The spread of lithography at the time made it easily possible to print these rings in colour – and soon after the introduction of the cigar band, ever more colourful examples were appearing. New works of art appeared almost daily to adorn the most diverse cigars, containing eye-catching symbols as well as gold-embossed lettering. The possibilities for designing an unmistakeable and individualistic cigar band definitely grew markedly.

This attracted the world's great and powerful and their hangers on, and cigar manufacturers were soon receiving numerous orders with the proviso that only cigars with cigar bands bearing the client's own portrait be sent.

This wish, born of vanity, continued far into the 20th century – King Farouk of Egypt, for example,

An Empress is Not Amused

If we are to believe some reports – which in this case is quite difficult to do – it was no less a person than Catherine the Great (1729–1796) in her capacity as Empress of Russia, who, according to legend, contributed decisively to the development of the cigar band.

It is well-known that this Empress of German descent was very broad-minded about many pleasures, and was also, it is said, not at all averse to smoking cigars. Once she fell prey to an earthly vice, she pursued it excessively – and so she quickly disappeared behind greater and greater clouds of smoke in her magnificent apartments in Saint Petersburg. This intensive indulgence in the royal pleasure of smoking cigars soon had the effect of staining certain areas of the Imperial Aficionado's blue-blooded fingers a dark colour, which in turn did not amuse the former Princess zu Anhalt-Zerbst at all. Rapid redress was required.

Somehow, the story of the imperial affliction must have spread, until, some decades later, it came to the ears of a certain Gustav(o) Bock. Sadly, however, it was not granted to Catherine the Great to experience the continuously rising popularity of the cigar band …

belonged to that group of people who only smoked a cigar when they saw their own image immortalised on its cigar band. Today, many bands are still colourful, but those bearing portraits are slowly dying out. One hardly needs to be a prophet, however, to foresee that the cigar band itself is not endangered.

Answering the question of whether a cigar should be smoked with or without its band demands tolerance towards the bad habits of those who think and act differently.

There is, however, a technical point to be considered. Whoever prefers to smoke a cigar without the band is well advised to remove the paper ring only after the cigar has been lit and developed a degree of warmth. The paper ring, which is fastened with a tasteless (and now also warm) vegetable gum, can then be more easily removed. Without this precaution, the wrapper leaf may be damaged – and no cigar enthusiast wants that to happen, irrespective of the strength of his opinion on this matter.

8-9-8 (Eight-Nine-Eight)

In earlier times, cigars were actually pressed into the wooden boxes when being packed. This explains the rectangular form they displayed soon afterwards. Eventually, the Cuban cigar manufacturer Ramón Allónes had the idea of packing the cigars in three rows, whereby they were arranged one on top of the other in a staggered fashion. Thus a method of packing arose that is often used for boxes of 25 cigars. Both the bottom and the top rows consist of eight cigars each, while the middle row contains nine.

Bundle

This is a particular form of packaging. Many producers offer certain formats of their brands in deep boxes containing 25 or 50 cigars bound together in a bundle by a silk ribbon. In Cuba, a bundle of 50 is called a *media rueda* or "half wheel". This is derived from a common Cuban colloquialism. Someone who is 50 years old is said to have reach the half wheel of life. Which goes to show that every Cuban intends to reach the age of 100 – no more, but also no less.

Media rueda – bundles of 50 cigars each await packing in a cabinet box.

Packaging

More appearance than reality – that's also the case with several brands of cigar. However, it can usually be said that the more elaborate the packaging, the better the content. All the same, there are exceptions to every rule – see above. One thing is nevertheless certain – if the packaging of a cigar is outlandish, then the price will be so too. Whether or not that is justified is another question. In the final analysis, it is the flavour that is decisive for the purchase of cigars – and, as we know, no one can argue with taste.

Even this brief outline shows how difficult it is to draw conclusions about a cigar's quality from its presentation. Nonetheless, if the packaging deviates from the standard (here the cedar wood cigar box serves as a benchmark) yet each cigar in a box of 25 is individually wrapped in cellophane, then the product cannot be all that bad – at least in the opinion of the producer – since from his point of view, it would really make no sense to try to elevate a product of inferior quality to the nobility of a premium cigar – the effort and expense would be too high. Apart from which, no experienced cigar smoker would allow himself to be dazzled by grandiose packaging, and he would most definitely not base his purchase on it. Here, one may well agree with Schiller, "Then whoso forms eternal bonds, Should weigh if heart to heart responds".

However, *aficionados* also know that cigars can be offered in cedar wood boxes, or perhaps wrapped individually in the thinnest of cedar wood or cellophane, sometimes they are packed in tissue paper and occasionally tucked individually into aluminium foil; at times they lie in aluminium or glass tubes (also available), or may even be presented wrapped individually in cellophane and placed in an aluminium tube which may in turn be lined with cedar wood – and they know that all this serves to preserve the freshness of the content for a while and thus guarantees the quality.

Of course, such measures are no substitute for a *humidor,* but that is another matter.

Cabinet boxes – here one of the Cohiba brands – are becoming ever more popular.

Puro

In Spanish, *puro* means nothing more than "cigar"
but, used as an adjective, it can further describe a
subject as "characteristic", "authentic", "pure in
nature", or "pristine". The expression *puro* is therefore used in the cigar world to designate a cigar
made solely from tobacco leaves harvested in the
producer's own country. A Havana is therefore
always a *puro;* numerous *puros* are also produced in
Honduras, Nicaragua and especially in Mexico,
while the first *puros* are also coming from the
Dominican Republic.

One comment is however necessary – the expression
puro relates to the origin of the tobacco used, and has
nothing to do with a cigar's quality properties. Furthermore, when the talk is of a "Pure Honduran",
this means that although the cigar has been made
solely from Honduran tobacco, the production itself
may have taken place in another country.

Belicoso

This is the name of a relatively thick cigar (usually
with a ring gauge of – at least – 52) displaying a

tapered head. The cigar is therefore counted among the *figurados,* and is fairly demanding of the *torcedor's* art.

Figurado

A cigar usually presents a rounded head connected to a tube with parallel edges that runs to the burning end. Cigar formats that deviate from this standard are called *figurados. Belicoso, culebra, pyramide* and *torpedo* are examples of such formats. An experienced *torcedor* with a command of his craft is needed to produce these formats.

Premium Cigars

These account for about 1.5% of cigars – and yet almost everything revolves around them. By "these" we mean the roughly 150 million premium cigars smoked annually worldwide that merit the title.

By contrast, the approximately 10 billion "normal" cigars almost pale in comparison. Whether that is justified or not may well be a matter of conjecture. One thing is certain – a premium cigar must fulfil three preconditions. Firstly, the product must consist of 100% tobacco; secondly, it must be made of long filler; and thirdly, it must be made by hand.

It is primarily cigars from the Caribbean, Central and Latin America, but also some from Indonesia and the Philippines, that meet these three criteria. In

*Torcedoras and torcedores
roll their cigars on a wooden
board.*

this respect, Europe – with the exception of the
Canary Islands – is out of the game. This is the reason: if the Old World manufacturers were to produce their cigars cost-intensively by hand, they
would have to charge a cigar price that would make
it practically impossible to compete with a comparable premium product from one of the aforementioned countries.

There is, of course, nothing better than a really good
cigar made exclusively by hand. In this respect, a
machine cannot come close to the ability of an
experienced *torcedor*.

On the other hand, a well-made cigar produced by
machine can sometimes be much better than a hand-
made one produced without sufficient care and
attention; for, in the final analysis it is principally

the quality and composition of the tobaccos used that is significant as well as – last, but not least – the technical method of production that is so important for a good draw and a satisfactory burning behaviour.

Not every premium cigar is worth the premium price demanded for it, which, of course, makes it necessary to be well-informed about the variety both before and during the purchase. Ultimately, no cigar smoker can avoid keeping to the three essential criteria of the cigar world – sample, sample, and sample again.

Duplicates

Let us establish this at once – duplicates are not forgeries. An example will clarify this. When a New York *aficionado* enters a tobacconist's and requests a box of Cohiba, he acquires it without problem (as long as the shop is relatively well stocked and, of course, as long as he can pay for it).

This transaction is entirely legal, for the *aficionado* has not been fobbed off with a forgery, but has bought Cohibas manufactured for the US General Cigar Company in the Dominican Republic. General Cigar is allowed to distribute these Cohibas because the United States business owns the rights to this brand name.

This somewhat convoluted affair goes back to a judgement of the International Court of Justice at The Hague in the mid 1970s. Exiled Cubans had gone to law to secure the right to give the cigars they were now producing in the Dominican Republic or

Honduras the same names they had had when produced in Cuba. This included those brands whose rights lay with an individual or a family.

Legal uncertainty often accompanies a legal decision. That seems to have been the case with the double brand names of Cuban and non-Cuban cigars, and several US companies (for example) took advantage of this.

For instance, Cohiba had never been the property of an individual or family, yet the General Cigar Company was licensed to produce and distribute cigars under that name. Eventually, it did indeed purchase the brand name from someone or other – most definitely not from Fidel Castro – perhaps from a former employee of the El Laguito factory who had years previously enjoyed a managerial position (not necessarily an executive one) in this "Temple of the Havana". Little can be reconstructed with certainty, but much can be surmised.

In any case, what used to be a curiosity has become rather important. Thus, the current tenuous situation is that there are two separate cigar brands on offer bearing the name Romeo y Julieta, two are sold under the name Partagás, and two are available as Montecristo – just to name a few. The table on pages 60 and 61 lists all the duplicates that are either currently on the market or were available in the recent past, thereby saving the *aficionado* from losing his or her bearings when faced with the difficult choice of deciding, for example, between two Bolívars.

In fact, such a choice should only be faced in a duty-free shop, for, a Partagás produced in the Dominican Republic should not be available at all in a country where a Cuban Partagás is on offer.

Hidden Messages

José Martí (1853–1895), was a Cuban writer who sought his island's independence from Spain, fought against injustice and inequality, and passionately resisted the USA's attempt to annex Cuba. Martí devised a unique and clever way of hiding the messages passed by courier between him and his fellow resistance fighters – he rolled them inside cigars!

Marketing agreements between Habanos S.A. and the respective duplicate brand owner – mostly US companies – make sure of that. This tenuous situation could with a single act be transformed into a volatile one – should the US government lift the embargo against some or all Cuban goods, then …

Duplicates of Current and Former Havana Brands

Belinda	*Honduras*
Bolivar	*Dominican Republic*
Cabañas	*Dominican Republic*
Cifuentes	*Jamaica*
El Rey del Mundo	*Honduras*
Fonseca	*Dominican Republic*
Fonseca Vintage Selection	*Dominican Republic*
Henry Clay	*Dominican Republic*
Henry Clay Habana 2000	*Dominican Republic*
Hoyo de Monterrey	*Honduras*
Hoyo de Monterrey Excalibur	*Honduras*
H. Upmann	*Dominican Republic*
H. Upmann Cabinet Selection	*Dominican Republic*
H. Upmann Chairman's Reserve	*Dominican Republic*
H. Upmann Special Selection	*Dominican Republic*
H. Upmann 2000	*Dominican Republic*
Jose L. Piedra	*Nicaragua*
La Corona	*Dominican Republic*
La Flor de Cano	*Dominican Republic*
La Gloria Cubana	*Dominican Republic/USA*
La Gloria Cubana Selección d'Oro	*Dominican Republic*
Montecristo	*Dominican Republic*
Montecristo Cigare des Artes	*Dominican Republic*
Partagás	*Dominican Republic*
Por Larrañaga	*Dominican Republic*

Punch	Honduras
Quintero	Honduras
Rafael Gonzales	Honduras
Ramon Allones	Dominican Republic
Romeo y Julieta 1875	Dominican Republic
Romeo y Julieta Vintage	Dominican Republic
Saint Luis Rey	Honduras
Saint Luis Rey Reserva Especial	Honduras
Trinidad y Hermano	Dominican Republic
Troya	Dominican Republic

1) The only duplicate brand that can be bought under the name of "Excalibur" in countries which also offer the Cuban "Hoyo de Monterrey".

Dutch-type

Sometimes, "dry type" is also used to indicate machine-produced short filler cigars. The expression "dry" is not quite accurate (the term "European" is more precise), because there are most definitely short filler for which storage in a Humidor can be helpful, for instance when Brazilian or Caribbean tobaccos form the body of a cigar.

The sloping walls, the old clinker floors and wooden pallets of the De Olifant cigar factory in Kampen, the Netherlands, are steeped in the fragrance of tobacco and cedar wood.

Solely those cigars made principally from Indonesian tobaccos – for example when a binder leaf from Java and a Sumatra sandleaf wrapper are used with Sumatra tobaccos (among others) in the bunch, and do not require a Humidor for storage over a longer period of time – are unproblematic in this respect. These include many European manufacturers' cigars, but especially those produced in Belgium, Denmark, Germany, The Netherlands, Austria and Switzerland.

The European cigar industry can look back on a long tradition – quite often a longer tradition than that of several Caribbean States (including the Dominican Republic, the country currently producing most premium cigars). In countries where the Industrial Revolution set in early, this tradition naturally included the use of machinery whenever appropriate. Thus it was precisely in Central and Northern Europe that the production of cigar by machine soon became common.

However, a machine can only process a bunch comprising short pieces of tobacco. Such pieces of tobacco were not (and still are not) analogous to "tobacco waste", but are rather strips of tobacco

The salesroom of the time-honoured firm, Hajenius, in Amsterdam is quite a "tobacco temple".

several centimetres long, usually – apart from the raw material for mass consumption cigars found in the low-price segment of the market – of relatively high-quality, both then and now.

Cigars produced in this manner, which allows a great deal of scope in the composition of the bunch, were well received by European smokers, and even became extremely popular – as they still are today among many European *aficionados*.

The term "Dutch type" or "European type" does not therefore provide an indication of a cigar's quality. Moreover, it is extremely difficult to compare cigars produced in Europe with those of Caribbean origin – apples and oranges come to mind.

It becomes even more problematic when HTL comes into play. This abbreviation stands for "homogenised tobacco leaf", a band of tobacco that serves as a wrapper for most cigars made by machine. To manufacture it, finely ground tobacco is mixed with a binding agent to create a tobacco substitute, whereby a mix ratio of 85% tobacco to 15% binding agent is generally used.

While it is true that a wrapper made from good tobacco band is always preferable to a miserable one consisting of 100% tobacco, the label "100% tobacco" in an indication of respectable quality.

In fact, many 100% cigars of excellent quality are now available. They are mainly offered to the market by extremely experienced European producers – experienced in the tradition of this production method. The result is short filler of high quality that promise unmitigated smoking pleasure.

"A cigar numbs sorrow and fills the solitary hours with a million gracious images."

George Sand – in reality, Aurore Dupin, French author and early feminist

The "Dutch type" designation of such cigars points out that Dutch cigar manufacturers have always been regarded as being among the leading producers in Europe, and that many developments from the land of tulips and windmills have positively affected the European cigar world.

Short Filler

Firstly, let us emphasize this: no short filler bears the label "Premium Brand". But we should add at once that there are numerous short filler, whose composition and production is significantly better than that

of many a long filler claiming for itself the above seal of quality.

If the tobacco used is of good quality, then a short-leaf cigar can provide a pleasant smoking experience, as long as it has been made in a satisfactory manner. If, in addition, the advantage of a short filler over a long filler is properly exploited, then nothing can stand in the way of the smoking pleasure that, for instance, a Brasil of European character can provide. To speak, in this case, of a premium cigar is really not as absurd as it may seem.

The advantage lies in the wider combination and composition possibilities provided by the many small tobacco pieces of a short filler, compared to the few leaves from which a long filler is formed.

Medium Filler

Table scrapes are typically used for cigars bearing the designation "medium filler". These are the clippings left over from the production of long filler, firstly after cutting the wrapper leaf to the right size, and secondly when the cigar is cut to the specified format length after rolling.

In contrast to a short filler, the tobacco is not chopped up into small pieces, but merely picked or plucked; creating tobacco strips of about 3 to 5 centimetres.

Tobacco leaves also used in long filler production are then added to provide the filler with better stability. The *torcedor* first makes the bunch from the filler and binder leaf with the help of a rolling aid, before finally rolling the wrapper leaf over the bunch by hand.

The leftovers mentioned above are therefore in no way of inferior quality but, in fact, the same tobacco specified for producing long filler. The use of this tobacco – which was originally used instead for short filler (at a relatively cheap price) – keeps medium fillers significantly less expensive than long filler cigars. That in turn is good news for cigar smokers who do not always have thick wallets at their disposal.

Following the start made by Davidoff roughly a decade ago with its Private Stock Medium Filler, more and more brands and series are now available as Medium Filler.

Long Filler

"Long filler" designates cigars made exclusively from long or whole tobacco leaves and (usually) rolled by hand. There are, indeed, long filler made by machine, but those cigars are the proverbial exception that proves every rule.

Another "rule" is that a hand-made long filler usually consists of five leaves. Three comprise the filler, or *tripa*, to which is added the binder leaf, or *capote*, and the wrapper leaf, or *capa*, the final crowning glory (we hope) of a cigar.

Good burning and draw properties characterise any long filler that justifiably bears the title "Premium

Cigar" – the key to which is the successful combination of the individual tobacco elements and their composition.

This job is assigned to the *ligador*, who carries a far greater responsibility than the generally better known *torcedor*, for even the best cigar roller cannot produce a satisfactory product if the mixture is wrong.

Tobacco leaves loose their excess moisture on drying racks following the second fermentation.

Havana

La Habana, capital of the República de Cuba as well as of the province bearing the same name (the city province known as Ciudad de la Habana), possesses a natural harbour in a bay in the Gulf of Mexico, stretches over 727 square kilometres, and comprises a little over 2 million inhabitants.

These few bald facts hardly do justice to a city whose name is synonymous with colour and glamour. Close by the modern residential areas, Old Havana blooms with colourful colonial buildings – including the *fábricas* – that line cobbled and brick-paved streets bustling with friendly, funloving people. Havana's historic life of art and music still burgeons alongside an inexhaustible nightlife, replete with with cinemas, historic theatres, cabarets, nightclubs and music venues to suit every mood and taste. And after all that activity, Havana's glorious beaches are perfect for relaxing in the shade of a palm tree while you enjoy a fine cigar.

San Cristóbal de La Habana – even the name of Cuba's capital brings the shimmering hustle and bustle of the city to life. Here resounds the music of

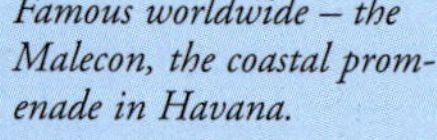

Famous worldwide – the Malecon, the coastal promenade in Havana.

the Salsa, the dance that combines elements of Afro-Cuban jazz, the Mexican Ranchera, the Rumba, and the Bossa Nova as well as Latin-American rock and Puerto Rican Jibaro music – which in turn have their roots in the popular Cuban dance music of the 1930s and 1940s.

Memories of that time are awakened: a time when the city drew numerous adventurers, rakes, potentates, gamblers and pleasure seekers like a magnet. The United States was not far away, and what was forbidden in Miami was not so in Havana – and when it was, it could be made legal by a bundle of dollar bills. The city was full to overflowing with bars and brothels, cafés and casinos, saloons and dance halls, and the patriarchal colonial buildings provided an incongruous backdrop to the hustle and bustle of the streets, alleyways and backyards.

Whoever thought themselves important – and there were many such – flaunted their wealth by being seen, for example, with a young Cuban girl on their arm, a bottle of liquor on the table, and a Havana protruding from the corner of the mouth.

Yes, the Havana had by this time long become a symbol of wealth and power. Anyone who could afford it, smoked one Havana after another to show the world that he had "made it". As a symbol of a refined savoir-vivre, the Havana also moved in "better circles", whether those circles consisted of bankers or industrialists, generals or ministers, notables, dignitaries, sculptors, composers, painters, musicians or authors.

Everything had begun about one and a half centuries earlier. It was in 1810 when production of cigars first began on North American soil, in Hartford,

"I always hold Cuba in my mouth."

Winston Churchill, English politician and author

Connecticut. That same year, a certain Bernardino Rencurrel appeared at the office for registering trade marks in Havana to register his name – which was also to be the name of his product – a cigar. The first Havana brand was born.

How many cigars Señor Rencurrel ever produced in his capacity as tobacco planter and cigar manufacturer, and for how long he sold the cigars that bore his name, tradition does not relate.

However, another cigar manufacturer who registered his cigars as a brand name that same year was, by contrast, very successful. His brand belonged to the best and most well-known Havanas to be had on the

market far into the 20th century – it was only Cas-tro's decision to produce (with the Siboney) a single cigar series in only four formats, which brought about the (temporary) end of the brand. Its name? – Cabañas y Carbajal. That name was missing from the list of long-established Havana brands that were reinstated when the *Máximo Líder* later corrected his mistake. The name has, in the meantime, been changed. Cabañas are now available in six (machine produced) formats.

At this time, that is, around 1810, there were already quite a few cigar manufacturers in Cuba, and esp-ecially around Havana, but Señores Rencurrel and Cabañas were the first to have their cigars registered

In the heart of the Vuelta Abajo: mist rises in a valley near Pinar del Río.

as a brand. The H. de Cabañas y Carbajal, to give it its full title, was also the eponym of the *fábrica* in which it was manufactured. An entry from this date can be found in the register of companies, recording a permit for a factory with an adjoining shop.

In this entry from 1810 – truly an historic year – can be read among other things, that, "Francisco Cabañas, born in Havana, bachelor, has opened a shop in the Jesus del Monte Avenida, which had previously been sited in the Calle Jesús María."

The next entry regarding a cigar in Havana's trade mark register was made more than 20 years later. Por Larrañaga was registered in 1834, and is the second oldest Havana brand still in production.

Further entries then followed at ever shorter intervals. Of the many brands registered, only the following have survived to the present: Ramón Allones (1837), Punch (1840), H. Upmann (1844), El Rey del Mundo (1848), Romeo y Julieta (1850) and Hoyo de Monterrey (1865).

The Cuban cigar industry experienced a boom at this time for several reasons. From about the middle of the 17th century, most of the raw tobacco from Cuba was shipped to Spain, where it was mainly processed in Seville.

About a hundred years later, tobacco cultivation in Cuba had improved so much that the descendents of the first Spanish colonists were now making cigars themselves. At that point, just after the middle of the 18th century, the cigar makers in Seville's Royal Cigar Factory discovered on receipt of some shipment that although the leaves from Cuba had survived the sea journey in their usual way, the

superlative quality of the ready-made cigars from Havana – of which a few had arrived on the same ship – exceeded anything they could make, and they were increasingly dissatisfied with the second rate.

As a result, cigar production in Spain gradually declined while a commensurate expansion took place in Cuba. The final demise of Spanish manufacturing came at the turn of the century.

In the following period, many Spaniards with a command of the art of cigar production turned their backs on their homeland and settled in Cuba to continue doing that which they do better than almost anyone else – making cigars.

However, the actual upsurge in Havana production that took place in the 19th century is primarily due to a decree by King Ferdinand VII of Spain that came into force in 1821. In this decree he granted the island, then still under Spanish rule, the right to trade freely. When, around the middle of the 19th century, the production technology in the *fábricas* was greatly improved – thereby continually increasing the quality of the cigars produced – a real Havana boom began.

One "stone witness" of this first great flowering played a part in shaping the upsurge, survived the temporary decline of the Havana, and today is again a pillar of Cuban cigar production.

This is the factory founded by Jaime Partagás that began working in 1845 (some sources mention 1827, others 1845) and has been producing Partagás ever since – a Havana that can look back on a long history, and which has always belonged to the figureheads of Cuban cigar manufacturing.

The full company title is Flor de Tabacos de Partagás y Compañía, to which the designation Fábrica de Cigarros Puros is added. The inscription Real Fábrica de Tabacos, to be seen, today as in the past, in oversized letters on the façade of the building – which remains a symbol of the Havana's chequered history – gives an idea of the pride the owner Don Jaime must have felt as the factory in the Calle de la Industria No. 520 on the outskirts of the city first opened its gates.

Today, the factory bears the name Francisco Pérez Germán – one of the repercussions of the Cuban Revolution, an event that has caused so many changes in the business sector of the tobacco and sugar cane island.

The new name is in memory of a Cuban freedom fighter, as are the names of the other five factories in Havana where cigars are produced for export.

Thus, the former El Rey del Mundo factory today bears the name Carlos Baliño, the Company logotype H. Upmann has been replaced by José Martí, the José L. Piedra factory has been transformed into the Héroes del Moncada factory, the production plant previously known as La Corona now operates under the name of Miguel Fernández Riog, while one of the most renowned early factories is no longer known as Romeo y Julieta but rather Briones Montoto. Only the El Laguito production plant has not

been renamed after a Cuban hero; however, its founding coincided with the beginning of Cohiba production.

A die-hard Havana enthusiast may well distain to speak the new trading names of these time-honoured factories. The previous titles belong, as in the past, to the parlance of almost all *aficionados,* and this book is no exception. When Havana's cigar factories – which are listed, incidentally, on UNESCO's World Heritage List, and are mostly found in the old part of the city – are mentioned, they will always be called by their historic names.

Two legends during the Festival del Habano, the annual cigar festival – Fidel Castro announcing the auction of Compay Segundo's hat. The singer became famous worldwide through the Wim-Wenders film Buena Vista Social Club.

The abbreviations of the individual cigar factories were, until a few years ago, added to the Havana boxes containing Cuba's gold, as part of a code that not only gave the name of the relevant production plant, but also made it possible to decipher the month in which the cigars had been packed. That has now been changed – only the month data remains from the old code.

But information regarding the month is not the only characteristic that a Havana box displays. Three embossed stamps can also be found on the box's underside.

Habanos S.A. stands for the Cuban state organisation mainly responsible for marketing and export. By the way, boxes bearing the stamp *Cubatabaco* are pre-1994, since it was the duty of this state body to foster and represent the interests of Cuban tobacco until then.

By contrast, the *Hecho en Cuba* stamp, denoting in large letters the land of origin, has been in existence since 1960, when it too replaced a previous stamp. Before Castro seized power, the English text "Made in Cuba" bore witness to the dependency of the tobacco and sugar cane island on the United States – not exactly one of the *Máximo Líder's* favourite countries, as is well known.

In 1989, the Cubans were forced to add the third stamp, *totalmente a mano,* to the underside of every box of Havanas. The European Union's Agricultural Commission had earlier decreed in its all too well-known regulatory zeal that cigars made only partly by hand could be called "hand made", thereby making the term "hand rolled" – which made plain that the wrapper alone had been rolled by hand around a

machine-made bunch – practically redundant. With this decision, Brussels's bureaucrats remained true to their policy of the lowest common denominator; and again did a great disservice to the quality demands many producers in this area of business make of their products.

These stamps and imprints are accompanied by two labels, rounding off the state's catalogue of information and intended to document the authenticity of the product.

Firstly, there is the guarantee seal of the Cuban government, first used in 1912 and resembling a United States dollar bill, and secondly there is the *Habanos* label – which means nothing more than "Havanas" – which is embellished with the depiction of a stylised tobacco leaf and, fixed to one of the two upper corners of the lid, has graced every box of Havanas since 1994.

Further insignia of Cuban lithographic art can be found on a Havana box, supplementing the state and semi-official quality and guarantee seals documented by these stamps, imprints and labels. On seeing a Havana box, the eye is first struck by the *cubierta*, the signet illustration of the producer or brand that adorns the centre of the lid.

Purely practical in nature, but no less stunningly colourful, are the long narrow strips of paper called *filetes* that rise up over the edges and corners of the box to seal them and preserve the aroma of the contents. The *tapaclavo* is the label (oval or rectangular) fixed over the nail or clasp, usually displaying a reference to the production company, which also serves as a seal.

Apart from other labels, there are two more large decorations inside the box that should be mentioned. The one is the *vista*, fixed to the inside of the

lid, while the other is the *bofetón* printed on the top paper that, with the bottom paper, envelopes and protects the Havanas, and which must first be lifted and folded over at the front before a cigar can be removed.

Both illustrations tend to be extremely colourful lithographs, often of a nostalgic romantic nature, illustrating special events in the brand's history. Only the cigar ring *(anillo),* which makes each cigar distinctive, remains to be discussed.

"If I cannot smoke in heaven, then I shall not go."

Mark Twain, American author

Havana Formats

There are significantly more Havana formats than those in common international use – and yet they are limited. This contradiction is easily explained.

Although there are only twenty formats listed in the table of non-Cuban formats on pages 102 and 103, almost every factory producing cigars uses the measurement for each format that it considers appropriate for each cigar. This gives rise, inevitably, to a multitude of formats within each size limit referred to in the tables. One example will make this clear.

The classical measurements of the Panatella format are a length of 6 inches and a ring gauge of 38. The metric length measurement is 152 millimetres.

Now, a cigar is also considered a Panatella when its length lies between 5 1/2 and 7 inches, that is between 140 and 177 millimetres, while the ring gauge may vary between 35 and 39.

This means (if we consider for simplicity's sake only millimetres) that it would be quite possible to find a cigar for every millimetre from 140 to 177 – which results in 38 Panatellas of different length. If this is multiplied by the permissible number of ring gauges (that is 5), then there could feasibly be 190 format variations of the Panatella alone.

As no cigar producer outside Cuba is bound by ring gauge specifications. For example, the diameter of a non-Cuban Panatella may measure precisely 13.7 millimetres and thus lie right between ring gauges 34 and 35 – the total number of possible variations in format lies considerably higher. If the other formats are now drawn into the equation, not forgetting the *figurados* – the potential number of variations easily becomes inconceivable.

The Cubans make it somewhat easier. There are about 85 Havana formats, and they are all specified to the millimetre. At the same time, a distinction is made between hand-made formats – and whether the subject is a long filler or short filler – and machine produced ones.

That 85 does not refer to the names under which the various formats are offered for sale (Cohiba Lanceros, for example), but to the production name (*vitola de galera*) – and that is the same in all *fábricas* in which Havanas are manufactured.

In practice, Cuban formats show a similarly annoying overlap. For example, it is quite possible to find the text, "25 Petit Coronas" in addition to the brand name on a box of Havanas.

This tells us, basically, that the producing company has given its cigars the commercial title (*vitola de salida*), Petit Corona. Unfortunately, this title can also cover several *vitolas de galera*, such as the (hand-made) Mareva format, in addition to the Petit Corona. Thus, this particular *vitola de galera* might be made entirely by hand or entirely by machine (*mecanizado*).

So it makes sense to pay attention to the stamps on the underside of the box. *"Totalmente a mano"* denotes hand-made long filler, while hand-made short filler is designated "TC" (*Tripa Corta*), and short filler produced by machine makes do with a simple *"Hecho en Cuba"*.

To help differentiate those *vitolas de galera* made by hand from those made by machine, the table on pages 83 to 86 lists them separately. It also distinguishes between long and short filler.

A further distinguishing characteristic is the weight of each type of cigar. This book does not cover that aspect. This is partly because too much information can be confusing, and partly because Caribbean cigars, in particular, are liable to change in weight fractionally, depending on how they are stored.

In any case, what *aficionado* would really take along a weighing machine capable of registering a hundredth of a gram when going to buy cigars? To be reasonably sure of acquiring a Havana that meets the established requirements it is enough to know what the format details mean, and to get one's bearings from the *vitolas de galera* rather than the *vitola de salida*.

Havana Formats: Long Filler Made by Hand
Totalmente a mano – Tripa Larga

Production Name	Length in Inches	(mm)	Ring gauge and Diameter		Frequency
Gran Corona	≈ 9 1/4	(235)	47	(≈ 18.7 mm)	seldom
Prominente	≈ 7 5/8	(194)	49	(≈ 19.5 mm)	often
Trinidad No. 1	≈ 7 1/2	(192)	40	(≈ 15.9 mm)	very seldom
Delicado	≈ 7 1/2	(192)	38	(≈ 15.1 mm)	seldom
Laguito No. 1	≈ 7 1/2	(192)	38	(≈ 15.1 mm)	less often
Delicado Extra	≈ 7 1/4	(185)	36	(≈ 14.3 mm)	very seldom
Paco	≈ 7 1/8	(180)	49	(≈ 19.5 mm)	very seldom
Julieta No. 2	≈ 7	(178)	47	(≈ 18.7 mm)	very often

Production Name	Length in Inches	(mm)	Ring gauge and Diameter		Frequency
Ninfa	≈ 17	(178)	33	(≈ 13.1 mm)	very seldom
Panetela Larga	≈ 6 7/8	(175)	28	(≈ 11.1 mm)	seldom
Dalia	≈ 6 3/4	(170)	43	(≈ 17.1 mm)	less often
Palma	≈ 6 3/4	(170)	33	(≈ 13.1 mm)	very seldom
Parejo	≈ 6 1/2	(166)	38	(≈ 15.1 mm)	very seldom
Cervante	≈ 6 1/2	(165)	42	(≈ 16.7 mm)	often
Cazador	≈ 6 3/8	(162)	43	(≈ 17.1 mm)	seldom
Delicioso	≈ 6 1/4	(159)	33	(≈ 13.1 mm)	very seldom
Taco (F)*	≈ 6 1/4	(158)	47	(≈ 18.7 mm)	very seldom
Pirámide (F)	≈ 6 1/8	(156)	52	(≈ 20.6 mm)	less often
Corona Grande	≈ 6 1/8	(155)	42	(≈ 16.7 mm)	often
Laguito No. 2	≈ 6	(152)	38	(≈ 15.1 mm)	less often
Palmita	≈ 6	(152)	32	(≈ 12.7 mm)	very seldom
Coñonazo	≈ 5 7/8	(150)	52	(≈ 20.6 mm)	very seldom
Exquisito (F)	≈ 5 3/4	(145)	46	(≈ 18.3 mm)	very seldom
Conserva	≈ 5 3/4	(145)	43	(≈ 17.1 mm)	very seldom
Corona Gorda	≈ 5 5/8	(143)	46	(≈ 18.3 mm)	often
Francisco	≈ 5 5/8	(143)	44	(≈ 17.5 mm)	very seldom
Carlota	≈ 5 5/8	(143)	35	(≈ 13.9 mm)	very seldom
Corona	≈ 5 5/8	(142)	42	(≈ 16.7 mm)	very often
Campana (F)	≈ 5 1/2	(140)	52	(≈ 20.6 mm)	less often
Gordito	≈ 5 1/2	(140)	50	(≈ 19.8 mm)	very seldom
Crema	≈ 5 1/2	(140)	40	(≈ 15.9 mm)	less often
Cosaco	≈ 5 3/8	(135)	42	(≈ 16.7 mm)	very seldom
Eminente	≈ 5 1/4	(132)	42	(≈ 16.7 mm)	seldom
Generoso (F)	≈ 5 1/5	(132)	42	(≈ 16.7 mm)	seldom
Almuerzo	≈ 5 1/8	(130)	40	(≈ 15.9 mm)	very seldom
Mareva	≈ 5 1/8	(129)	42	(≈ 16.7 mm)	very often
Petit Corona	≈ 5 1/8	(129)	42	(≈ 16.7 mm)	often
Petit Cetro	≈ 5 1/8	(129)	40	(≈ 15.9 mm)	seldom
Hermoso No. 4	≈ 5	(127)	48	(≈ 19.1 mm)	often
Conchita	≈ 5	(127)	35	(≈ 13.9 mm)	very seldom
Londres	≈ 5	(126)	40	(≈ 15.9 mm)	very seldom
Seoane	≈ 5	(126)	33	(≈ 13.1 mm)	seldom
Belvedere	≈ 5	(125)	39	(≈ 15.5 mm)	seldom

Production Name	Length in Inches	(mm)	Ring gauge and Diameter		Frequency
Placera	≈ 5	(125)	34	(≈ 13.5 mm)	seldom
Robusto	≈ 4 7/8	(124)	50	(≈ 19.8 mm)	often
Carolina	≈ 4 3/4	(121)	26	(≈ 10.3 mm)	very seldom
Favorito (F)	≈ 4 3/4	(120)	42	(≈ 16.7 mm)	very seldom
Coronita	≈ 4 5/8	(117)	40	(≈ 15.9 mm)	less often
Sport	≈ 4 5/8	(117)	35	(≈ 13.9 mm)	very seldom
Panetela	≈ 4 5/8	(117)	34	(≈ 13.5 mm)	very seldom
Franciscano	≈ 4 5/8	(116)	40	(≈ 15.9 mm)	less often
Cadete	≈ 4 1/2	(115)	36	(≈ 14.3 mm)	seldom
Laguito No. 3	≈ 4 1/2	(115)	26	(≈ 10.3 mm)	less often
Minuto	≈ 4 3/8	(110)	42	(≈ 16.7 mm)	less often
Trabuco	≈ 4 3/8	(110)	38	(≈ 15.1 mm)	very seldom
Epicure	≈ 4 3/8	(110)	35	(≈ 13.9 mm)	very seldom
Petit Bouquet (F)	≈ 4	(101)	43	(≈ 17.1 mm)	very seldom
Perla	≈ 4	(102)	40	(≈ 15.9 mm)	often
Entreacto	≈ 4	(100)	30	(≈ 11.9 mm)	less often

* F = Figurado

Havana Formats: Short Filler Made by Hand
Totalmente a mano – Tripa Corta (TC)

Production Name	Length in Inches	(mm)	Ring gauge and Diameter		Frequency
Cazador TC	≈ 6	(152)	43	(≈ 17.1 mm)	very seldom
Cristales Mano	≈ 5 7/8	(150)	41	(≈ 16.3 mm)	very seldom
Conserva TC	≈ 5 1/2	(140)	44	(≈ 17.5 mm)	very seldom
Nacionales Mano	≈ 5 1/2	(140)	40	(≈ 15.9 mm)	very seldom
Crema TC	≈ 5 3/8	(136)	40	(≈ 15.9 mm)	very seldom
Nacionales	≈ 5 1/4	(134)	42	(≈ 16.7 mm)	very seldom
Breva	≈ 5 1/4	(133)	42	(≈ 16.7 mm)	very seldom
Petit Cetro TC	≈ 5	(127)	38	(≈ 15.1 mm)	very seldom
Veguerito Mano	≈ 5	(127)	37	(≈ 14.7 mm)	less often
Standard Mano	≈ 4 7/8	(123)	40	(≈ 15.9 mm)	less often

Havana Formats: Short Filler Made by Machine
Mecanizados (M)

Production Name	Length in Inches	(mm)	Ring gauge and Diameter		Frequency
Cristales M	≈ 5 7/8	(150)	41	(≈ 16.3 mm)	very seldom
Culebra (F)	≈ 5 3/4	(146)	39	(≈ 15.5 mm)	very seldom
Nacionales M	≈ 5 1/2	(140)	40	(≈ 15.9 mm)	very seldom
Universales	≈ 5 1/4	(134)	38	(≈ 15.1 mm)	seldom
Petit Corona M	≈ 5 1/8	(129)	42	(≈ 16.7 mm)	very seldom
Perfecto (F)	≈ 5	(127)	44	(≈ 17.5 mm)	very seldom
Veguerito M	≈ 5	(127)	36	(≈ 14.3 mm)	very seldom
Belvedere M (F)	≈ 5	(125)	39	(≈ 15.5 mm)	often
Standard	≈ 4 7/8	(123)	40	(≈ 15.9 mm)	often
Coronita M	≈ 4 5/8	(117)	40	(≈ 15.9 mm)	seldom
Sports	≈ 4 5/8	(117)	35	(≈ 13.9 mm)	very seldom
Epicure M	≈ 4 3/8	(110)	35	(≈ 13.9 mm)	very seldom
Petit	≈ 4 1/4	(108)	31	(≈ 12.3 mm)	very seldom
Chico	≈ 4 1/8	(106)	29	(≈ 11.5 mm)	often
Demi Tasse	≈ 4	(100)	32	(≈ 12.7 mm)	seldom
Infante (F)	≈ 3 7/8	(98)	37	(≈ 14.7 mm)	very seldom

Clear Havana

"Pure" Havanas, that is, cigars made exclusively from Cuban tobaccos, are produced today as they always have been; however, "Clear" Havanas are no longer manufactured. This term was used for cigars made, from the end of the 19th century, by Cuban exiles in Florida.

During this period of bad economic and uncertain political conditions on the tobacco and sugar cane island – the 1895 Cuban insurrection against the descendents of the *Conquistadores* led, in 1898, to war between Spain and the United States – many cigar manufacturers left their homeland and settled mainly in the area in and around Key West and Tampa, but also in Ybor City.

In this last community, now a part of West-Tampa but then located beyond the city boundary, hardly a month went by without a new Cigar manufacturer opening for business. By the end of the 19th century there were more than 500 such companies in these three communities and their surrounding area. In respect to cigar production, Florida had become a second Cuba, with Ybor City as its capital.

The town was founded in 1885 by Vincente Martinez Ybor, a Cuban exile. In view of this background, it is no wonder that the Ybor City of the time could boast the greatest concentration of cigar factories in the world, employing more cigar rollers per acre even than the manufacturers of Havana.

Clear Havanas experienced a second boom after the Castro revolution when many cigar manufacturers left the island state for Florida, where they continued the occupation they had pursued in their homeland.

At the time, the cigar manufacturers of this, the most south eastern state, were ordering almost every bale of Cuban tobacco available, as there was already talk of an imminent US embargo against Cuba.

As a result, the US cigar factory warehouses, especially those in Florida, were full to overflowing with bales of Cuban tobacco when the embargo finally came into force.

However, every reserve is sooner or later exhausted. Thus, to all intents and purposes, no Clear Havanas are produced any more.

Non-Cuban Caribbean

This is the term for all cigars originating from the Greater Caribbean Area, but not produced in Cuba.

The area includes not only the countries which lie in the Caribbean itself, such as the Dominican Republic and Jamaica, but also those that belong to the mainland, such as Honduras, Mexico and Nicaragua. However, other areas, such as Brazil, are excluded.

The United States is also excluded, although the coast of Florida – the US's most southerly state and home to a considerable number of cigar factories – is indeed subjected to the tides of the Caribbean.

Forgeries

Yes, there are imitations, designed primarily to be palmed off as Havana forgeries on a trusting *aficionado* for the price of genuine ones.

An experienced forger can easily produce deceptively good counterfeits of all the distinguishing characteristics to be found on a Havana box, such as labels, seals and stamps, that confirm it to be the container of genuine Havanas.

Although Habanos S.A. specialists have the requisite skills, based on over 150 distinguishing criteria, to differentiate between genuine goods and imitations (for example, by subjecting the positioning and printing of cigar rings and stamps, or the colour and consistency of wrapper leaves to close scrutiny), most of these quality criteria are missing from a cigar enthusiast's general knowledge.

The enthusiast should, however, pay special attention to several useful distinguishing marks. Whereas, the even, smooth varnish of a box of genuine *Habanos*

catches the eye, the varnish on a counterfeit box is often uneven; in addition, Habanos S.A. uses exclusively brass hinges and clasps, which is not always the case with imitations; and while genuine imprints are relatively clear thanks to a special procedure, those of forgeries are often blurred.

Furthermore the *escogedores* of Habanos S.A. – that is, those *tabacaleros* who sort the rolled cigars according to the nuances in colour of the wrapper leaves – lay the cigars in the boxes according to a strict principle, by which, the lightest in colour is always placed at the far right, then the next light, and so on until the darkest is to be found on the far left.

Forgeries, on the other hand, are often sorted in an irregular fashion. Finally, the cigar rings of genuine *Habanos* are all located at the same level and are practically immovable, whereas the *anillos* of forged cigars are usually quite loose and are seldom in line.

In addition, all cigars legally imported into England have a colourful Hunters and Frankau English Market Section (EMS) sticker applied to the top left corner of the box. The stamps are printed on glossy stock with a watermark design, a gold foil lion crest, and a serial number. The colour of the stamp changes every year. Boxes from Gibraltar have a small green Hunters and Frankau stamp, in which the letters H&F replace the EMS and the lion crest is replaced with the text, "imported directly from Cuba".

Even if a box of Havanas does not display either of these guarantee seals, it may still be genuine; for example when imported from another European Union country, such as Spain, Holland, Germany, or even from Australia. This sets the seal on the whole confusing affair. For this reason, the appropriate advice of this book and of others is that the best guarantee is a reliable cigar dealer.

If one disregards the case of Havana forgeries, the *aficionado* of Central and Western Europe really has little cause for concern.

The final phase of cigar production – attaching the cigar ring and packing the finished product in a cabinet box.

For one thing, it is only worth forging high priced cigars. No one would bother to counterfeit a 1-pound, 2-euro or 3-franc cigar, since the expected gain fails to justify the effort involved. With few exceptions, therefore, forgers tend to concentrate on the Havanas and the Davidoffs.

For another, as a result of the embargo against Cuba coupled with the strong demand for premium cigars, by far the most fakes are to be found in the USA, where the eyes of almost every *aficionado* mist over at the sight of a box of Havana cigars for sale – despite the fact that they are illegal.

Furthermore, besides tobacco growing, there also thrives a black market in cigars in Cuba, promising the forger a considerable profit – and that in the US dollars that most tourists are more ready to part with on holiday than their pounds, francs and euros at home. When the cigar-smoking tourist buys a box of Havanas and then falls back on the contents to smoke during his stay (so as not to have to smuggle them through customs) he or she is usually disappointed.

The explanation is obvious. Only about 10% of all cigars available illegally are stolen originals. The rest have been produced in a back yard somewhere from any old junk tobacco. Cigars of this dubious quality are also mostly available in the United States.

The situation in Europe is by no means so worrying. Here, the cigar enthusiast is most unlikely to encounter any reputable dealer who would pass off an apparently genuine box of Havanas filled entirely with imitations. It is usually tourists, flight personnel and diplomats who bring these with them in their baggage, and then turn to the trade to try to dispose of their "hot" goods. No reputable cigar dealer would ever get involved with such a deal, for an *aficionado* values a Havana highly (and, with time, can also evaluate it).

Yet even in Europe, an *aficionado* can become a victim of forgery – it can happen when a friend, on returning from a Caribbean holiday, cheerfully presents him with a box of "genuine" Havanas as a present.

We repeat, therefore, that the best guarantee when purchasing cigars is a well-established, reputable tobacconist, wholly intent on justifying his good name.

The point bears repeating – good advice and guidance from trained personnel is highly recommended when buying cigars.

Formats

The above title should actually read "Common International Formats", since that is the subject of this section. Although the tables on pages 102 and 103 only list 20 such formats each, this is (almost) sufficient to cover the entire spectrum of formats available worldwide.

Let us start by explaining that the *figurados* are not included in these tables, as that would entail considering too many peculiarities regarding ring gauge and length.

For instance, a cigar that is known for its pyramid format, might have a ring gauge 36 at its head (or even a size 40), while the burning end may be a size 50 (or may even reach a magnificent 54). The same is true for the cigar's length. Although one of 5 inches, that is 127 millimetres, would make little sense, since it would not be long enough to allow the body to develop, lengths of between 6 1/2 and 7 1/2 inches (165–191 mm) are often encountered.

The same is true for the torpedo. Here the measurement of thickest section might amount to ring gauge 44, but it could also reach a size 54, while a length of 6 inches (152 mm) is just as conceivable as one of 7 inches (178 mm).

The tables are intended as approximate guides only, because where format specifications are concerned there are significant exceptions (the idea of a jungle would be quite appropriate in this context).

If an *aficionado* has quickly grasped that format terms such as "Diplomat" or "Minister" are merely *vitola de salidas*, that is, trade names, then "Corona" can just

as well be a trade name as production name. The latter (the *vitola de galera*) makes it a little easier for the
aficionado to negotiate the undergrowth of format
terminology.

A "Lonsdale" offered under this name, does not, by
any means, have to correspond to the internationally
common format for a Lonsdale. Even the conceivable
information "25 Coronas", featured on a cigar box as
the product name below the trade name, is no guarantee that the format is identical to the common
international one. Should the cigar concerned be
about 6 inches long while displaying a ring gauge of
42, then it is neither a corona nor a Lonsdale, but
rather a Long Corona. Any questions?

The tables will, however, certainly help to minimise
recurrent irritations. They should particularly serve
to provide those interested with appropriate advice
for identifying their preferred format.

The Right Cigar for the Right Moment

*The great cigar connoisseur, Zino Davidoff, always recommended certain formats
for the following situations and occasions, bearing in mind the length of time
available …*

Cigarillo, Panatella: for the quarter-hour coffee break
Petit Corona, Corona: for free time at midday lunch
Gran Corona: for an hour-long leisurely stroll
Double Corona: to crown an evening meal
Giant Double Corona: exceptional, for that special moment

A cigar intended for smoking during a tea or coffee break should certainly not have the Churchill format and even a Long Panatella may be out of place, while a Small Panatella or a not–too-long Short Panatella could be ideal in this case.

The tables do not include the Havana formats either – those are dealt with separately (see pages 83 to 86). Instead, these tables cover cigars of non-Cuban origin.

The inch measurements are restricted to quarters and halves to prevent an already dense jungle becoming even thicker. The measurements are in both inches and millimetres, for the simple reason that many overseas manufactures work either exclusively in inches or generally in millimetres.

Slight discrepancies that arise in the conversion of the one unit of measurement into the other are a result of the conversion process.

Such discrepancies are solely in the order of tenths or hundredths of millimetres. Again, this makes things more manageable, for the main object is to provide the reader with as many landmarks as possible for navigating the format jungle.

The following is a description of the best-known and commonest formats, i.e. *vitolas,* often requested by *aficionados.*

Churchill. This eminent British statesman's name is ubiquitous in the cigar world, especially where one of the really large formats is concerned. For many *connoisseurs,* a Churchill is exactly the right format for a quiet evening's reflection on the day's activities accompanied by a really large-sized cigar – in any case, it is ideal for an extended smoke.

Corona. "Corona" means "crown" in translation, and many cigar enthusiasts are convinced that this format justifiably bears the name due to its ideal size. For it possesses sufficient length, in combination with a respectable ring gauge, to allow the aromas of a cigar to develop fully. This provides a smoking pleasure which, although it may not last for hours, nevertheless meets the requirements of a good smoke.

When choosing a format, the same is definitely true as when choosing a cigar brand. It is a matter for the individual *aficionado* to discover his preferred format for himself. Nonetheless, the Corona belongs among the classical cigar formats and is still one of the most common.

Culebra. This is indeed the rarest format of all, but should under no account be left out this list due to its unusual form.

Culebra is the Spanish word for snake, and this format looks the way three writhing grass snakes usually appear – twisted together and bound by ribbons to form a unit. Although there is a very wide variety of *figurados* available, the Culebra is without a doubt the most interesting (handrolled) format of this extraordinary species.

This format has a particularly long tradition. Towards the middle of the 19th century, the *torcedores* in Spanish factories were instructed to roll their daily personal ration of cigars in this way. The set of three corresponded to the daily ration. This was done to make it more difficult for the cigar roller to resell his ration and thus prevent the resulting reduction in receipts for the tax authorities. Such measures are no longer taken, but the art of rolling cigars in this format has survived over the decades.

As mentioned above, this format is typified by three small-bundle Culebras twisted together. Each cigar practically twists around its own axis.

Partagás is the only brand in Cuba to include this particular small bundle in its portfolio. But the *torcedores* of this time-honoured *fábrica* appear to have lost this aspect of the high art of rolling *figurados;* for the Culebras of Partagás – 5 3/4 inches (about 146 mm) in length with a ring gauge of 39 (about 15.5 mm) – are produced by machine.

Several cigar rollers in the Dominican Republic, however, have indeed mastered the art of this format. At any rate, Davidoff resurrected this cigar form in the middle of 1997, and includes it in its range under the trade name, Special C (where the "C" clearly refers to "Culebra"). It should, however, be noted that it differs from its Cuban counterpart in size. Every Special C has a respectable length of 165 millimetres and a diameter of 13.1 millimetres.

Double Corona. Any smoker unwilling to settle for a Churchill is best served by this common international format, which is about 20 millimetres longer and also boasts a somewhat larger ring gauge (49 to 47).

Gran Corona and **Grand Corona.** The "Great Crown" (Gran Corona) really does have an impressive size – this Havana format enjoys the stately length of 9 1/4 inches (about 235 mm) and a ring gauge of 47 (about 18.7 mm). As a cigar of this calibre is not everyone's cup of tea, the Gran Corona format is not much in demand, so this *vitola* is only to be found in two Havana brand ranges – Montecristo and Sancho Panza.

The Gran Corona format is extraordinary in every way; it corresponds neither to the Giant (for it displays a considerably smaller ring gauge) nor to the Churchill (for it is considerably longer). In fact, it is the longest of all Havana formats. Despite the similarity in name, it should by no means be confused with the standard international Grand Corona format – which may have the same ring gauge but is considerably shorter than the Gran Corona.

Lonsdale. The specifications for this classical format – length: 6 1/2 inches (about 165 mm), ring gauge: 42 – were the result of the Earl of Lonsdale habitually ordering the brand, Flor de Rafeal González, in large containers during the 1830s. The required format did not exist at the time – but the customer's wish was naturally the supplier's command. Thus, this format owes its being to the amiable eccentricity of a British aristocrat, who could not be dissuaded from smoking only cigars of the format he had invented bearing cigar rings with his image – for him a matter of course.

The Lonsdale is the cigar format par excellence for many cigar smokers. Although it shares the same ring gauge as the Corona, its significantly longer length lends it a far more elegant appearance.

Panatela. Irrespective of whether it is called a "Panatela" or "Panatella", "Panetela" or "Panetella", the meaning is the same. This format seems custom-made for the elegant hand of a lady, with its narrow ring gauge and its respectable length. On the grounds that hands are usually slightly more slender in the morning as a result of sleep than in the late evening, many dyed-in-the-wool *aficionados* reach for a Panatella in the morning – at all events, this is the preferred format for their daily breakfast cigar.

Of course, there is nothing to confirm a connection between early morning, slender hands and a slim cigar, but it is quite conceivable …

Petit Corona. Although often bearing the same ring gauge, the Petit Corona – known as Half Corona – is considerably shorter than its big sister, the Corona, and is therefore ideally suited for a short smoke (for example during the lunch break). It is precisely because it is so very versatile that the Petit Corona is one of the most common formats.

Pyramid. This interesting format is experiencing a renaissance after being almost forgotten in the past because of its rarity and the scarcity of *torcedores* who knew how to roll it. Today, almost every renowned brand offers a Pyramid. This is a pleasing development, for most large volume Pyramids promise an agreeable smoking experience.

Robusto. This increasingly popular format certainly looks strong and robust. That may well be so, but the compact appearance of a Robusto with its large ring gauge and less than generous length, certainly communicates a type of cigar whose full body promises to provide considerable content and an interesting diversity of aromas.

Customary International Formats
(Approx. Specifications in Inches)

Production Name	Classical Measurements	Variation in Length	Variation in Ring gauge
Giant	9 × 52	8 + > 8	46 + > 46
Double Corona	7 3/4 × 49	6 3/4 – < 8	49 + > 49
Giant Corona	7 1/2 × 44	7 1/2 + > 7 1/2	40 – 45
Long Panatela	7 1/2 × 38	7 + > 7	35 – 39
Churchill	7 × 47	6 3/4 – < 8	46 – 48
Grand Corona Special	7 × 45	6 3/4 – < 7 1/2	45
Grand Corona	6 1/2 × 46	> 5 1/2 – < 6 3/4	45 – 47
Lonsdale	6 1/2 × 42	6 1/2 – > 7 1/2	40 – 44
Toro	6 × 50	> 5 1/2 – < 6 3/4	48 – 54
Long Corona	6 × 42	5 3/4 – 6 1/2	40 – 44
Panatela	6 × 38	5 1/2 – < 7	35 – 39
Slim Panatela	6 × 34	5 + > 5	28 – 34
Corona Extra	5 1/2 × 46	4 1/2 – 5 1/2	45 – 47
Corona	5 1/2 × 42	5 1/4 – 5 3/4	40 – 44
Robusto	5 × 50	4 1/2 – 5 1/2	48 + > 48
Petit Corona	5 × 42	3 3/4 – < 5 1/4	40 – 44
Short Panatela	5 × 38	3 3/4 – < 5 1/2	35 – 39
Small Panatela	5 × 33	3 3/4 – < 5	28 – 34
Short Robusto	4 × 48	< 4 1/2	45 + > 45
Cigarillo	4 × 26	5 + < 5	27 + < 27

Customary International Formats
(Approx. Specifications in Millimetres)

Production Name	Classical Measurements	Variation in Length	Variation in Ring gauge
Giant	229 × 20.6	203 + > 203	18.3 + > 18.3
Double Corona	197 × 19.5	171 – 202	19.5 – > 19.5
Giant Corona	191 × 18.3	191 + > 191	15.9 – 17.9
Long Panatela	191 × 15.1	178 + > 178	13.9 – 15.5
Churchill	178 × 18.7	171 – 202	18.3 – 19.1
Grand Corona Special	178 × 17.9	171 – 190	17.9
Grand Corona	165 × 18.3	141 – 170	17.9 – 18.7
Lonsdale	165 × 16.7	165 – 190	15.9 – 17.5
Toro	152 × 19.8	141 – 170	19.1 – > 19.1
Long Corona	152 × 16.7	146 – 164	15.9 – 17.5
Panatela	152 × 15.1	140 – 177	13.9 – 15.5
Slim Panatela	152 × 13.5	127 + > 127	11.1 – 13.5
Corona Extra	140 × 18.3	114 – 140	17.9 – 18.7
Corona	140 × 16.7	133 – 145	15.9 – 17.5
Robusto	127 × 19.8	114 – 140	19.1 – > 19.1
Petit Corona	127 × 16.7	95 – 132	15.9 – 17.5
Short Panatela	127 × 15.1	95 – 139	13.9 – 15.9
Small Panatela	127 × 13.1	95 – 126	11.1 – 13.5
Short Robusto	102 × 19.1	< 114	45 + > 45
Cigarillo	102 × 10.3	127 + < 127	10.7 + < 10.7

Inches

The term for the common unit of measurement used in England and America, the inch, is derived from the Latin word *uncia,* meaning "a twelfth of a foot". An inch is therefore a twelfth of that other unit of measurement, the foot, and a 36th of yet another, the yard (comprising of three feet). The metric equivalent of one inch is 25.4 millimetres.

The measurements in the format tables are given in inches for a specific reason. The countries of the Caribbean and Central America have been under the strong influence of the United States since the end of the 19th century, and their businesses – either co-operating with companies from the Unites States or owned by them – have tended to abide by the specifications in common use there.

This strong influence is still felt in many Central American cigar producing countries. It is augmented by the fact that Britain was the main country of consumption during the first great boom period for Havana cigars in the second half of the 19th century. So cigar measurements in relation to length and ring gauge are always given in inches in this region.

Another reason is that many enthusiastic European cigar smokers have become so used to such measurements that they can visualize the length of a cigar more easily when the details are provided in inches than when they are given in millimetres.

Ring Gauge

As explained above, many manufacturers customarily give the size of a cigar in inches. This is also the case with the thickness, diameter or circumference of a cigar.

Many ring gauges therefore also take the inch as their basis. In figures, for instance, a ring gauge of 50 should actually be given as 50/64, for the diameter is 50 times larger than a 64th of an inch.

Staying with this example, as one inch is the equivalent of 25.4 millimetres, the diameter of a ring gauge of 50 amounts to 19.84 (rounded) millimetres (50 ÷ 64 × 25.4). Thus, the diameter of ring gauge 32 measures exactly 12.7 millimetres.

Ring Gauges (Ø in mm)

25 = 9.92	34 = 13.49	43 = 17.07	52 = 20.64
26 = 10.32	35 = 13.89	44 = 17.46	53 = 21.03
27 = 10.72	36 = 14.29	45 = 17.86	54 = 21.43
28 = 11.11	37 = 14.68	46 = 18.26	55 = 21.83
29 = 11.51	38 = 15.08	47 = 18.65	56 = 22.23
30 = 11.91	39 = 15.48	48 = 19.05	57 = 22.62
31 = 12.30	40 = 15.88	49 = 19.45	58 = 23.02
32 = 12.70	41 = 16.27	50 = 19.84	59 = 23.42
33 = 13.10	42 = 16.67	51 = 20.24	60 = 23.81

Editions

The numerous editions issued every year, for instance the *Cuban Edición Limitadas* (Cohiba, Hoyo de Monterrey, and Partagás, among others), and also those from Davidoff and other premium brands, are not discussed in this book – nor could they be, for they are always released in limited numbers.

Bearing in mind that this book can never be as up-to-date as a magazine or newspaper, it is quite conceivable that an edition discussed here would no longer be available before the ink on this page had dried sufficiently to allow the further production of the book.

Davidoff
Short Perfecto
Hecho a mano
República Dominicana
Davidoff
Special «B»
Made by Hand
in the Dominican Republic
Davidoff
Short «T»
Hecho a mano
República Dominicana
Davidoff
Special «R»
Hecho a mano
República Dominicana
Davidoff
Special
Davidoff
Double «R»
Made by Hand in the
Dominican Republic
Davidoff
Special «C»

Consumption,
Purchase, Care

Aficionado, Aficionada

Afición is the Spanish word for fondness, passion or soft-spot, so an *aficionado* can quite well be someone who pursues a matter – such as smoking cigars, for example – with passion. Where the term *aficionado* is used in this book, it refers, therefore, to the devoted cigar smoker.

Whereas a *connoisseur* is not necessarily an *aficionado*, the latter is definitely to be regarded as belonging to the *connoisseur* species, for an *aficionado* is someone who prizes the enjoyment of his beloved cigars above all else.

Apart from this, he possesses excellent knowledge of the world of cigars, and knows precisely the formats, characteristics and properties of cigars he considers worthy of meeting his anticipated pleasures. But he is also well-informed about the wider subject of accessories and paraphernalia, making sure he handles and looks after his beloved cigars with the necessary care.

An *aficionado* is more than a cigar smoker or fancier – he is, in a manner of speaking, a cigar gourmet.

All this is also true of a passionate *aficionada*. Female cigar smokers may still be in the minority compared to their male counterparts, but their numbers are growing – not only in the United States, where there are several clubs exclusively reserved for *aficionadas*, but also in the Old World.

A brief comment is called for at this stage. For ease of writing, this text consistently refers to the *aficionado*. To use conscientiously such cumbersome and unwieldy concoctions as "*aficionado* and/or *afi-*

A staunch aficionado as torcedor during a visit to the Davidoff factory in the Dominican Republic – the German actor Fritz Wepper makes a convincing cigar roller.

"When I was twenty, I fell in love with the wide tobacco plantations of Cuba. This love of my youth has never died. From today's view of things, I can say that my whole life has stood in the service of those – young and old – who have remained loyal to the cigar. Yes, my life really belongs to the cigar. I can thank it for everything – joy and sorrow, enjoyment of work and the pleasurable leisure hours that it can create for one, and I thank it for a whole row of philosophical insights which I have gained during my life."

Zino Davidoff in a retrospective

cionada" would simply be a repetitive burden on the reader, and would do no service to the flow of the text and ease of reading.

An *aficionado* is well aware that there are two genders, and therefore holds an *aficionada* in the same high regard as he would a male counterpart, showing at times perhaps even more respect for the former than the latter.

Connoisseur

According to one definition, a *connoisseur* is an enthusiast, expert or *gourmet*. The latter corresponds most closely to the use of the term *connoisseur* in this book, although the word gourmet falls a little short in this context.

The term *hedonist*, i.e. a person whose highest ethical principle is insatiable sensual desire, would, however, be an exaggeration. The definition *enjoyer of pleasure* comes closest to describing someone who claims to be a *connoisseur*.

The great *connoisseur*, Zino Davidoff, once said the following to a journalist interviewing him, "People I'm fond of make me hungry." This is the comment of a true enjoyer of pleasure. He literally takes most pleasure in their stimulating conversation over a well-laid table (providing pleasure for the eye) and a good glass of wine, before rounding off the experience most pleasurably with a mature cognac (or whisky, etc.) and an excellent cigar – although in this case the *aficionado*, another possible face of a *connoisseur*, also makes an appearance.

There are significantly more types of pleasure than those mentioned above, but they should suffice to explain, as closely as possible, how the term *connoisseur* is to be understood in the context of this book.

Cutting

The cutting of a cigar is a philosophy in itself. Whereas one *aficionado* may swear by cigar scissors, another puts his trust in a razor blade (which is rather odd, but perfectly understandable), while a third – usually a Cuban – uses his teeth to prepare a cigar head appropriately prior to lighting-up.

Of all methods, this last is seldom observed in European circles and really does seem to be restricted to smokers who have grown up around wide-ranging tobacco plantations.

During a smokers' night over here, it would be more than crass if someone were to rip off a piece of cigar head with his choppers and then spit it out in a wide arc – it could also be disastrous. Who knows where it might land?

A guillotine is therefore more highly recommended. This once-menacing piece of equipment, primarily known for its frequent use during the French Revolution when its sole purpose was to separate an undesirable's head from his body, has now lost its terror – at least for *aficionados*.

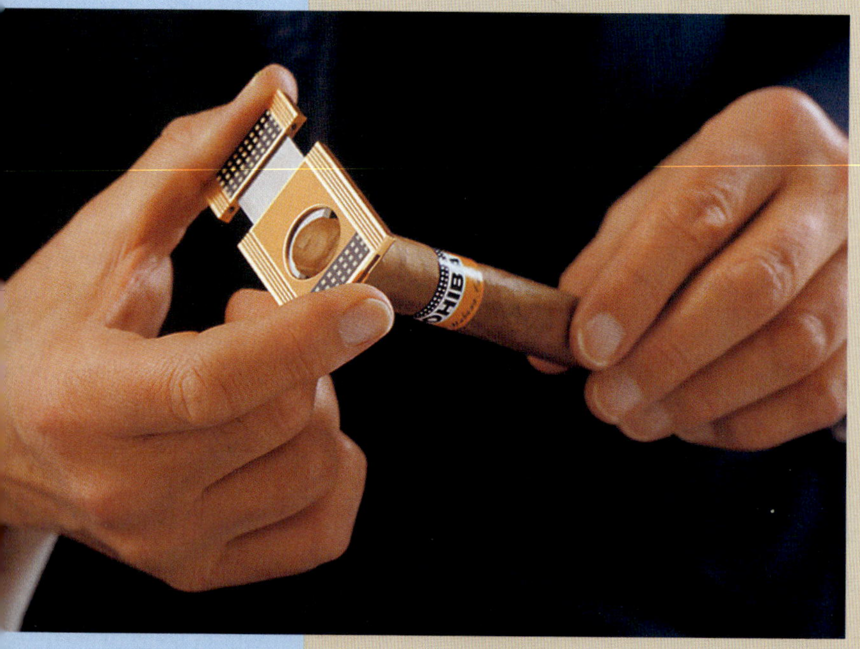

The proper cut guarantees unspoiled smoking pleasure.

They treasure the guillotine for its property of cleanly and smoothly slicing – here memories of the French Revolution are re-awoken – a cigar head from its rump. This clean cut matters a great deal, for it is one of the most important factors affecting the burning performance of a cigar. Should the cut be less precise, the burn may become uneven.

This in turn has an unpleasant effect on the pleasure gained from smoking. Moreover, anyone who doesn't take the necessary care when cutting, risks damaging the wrapper leaf. Apart from the evenness of burning, a clean cut also guarantees a faultless draw and helps heighten awareness of a cigar's aromas.

But the guillotine is not the only viable tool for cutting cigars. For example, many *aficionados* use a punch cutter, an accessory that has become increasingly available for quite some time. Here, a circular blade punches a hole of approximately 1.5 millimetres deep into the cigar cap, and removes the loose tobacco when it is withdrawn.

Alternatively, many use cigar scissors, the use of which was preferred by none other than Zino Davidoff himself. If the remarks of this great cigar enthusiast are to be believed – and who could doubt them?

– the advantage of good cigar scissors lies in their clean circular cut irrespective of a cigar's diameter.

There are, as mentioned, several possible ways of cutting a cigar head perfectly. Where one person is better served by one tool, another may prefer quite a different one, finding it easier. As with choosing cigars – whichever comes closest to meeting the penchant and preferences of the individual will prevail.

Lighting Up

The enjoyment of a cigar begins with lighting it up properly. The open burning end of the cigar is slowly turned over the flame of a lighter or match to warm it. During this process, the flame should not come into direct contact with the cigar. This prevents singeing and the resulting strong taste. This process is called *toasting*.

Gently puffing, while the cigar is still being revolved and the tip of the flame is held directly underneath the burning end, draws the flame to the cigar and ensures the burning end is evenly lit.

There is just as great a division of opinion about the right tool for lighting a cigar as there is about the removal of the cigar ring. This time the question is whether a lighter should be used or a match. A true *connoisseur* would never pose the question at all – he would always use a long wooden taper, preferably of cedar wood. This implement is not always readily at hand, but there are alternatives …

The match or taper is without question one of a cigar smoker's most important utensils. However, it should either be somewhat longer to enable the sulphur fumes to dissipate before lighting a cigar, or have a head that contains no sulphur whatsoever (available in specialist shops).

It should be emphasised that the matches be of wood, and not made of waxed material as some are. Such matches only cause a nasty taste and considerably impair the pleasure of smoking.

A match or taper is not always the appropriate instrument to initiate the flavour experience so essential for an *aficionado*. A gas lighter is an absolute advantage when travelling for example, since a large box of long matches would cause an unsightly bulge in the smoker's jacket. Anyway, a good gas lighter fulfils practically the same purpose

Whether with a match or – as here – with a gas lighter, lighting properly is essential.

as a match or taper – only the atmospheric feeling created by the use of a lighter differs from that generated by the latter.

If the emphasis is on wood with regard to matches, then it is on gas in the case of lighters. A cigar lit by a petrol lighter will deliver a nasty aftertaste lasting the whole of the smoke – not at all pleasant for a *connoisseur*.

A candle also promises little smoking satisfaction. Anyone who even thinks about the absurd idea of

The height of sophistication: lighting a cigar with a cedar wood taper.

using such a flame to light a quality cigar should remove the word "cigar" from his vocabulary and never let it ever cross his lips again.

Aroma

When aroma is mentioned in this book, it usually relates to a cigar's strength. Every aroma develops a certain strength, irrespective of whatever nuance of fragrance a cigar may give off and whatever nuance may be dominant, sometimes even masking others.

"Aroma" is used to indicate, as it were, the strength of a cigar's aroma in its entirety, avoiding the continual use of the term body. Aroma has, in this case, nothing to do with flavour – just as taste has little to do with strength.

For example, a relatively mild cigar tastes comparatively bitter when more than two thirds have been smoked. Many *aficionados* therefore only smoke two thirds of a cigar, because the bitterness arising thereafter – even when it is only slightly noticeable – masks the fragrance nuances and impairs their full appreciation.

Aromas

Aromas are often mentioned in this book, for example when a cigar is said to surprise the smoker with "sweet aromas". In that case, the term aromas specifically relates to a cigar's nuances in flavour, and not the strength of its body.

A needful comment may be made in this context. Anyone who expects to find detailed descriptions of individual cigar characteristics, such as "the Corona's beautiful fragrance of leather, paired with the bouquet of honey, is actually reminiscent of the traditional flavour where a spiciness evocative of tree bark develops in the last third", that are found in some cigar evaluations will be disappointed.

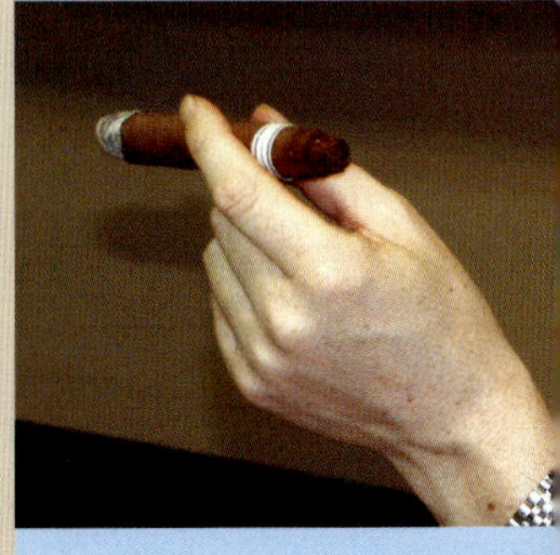

It cannot and should not be the job of this lexicon to expound upon and document individual types of aroma, and to explain which cigars develop which flavour, at what stage and to what intensity.

That should be the domain of experts, and those *connoisseurs* who discover and learn through smoking experience which aromas greatly broaden their enjoyment of a cigar, and which remain less memorable.

"With a well-chosen cigar, one is always strongly fortified against the rigours of life. A little blue haze dispels all worries in a most mysterious way."

Zino Davidoff in a retrospective

Strength

In contrast to the intensity of certain aromas emitted by a cigar during smoking, a cigar's strength can be determined with relative accuracy. While it is true that an experienced *aficionado* will perceive the strength of a robust Havana differently from someone who has recently taken up cigar smoking, the strength of a particular cigar remains constant.

It goes without saying that there is no arguing with taste – despite the fact that one can easily be drawn into conflicts concerning some cigar or another. But since this lexicon is primarily intended, not to foster a culture of controversy among *connoisseurs* but, rather, to provide factual information, observations such as "strong in flavour" or "possesses a strong aroma" always refer to a cigar's strength.

Burning Performance

An ideal burning performance is the mark of a really good cigar. There are two points to be made in this context. It should be possible to draw on the cigar effortlessly and without problem, and the burn itself should be even.

The colour of the ash is effectively irrelevant as far as quality is concerned. Regardless of whether it is white, light grey or simply grey, the colour is no indication of a cigar's quality – contrary to popular

opinion. And while on the subject of ash, cigar smoking should not be transformed into a sports event with the smoker attempting to hold the ash as long as possible. That is definitely not necessary; besides, the only outcome of this "sport" is usually soiled clothing – apart, that is, from ugly stains on furniture covers.

Of course, good burning performance also depends on the care taken of a cigar. Anyone who stores his cigars in an open dish next to a burning fire, "cuts" them the Cuban way by ripping off a piece of the head with his teeth, and lights them with a candle, possibly holding the burning end directly in the flame, can only expect a miserable burning performance.

Flavour

Since there is no arguing with taste, no appraisals or evaluations of flavour are to be found in this book.

The occasional remarks referring to the burning performance and the strength of individual cigars alone should provide the beginner with some orientation in choosing his or her preferred brand or format, while also helping the *connoisseur* to discover previously unfamiliar brands.

It cannot be said often enough that cigar smokers are individualists who will develop their own taste in cigars, assuming they have not already done so.

An Unusual Wish

As Franz Liszt, the great Hungarian pianist and composer, entered a monastery towards the end of his life, he asked to be allowed to smoke his cigars at will for as long as he lived. His wish was granted.

Storage

Few premium cigar owners have a cellar at their disposal that not only boasts a constant air humidity of about 70% and a temperature not exceeding 20 °C, but is also free of foreign odours. Cigar boxes are

After lighting up: Blowing a little air cannot be detrimental to an even burn.

intended for storage in such a cellar and this "brown gold" should certainly not be kept in a cramped place alongside other brown goods, i.e. potatoes, as well as possible strings of garlic, peppers, dried fish and onions.

Other solutions are available – strings of garlic, for example, are best nailed to the window frame (to deter vampires), and cigars are best stored in a humidor (to preserve their enjoyment value).

The humidor should have a humidifier that not only guarantees, at all times, the relative air humidity of 70% mentioned above, but also absorbs any excess moisture. That would be ideal, in fact. An efficient humidor ensures a constant tropical humidity for the cigars and thus contributes to unsullied smoking enjoyment.

However, this enjoyment would be impaired should the humidor be kept on a window sill or stand directly in front of a radiator that constantly belts out heat. That wintertime habit of keeping it near the fireplace, or even on the mantelpiece – where an expensive humidor naturally catches the eye of every visitor – is vehemently to be discouraged.

For one thing, a true *connoisseur* considers such exhibitionism gratuitous. For another, although the exotic wood used predominantly in humidor production and the air-tight seal ensure that practically no external influence can affect the contents, that

In this table-top humidor four generations of Havanas wait to go up in smoke at some point.

dense tropical wood does adapt to its surrounding temperature (as all woods do).

So the interior of a humidor subjected to a relatively high external temperature can become several degrees too warm for the cigars contained within. As already indicated, humidity is not the only important factor in the proper storage of these "tropical treasures": temperature also matters. Where possible, it should not exceed 20 °C – a humidor should therefore be kept in a relatively cool place.

All Caribbean cigars belong in a humidor; but Dutch-type cigars with a relatively small proportion of Sumatra tobacco are also grateful when entrusted by their owners to such a climatised cabinet.

The premises of a cigar dealer should also be fitted out with an appropriate number of such cabinets, or, better still, a special climatised room. It is important to note that even the best home humidor can never make up for bad interim storage.

Humidors can be purchased in every good specialist shop or ordered from mail-order businesses that specialise in cigars. Price range is very wide. Humidors made from exotic woods which entirely fulfil the requirements made of them are available for a little more than a hundred pounds – but veritable works of art also await a buyer. The prices expected for these may reach as much as five digits.

Ultimately, as with so many things, there are no limits. For example, there is a special cabinet available which provides room not only for high quality cigars, but also for selected wines – for which, of course, different climatic systems are incorporated – and it is constructed purely of Markassa ebony.

Smoke less, but better and longer – make it a cult, a philosophy!"

Zino Davidoff, Grand Seigneur of cigars

This "wood of kings", incidentally, is the only exotic wood that a carpenter pays for by weight. Equally, there are certain cigars that a European on an average income would be well advised to limit to a single one per week.

Cigar Aficionado

Cigar Aficionado is the leading voice concerning cigars. First brought on the market by the publisher Marvin Shanken in September 1972, this US magazine contributed considerably to the run on premium cigars that began towards the end of the 1980s in the United States, and which, in the course of time, also spilled over to Europe.

European cigar enthusiasts suffered considerably from this US run for some time, as the availability of non-Cuban Caribbeans was seldom able to meet the increased demand (which is now no longer the case).

Own-brands

Every self-respecting cigar dealer has them in his range – own-brands. These are by any measure good quality cigars, available in a variety of formats. They could be Brazil or Sumatra cigars produced in

Europe, and possibly also those produced in the Dominican Republic or Honduras.

Own-brand cigars are usually found in a very acceptable price category. They are usually more than value for money.

Since products like own-brands incur no marketing costs and less presentation outlay, the interested customer receives a thoroughly good quality product at a very reasonable price – because, ultimately, a well-established tobacconist business has a reputation to maintain, and is hardly likely to offer its customers an own-brand that might be stigmatised as "unsmokeable".

For several years now, cigar dealers with large turnovers have also been offering direct imports from Caribbean countries (with the exception of Cuba) and the Canary Islands. These are thoroughly good cigars that can only be bought under the dealer's own name.

As a rule, an importer is still involved, but he is solely responsible for transport (custom formalities, etc.) and interim storage, thereby guaranteeing the exclusivity of the brand. Such cigars are chiefly hand-made long filler from the Dominican Republic, but some are also imported from Honduras, the Canary Islands and Nicaragua.

La Casa del Habano

Worldwide, there are (as of mid 2005) almost 90 Havana houses to make the eyeballs roll of every

"Gentleman, you may smoke."

Edward VII after his coronation as King of Great Britain and Northern Ireland

aficionado who is a die-hard Havana fan. These "tobacco temples" deal only in Havanas, with the exception, that is, of all those accessories needed for a proper smoke.

The Cuban state-owned company, Habanos S.A., which looks after the interests of the indigenous cigar industry, founded these *Casas del Habano* quite a while ago to ensure the worldwide presence of the Cuban art of cigar manufacturing.

It is not the newcomers on the market – Cuba constantly plans to introduce further formats – that make the *Casas del Habano* appear so interesting, for after all, newcomers are usually available in normal specialist shops after only a short introductory period; but rather the special editions and individual brands and formats that are only available there, for each and every *Casa* strives to have the complete *Habano* range in stock – an El Dorado for the Havanaphile that can quickly become a veritable Mecca.

Accessories

The necessary accessories, those indispensable utensils without which a true *aficionado* is lost, are available in every conceivable form, fashion and price category.

Whether it is the long matches from Cohiba or Dunhill or the humidor made of either acryl glass or root wood from Davidoff, the cigar cases of exotic wood or finest leather, the cigar tubes of acrylic, tinted plexiglass and tinted glass, the cigar cutter whose stainless steel blade has a diagonal cut and a casing available in gold plate or burnished steel, the chrome- or silver-plated cigar scissors, the cigar cutter with either a double blade or a circular one, with or without a leather case, or whether it is the traveller's humidor, made of stitched leather and lined with cedar wood, or perhaps the root wood and velvet designs by Guy Janot – these are all accessories that don't have to belong to a cigar smoker's basic equipment, but without which a *connoisseur* could not get by.

It is true that a simple match, costing a fraction of a penny, or an ordinary disposable gas lighter that lands in the dustbin after use, will also do to light a cigar.

And it is also true that the guillotine sometimes given away free when a box of cigars is bought will also do to behead a cigar. But, realistically, what *aficionado* could bring himself to mistreat a Montecristo A with such "tools"?

Granted, it doesn't have to be a walk-in humidor, but a certain ambience does belong to a pleasant smoke.

And that is why cigar dealers and mail-order firms also stock further outlandish accessories besides those mentioned above; they are all intended to enhance the experience of smoking a cigar.

Outlandish accessories catch the eye immediately. Here is a noble cigar stand by Chambrair.

Areas of Cultivation

Although tobacco is cultivated in several African countries, such as Tanzania and Uganda, and cigar producers do sometimes use these for the filler, when excellence is required, only the wrapper leaf grown in Cameroon meets the need.

Cameroon

After a marked decline in production and export, the supply of wrapper leaves from the West African state increased again recently. This is more than welcome, since wrapper leaves from Cameroon are among the best in the world.

Mount Cameroon, an active volcano approximately 4,000 meters in height and situated near the coast, is

There is no doubt that smoking endangers health. But not smoking also endangers the economy. In parts of Africa where tobacco is grown almost every second person earns their living from what others smoke.

The workers on a tobacco plantation push a wagon of dried tobacco leaves into a steam room. The additional moisture gives the leaves the necessary elasticity for further processing.

the natural emblem of the country. The western slopes of this mountain with their 10,000 millimetres of rainfall per year are among the rainiest regions in the world.

Apart from this, the extremely lush vegetation of the country is also rich in diversity. The wide ranging grassy meadows of the north give way to dry savannahs towards the south, which in turn are replaced by wet savannahs bordered in the coastal lowlands by tropical rainforests. Apart from the already mentioned Mount Cameroon, there are several highland areas further inland lying between 600 and 1,200 meters above sea level.

The diverse forms of vegetation found in this country (half of which is covered in forest) ensure rich rainfall for the coastal area, which is why the climate is characterised as equatorial rainforest. This climate –

relatively dry in the north, becoming increasingly rainy to the south – is naturally ideal for the cultivation of numerous agricultural crops such as bananas and beans, cotton, peanuts, millet and maize, coffee and cacao, rubber, tapioca and oil palm trees, rice and sweet potatoes and, of course, tobacco.

Growing in rainforest clearings, it produces wrapper leaves characterised by a greenish-brown to brown colour and distinguished by a flavour rich in aroma. Moreover, their extreme thinness also makes them excellent for further processing.

Tobacco dealers check the quality of the goods on offer at a tobacco auction.

"Made in EU" is often seen on cigar packaging. Clearly, that is a very general pointer to the country of production. Concealed behind it may lie, for instance, Italy or Spain, Denmark or Ireland, Germany, Austria or Switzerland, and more recently, Poland or the Czech Republic.

This practice is not necessarily a sign of inferior quality, and is entirely legal. But it is still advisable to ask about the country of production when making a purchase. A well-informed cigar dealer will provide the answer.

Classic short filler production is an important characteristic of the European tobacco world. Dutch cigar makers have made no small contribution to this. On the far left a peak into the climatised room of the traditional cigar house "Hajenius".

Although several European countries – including Denmark, Germany, the Netherlands and Switzerland – can look back on a remarkable cigar-making tradition, only one county (or more accurately one group of islands) is considered in any depth here.

*Seville Makes
a Start …*

*It was in the year
1676 that the first
cigars in Europe were
produced in Seville.
Thus, the Andalusian
University City is, in
effect, the birthplace
of cigars as we know
them in their present
form and appearance.
More than half a
century later, the
Spanish state re-
cognised that the
laborious task of
filling the state coffers
could be made easier
by cigars – and more
so by raising a tax on
tobacco. In 1731, the
Royal Cigar Factories
were set up in Seville.*

Canary Islands

The Canary Islands played a significant role throughout the discovery and later development of the Americas. This group of islands off the North African coast
was the last port of call for both Christopher Columbus and the *Conquistadores* that followed him, before
they sailed out into the endless expanse of the Atlantic
Ocean; and La Gomera, an island to the west of
Tenerife, was always the first goal of every ship on its
return journey from the New World.

The following period saw several "exchanges of
human capital", to use the dreadful language of today,
between the Canary Islands and Cuba; in some cases
Spaniards resident on the islands emigrated to Cuba,
in other cases descendants of émigrés returned seeking
their luck in the Old World, beginning with this
Atlantic island group (and at times also ending here).
The latter was usually the case when the barometer of
the largest Caribbean island was pointing to storm,
that is, when the economic position was abysmal or
the political situation provoked the rise of radically
opposing points of view with consequent risk to life
and limb.

The most recent notable wave of emigration happened when numerous Cubans left their homeland
after Castro took power. Most resettled in the region
of Central America, but there were those who did as
their forefathers had done and risked the leap over the
great pond. These included the García and Menéndez
families, descendents of veritable tobacco dynasties
and whose names were (and still are) of high status in
the world of cigars.

One of the most important factors encouraging this
process was the considerable tax relief that the

Spanish state granted at that time to firms settling on the islands, thus creating important jobs.

More or less settled in on the Canary Islands, it was not long before Pepe García and Benjamín Menéndez created the Montecruz, a cigar made from non-Cuban tobaccos intended to be evocative of the Cuban Montecristo, whose production had been their responsibility in Havana.

In the meantime, the Garcías and Menéndez are also following their passion in other parts of the world. In the mid 1970s, the US General Cigar company offered Benjamín Menéndez the job of managing the production of Partagás in the Dominican Republic following the company's acquisition of the brand rights.

Just over a decade later, several cigar manufactures decided to leave the Canary Islands again. The reason was Spain's accession to the EC on 1ˢᵗ January 1986 and the resulting harmonisation of sections of its tax legislation with that of the community. Several tax incentives were revoked as a result – including those that had until then pertained to cigar manufactures.

The situation has improved only recently. The buzz-word is now "offshore". As in many parts of the world, the Canary Islands lately become home to off-shore companies: companies that settle in free-trade zones and pay practically no tax but create badly needed jobs. That is to the benefit of everyone – the state and the companies concerned.

Clearly, the companies currently producing cigars on the Canary Islands have the requisite expertise in cigar-making – for it has developed on the island group over several centuries, resulting in a level of skill

... and Hamburg Follows Through

It was Heinrich Schlottmann who founded the first cigar factory in Germany in 1788. The merchant had previously studied the cigar trade in Seville – the European "cigar metropolis" of the day. Soon Schlott-manns were both renowned and popular beyond the country's borders.

A Waft of Blue Haze for a Genius

It is hard to say whether the following story is really true. But if so, then it would have happened on the 25th of October 1881, in the southern Spanish harbour of Málaga …

On that day a child was born. It was in effect a birth like all others. The doctor had hurried to the house of the parents on being informed that the first labour pains had set in. Towards evening, the pains began anew, but were not so strong as to cause concern. However it took some time before the child entered the world. It was a boy. But he did not move, even when the doctor gave him a light slap on the bottom. A stillbirth? The doctor didn't want to believe it. He lit a cigar, drew strongly several times and held the smoke of the last draw in his mouth before blowing the blue haze into the baby's face. Incredibly, a wailing cry immediately echoed around the room.

The cry had, of course, come from the newborn child. Had the healing properties attributed to tobacco ever since its arrival in the old world really helped in this case? If so, it was surely divine intervention, for the baby would become one of the greatest artists of the 20th century.

According to the story, the boy was christened Pablo a few days after this memorable event. It was Pablo Picasso, who entered this world on the 25th of October 1881 in Málaga, Spain.

capable of satisfying the highest demands made upon it.

With this background, it is easy to understand why several brands from the Canaries are highly regarded by cigar smokers. Condal, Goya, Hacienda, Peñamil, Vargas – these brands may not be well known by all *aficionados*, but where available, each has gained a loyal circle of customers, not least because each can also claim for itself the title *Hecho a mano*.

Incidentally, of the seven islands of the group, La Palma is considered the centre of cigar production on the Canaries.

Canary Island tobacco is still grown there, too, although the area of cultivation only amounts to about five hectares (and declining) and is barely large enough to provide the various filler mixtures with indigenous tobacco.

This tobacco is an essential part of at least those cigar fillers composed for the home market, for the "Palmeros", as the inhabitants of La Palma are called, swear by their strong dark tobacco.

Administrative assistance – the Social Democratic mayor of El Paso on the Canary island of La Palma devised this gift for the designated German chancellor and cigar fan following the 1998 federal elections in Germany. Whether they were smoked during the nights of negotiations needed for the coalition agreement with the Greens has not been passed down.

Tobacco is grown in many countries of this largest continent, for instance China and India. However, only two are of interest in relation to cigar tobacco – the Philippines and, in particular, Indonesia.

Indonesia

The Southeast Asian republic of Indonesia stretches over a total of 13,677 islands. The interest of all those connected with cigars is focused on only two of the 6,044 inhabited islands, Java and Sumatra, which along with Borneo and Celebes, belong to the Sunda Islands.

Cigar tobacco has been cultivated on these two islands for centuries. The resulting expertise has contributed decisively to the high quality of Indonesian raw tobacco. But this expertise would be useless if the climatic and topographical conditions so important for the development of tobacco seeds into fully matured plants were not right.

However the above-mentioned conditions are certainly present on Sumatra. An annual average temperature of 27 °C can be measured on the extreme north of the island, where the fertile soil is partly of volcanic origin and partly of sandy clay, where abundant rain falls and the skies are constantly overcast by numerous clouds, weakening the sun's rays. This interaction of climate and weather is an ideal prerequisite for the cultivation of cigar tobacco.

The most outstanding conditions for an appropriate plantation economy are found in the region of Medan, named after the metropolis bordering on the southern part of the cultivation area. This area also

*A Stronger
Structure*

*In places, Javan
wrapper leaves are
somewhat browner
and and stronger
than those from
Sumatra. This
happens when the
plants are not covered
by shade nets.*

produces one of the most precious wrapper leaves this world has to offer – the Deli-sandleaf.

However, these wrapper leaves cannot be purchased on Sumatra itself, but only in Bremen. This fact demands an explanation. The cultivation of tobacco was (and still is) carried on by state-owned companies following the dispossession in 1958 of the Dutch businesses in control of the tobacco industry on Sumatra. However, marketing this important raw material was more problematic than had been hoped.

It was taken over by the *Deutsch-Indonesische Tabak-Handelsgesellschaft,* or *DITH* for short, founded as early as 1959. This is still the case – cigar manufacturers wishing to obtain Sumatra tobacco must attend the annual tobacco exchange in the Hanseatic city of Bremen. It is only here that the coveted raw material can be ordered.

Javanese tobacco is another matter. Interested dealers can also purchase it locally. Tobacco cultivation here is also under state control, but it is possible – and now customary – to buy it locally without having to go via the Bremen tobacco exchange.

An interested dealer does not necessarily have to travel to East Asia to obtain Javanese tobacco. A large proportion of Java's tobacco bales can be bought in Germany – at the Deutsch-Indonesischen Tabak-Handelsgesellschaft tobacco exchange held annually in Bremen.

Since tobacco production has decreased noticeably on Sumatra in the last few years, an attempt has been

made on Java to repair the loss through intensive cooperation between the state bodies responsible for running the plantations and renowned cigar manufacturers – with success. Both the Besuki region in the extreme south of the island, and the Vorstenlanden region stretching to the north of Besuki, now yield cigar tobaccos used for filler as well as binder and wrapper leaves.

The Philippines

The Cigar industry of the Philippines has for decades been something of a Sleeping Beauty. The international cigar world took little notice of its meagre existence. It had once possessed a cigar culture of which it could be proud.

Renowned manufactures in and around Manila delivered their produce to top addresses around the globe. There, as elsewhere, the great skill of Philippine cigar manufactures was treasured. The Islands could look back on a tradition originating from the end of 16th and beginning of the 17th century.

This tradition has been revived in recent years, giving rise to several premium brands capable of meeting international comparison.

Leaf for Leaf

The plucking of individual leaves is the custom on Sumatra. After a drying phase of about 30 days, there then follows a six-month-long fermentation process during which the temperature in the tobacco bales may not exceed 48 °C to prevent damage to the aroma and colouring.

The Italian Toscano – quite an unusual cigar – uses a tobacco grown in the east central region of the United States, in Kentucky. But the subject of our attention lies to the north east, where cultivation predominantly centres on the growing of wrapper leaves.

Connecticut

With the exception of Rhode Island and Delaware, Connecticut is the smallest state in the USA, but in many respects is also one of the most eminent. Connecticut, settled at the beginning of the 17th century firstly by the Dutch then increasingly by the English, was founded in 1635, and became the fifth state to ratify the constitution of the USA and join the community of states.

That was on the 9th January, 1788. Today, the economy of Connecticut is dominated by shipyards and, to an even greater extent, by the space and armaments industry. Agriculture, however, also plays significant role in the New England state.

Whereas dairy farming, chicken rearing and the cultivation of fruit and vegetables is primarily oriented towards meeting the needs of the surrounding urban areas and is therefore more of regional importance, another branch of crop-growing is clearly intended to supply numerous producers, in part indigenous but chiefly from overseas, with a really excellent raw material.

These are the top ranking tobacco leaves of cigar production – the wrapper leaves. In fact, those grown in New England are among the best of their kind worldwide.

Generations of tobacco farmers have been carrying out their profession on many tobacco farms in Connecticut.

At the beginning of the 20th century, the use of child labour during the tobacco harvest was common in the United States, too. Two young boys carry harvested tobacco leaves into a shed in this photograph from the year 1916.

Yet, the first attempts to grow wrapper leaves in Connecticut that would rival those grown in Cuba and on Sumatra were not crowned with success. The efforts of numerous tobacco growers towards the end of the 19th century, to grow wrapper leaves from Sumatra seeds in the fertile valley of the Connecticut River, failed to yield anything like the promised results.

Another attempt was made several years later, this time with better results. Apparently, the sandy clay soil of the Connecticut River Valley stretching up to 30 kilometres wide north of the state capital, Hartford, was ideal for the Cuban seeds used this time. This beginning could be built upon, and as time went on the tobacco farmers continually improved the development and cultivation of their plants.

Connecticut Shade, as this tobacco grown in shade is known, has become a synonym for one of the world's best wrapper leaves. Actually, it is not grown "in shade" so much as "in the shadow of plastic covers", since Connecticut has neither tropical wetness nor low-hanging clouds to provide natural shade from the sun.

If nature is not given a helping hand and covers are not used, the result is the *Connecticut Broadleaf,* a dark wrapper leaf covering the section of the wrapper leaf colour spectrum that begins with *Colorado Maduro* and ends with *Oscuro.*

Regardless, *shade* or *broadleaf,* Connecticut tobacco is among the world's most coveted wrapper leaves – and also one of the most expensive. For example, where a kilogramme of *Connecticut Shade* cost 28 US-dollars in 1996, the same amount was fetching an astronomical 145 dollars one year later – an exorbitant increase of more than 500 percent. The US General Cigar Company was no doubt pleased, since it controls about two thirds of tobacco cultivation in the Connecticut River Valley through its daughter company, Culbro.

The price increases for tobacco from Connecticut have abated significantly in the last few years. This is also due to the recent development of equally good wrapper leaves in Ecuador – and their considerably lower price. The laws of supply and demand are still effective.

Central America

In addition to the island states of the Caribbean, this "third" American continent is made up of the countries on the isthmus linking North and South America that divides the Caribbean and the Pacific Ocean. We will start with the mainland.

Mexico

The land of the Maya and the Aztecs was long considered the only country outside Cuba capable of producing *puros*. That is mainly due to the San Andreas Valley, whose first class soils allow all conceivable types of tobacco plant to thrive, irrespective of whether grown from Brazilian or Cuban seeds or those of Connecticut or Sumatran origin.

Of course, indigenous plants also grow here, producing, for example the (wrapper leaf) tobacco known as *Negro,* which is, as its name suggests, a rich black colour that gives rise, for some, to the inference that they are faced with a cigar that will bowl them over when smoked. The truth is that most such cigars are relatively mild.

But there is another, very good reason why Mexico is a land of *puros*. A law existed, quite recently, which forbade the manufacture of cigars not made 100% from tobacco leaves grown in Mexico. *Puros* by order of the state, as it were.

The method of production, by contrast, is subject to no such requirements whatsoever. Nevertheless, several long filler that meet the premium criteria are produced in Mexico. In fact, Mexico can boast of quite a range of premium cigars. There are currently about a dozen, including the Santa Clara 1830 and Te-Amo brands, to name the best-known.

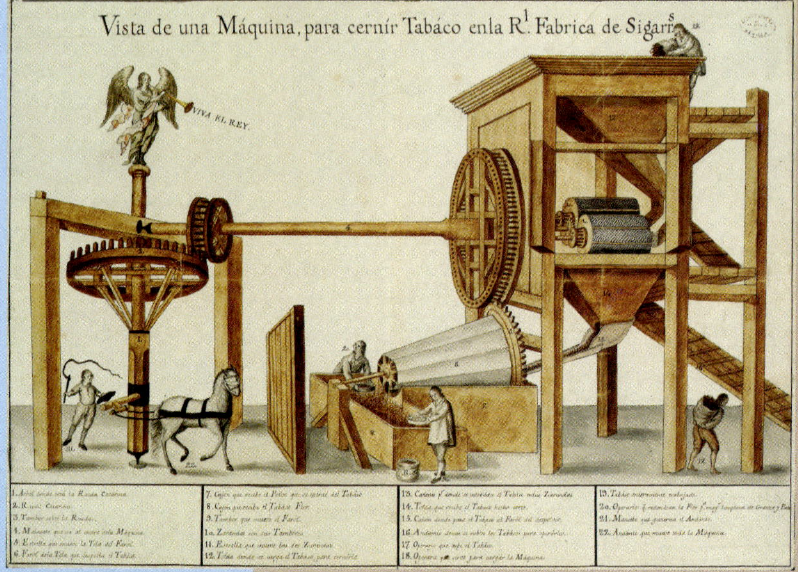

This 18th-century water-colour illustration of a tobacco mill at the Real Fábrica de Mexico demonstrates the leading role Mexico played from the earliest times in the tobacco industry.

Premium cigars are almost exclusively produced in the aforementioned San Andreas Valley, which lies in the state of Veracruz, a little more than 150 kilometres to the south of the harbour on the Gulf of Mexico that also bears the name of Veracruz.

The fertility of the soil of the San Andreas Valley – the cigar centre of Mexico – is extraordinary. It enables two harvests a year. In March, during the Central American country's dry season, the tobacco farmers can harvest the tobaccos grown from Sumatran seeds, while other types including those of indigenous origin are harvested in wetter June.

Not only numerous tobacco fields are to be found in this valley – the small city of San Andreas Tuxtla is also the centre of the Mexican cigar production.

For example, San Andreas Tuxtla is home to both the country's largest cigar producer, Nueva Matacapan Tabacos (Te-Amo), as well as the country's producer richest in tradition, Tabacos San Andreas S.A. (Santa Clara 1830).

Although the law already mentioned no longer bindingly prescribes a cigar's composition, there will still be many *puros* made in Mexico. Why should a country whose first major cigar manufacturer began work in the 1830s and for many years produced (and was allowed to produce) solely *puros,* break with this tradition, especially when such cigars are enjoying increasing popularity among *aficionados* around the world.

Honduras

The current situation of the Central American cigar industry, characterised as it is by the production of numerous premium cigars, can be primarily ascribed to thee interrelated events – the Cuban Revolution, the nationalisation of industry there and the subsequent embargo by the USA.

As a result of these events, which also had a lasting effect on the social conditions on the main island of the Greater Antilles, many Cubans left their homeland. Numerous tobacco planters were also among the émigrés who finally, often after a veritable Odyssey, settled on one of the Caribbean islands or sought their luck in one of the countries of Central America. The preferred destinations were the Dominican Republic, Jamaica, Nicaragua and Honduras.

This country, lying between the Caribbean and the Pacific Ocean, is predominantly shaped by agriculture and is one of the poorest states of Latin America – the gross national product for 1995 was a mere 600 US-dollar per head. Although staple foods such as beans,

millet, maize and rice are cultivated here on, for the most part, small farms, and while livestock farming is also not insignificant, nevertheless the banana industry makes up the largest section of the agricultural economy – and that is mainly in the hands of US concerns.

Although Honduras is rich in natural resources, the deposits of lead, gold, silver and zinc, to name but a few, have hardly been tapped. Tourism is also slumbering like a Sleeping Beauty – only the former Mayan stronghold Copán attracts several tens of thousands of cultural tourists every year. The massive ruined city, situated in the west of the country near the border with Guatemala, has in only the last 25 years been wrested from the tropical rainforest and uncovered. In many respects Honduras is reminiscent of a sleeping giant.

This is not the case, however, with the cigar industry. Although the first cigar factories were founded in Honduras as early as the 18th century, it was the arrival of numerous Cuban exiles who settled here that began the upsurge of the Honduran cigar industry, a boom which continues today.

It was the Cuban exile Ángel Oliva, one of the most significant tobacco farmers and cigar manufacturers of the previous century, who grew, in 1962, the first plants on Santa Luz, a *finca* near Copán, from seeds he had brought with him from the Vuelta Abajo.

Oliva was certain that his efforts would be successful, since he was more than happy with the soil he found here. He was right. Today the Oliva's – the great man himself, Ángel, died in 1993 – run a tobacco plantation in the east of the country near the border with Nicaragua.

More than 150 kilometres to the west of the Mayan city lies a small city that also bears the name Copán – Santa Rosa de Copán. A cigar factory bearing the name, Fábrica de Tabacos La Flor de Copán, can be found here. Founded in 1785, it can look back on a tobacco tradition more than 200 years old; however, the real upswing in its fortunes began in the mid 1970s and led to it acquiring an international reputation. For it was lucky enough to be awoken from its Sleeping-Beauty slumber.

Thereafter, it has significantly contributed to the triumphant success that Honduran cigars have experienced in the last few years. Since 1977, cigars of the Zino brand have been made here, cigars with which Davidoff hoped to gain a foot in the door of the profit-rich US market.

Mayan ruins in Honduras. Excavations have revealed something extraordinary – several stone witnesses show that pre-Columbian priests inhaled tobacco during ritual events until they fell into a trance, in which they imagined themselves to be nearer their gods.

Because of the US embargo, this had not been possible for the Havanas of this resourceful Connoisseur's concern.

The manager of La Flor de Copán is Jorge Portillo, while Dr. Jorge Bueso Arias is the business' president – both Hondurans, i.e. locals, which is in no way a common occurrence in the cigar world of Central America.

Arias has even run for president of his homeland, but that was quite a while ago, in 1971 actually, just over a year after the disastrous "Football War" between Honduras and El Salvador. He failed by only a small margin. Since then, Dr. Bueso Arias has devoted himself primarily to the cultivation of tobacco.

Soon after Ángel Oliva's arrival, a further Cuban exile livened up the tobacco and cigar scene in Honduras with gusto. Frank Llaneza, who grew up with cigar tobacco and is today still closely associated with it in as much as he manages, among other things, the production of numerous premium brands, worked at the time for the US-company, Villazón. He soon recognised the possibilities Honduras had to offer – and began cooperating with Oliva.

Villazón and Honduras American Tobacco (the name of Oliva's company), jointly set up a factory in Cofradia, not far from San Pedro Sula, the most important industrial area after the capital Tegucigalpa, and also a centre of the indigenous Honduran cigar production.

The Hoyo de Monterrey Excalibur, created by Frank Llaneza, who proved with it that an excellent businessman can also be an outstanding cigar maker, is still produced in Cofradia – together with other premium brands.

And here an observation. As the first Hoyos de Monterrey Excalibur were being smoked in the United States the editor of a renowned specialist magazine enthused over the quality of these cigars: "The Hoyo de Monterrey Excalibur is the best strong cigar that can be bought in America [...] In flavour tests, it proved to be the best cigar of all, even better than Cuban cigars ever were (or are)."

It cannot be denied that the Excalibur belongs to the absolute top premium brands, but the chauvinism of some Americans is at times amazing.

Soon after Cofradia began production, Llaneza set up a further plant for Villazón – this time in Danlí, a medium-sized city lying to the west of Tegucigalpa, near the border with Nicaragua. The factory in Danlí is in the meantime being managed by Estelo Padrón, another – how could he be anything else – Cuban exile. And meanwhile, Frank Llaneza also has another job – he is president of Villazón & Co. the company for which he previously opened new markets in Honduras.

Further Cuban exiles, in addition to those already mentioned, were responsible for revitalising other elements in the Honduran cigar industry. Two such exiles are Ramón Martínez and Rolando Reyes. They are mentioned here as representative of the many development helpers who were forced at one time to leave their homeland and have since firmly established themselves in Honduras.

Today, the above-mentioned city of Danlí is also considered a centre of cigar tobacco cultivation and processing, and has since developed to become the epicentre of a region that is expanding strongly in the field of tobacco growing and cigar production.

Don Jorge Bueso, President of the legendary Fábrica de Tabacos La Flor de Copán factory.

Here, Néstor Plasencia, considered by many to be the doyen of the Central American cigar world, is also to be found. A wanderer between different worlds – that is, between Honduras and Nicaragua – he manages the production of a range of premium brands.

All these activities have resulted in numerous top-quality leading brands being produced in Honduras – with an upward tendency – and, after the Dominican Republic, this land now manufactures the largest number of cigars in this field. Quite a few of these cigars belong to the *puro* category – which also goes to show that the Honduran cigar industry has by no means reached the limit of its potential.

Nicaragua

"Cigars from Nicaragua are almost on a par with those from Cuba" – "what the Vuelta Abajo is for Cuba, is the area around Estelí and Jalapa for Nicaragua. Here excellent tobacco is grown" – "it will not be long before one can hardly tell Cuban and Nicaraguan cigars apart with regard to their aroma and quality".

How destructive a civil war can be! Here, a branch of business in the agricultural sector is experiencing a breathtaking upsurge, and within half a decade the effort and dedication of almost twenty years is sacrificed on the altar of power politics, destroying hopes and visions for the future.

Anyone giving utterance to one of the comments above in the middle or even towards the end of the 1970s would not have been rewarded with pitying shakes of the head or vehement protests of disagreement, but would have been taken quite seriously, as long as the other party understood something about tobacco and cigars – at that time, Nicaraguan cigars were generally considered the nearest thing to Havanas.

The civil war completely destroyed this dream. It all began at the start of 1978, with the murder of opposition politician Chamorro during an election rally by

Common Ground

If you open an atlas and turn to a map of the Caribbean, you will observe that both the Vuelta Abajo region and area around Jalapa – both centres of their respective cigar tobacco cultivation – lie on more or less the same degree of latitude. Could this explain the excellent climatic and topographic conditions that dominate both countries and which appear so ideal for growing tobacco?

supporters of the dictator Somoza. The national uprising that followed quickly turned into a bloody civil war. When the hated dictator left Nicaragua in July 1979, he left behind him a country in which not only the fields and buildings had been destroyed, but the very soul of the people had been seriously wounded.

When the Sandinista government of Daniel Ortega began the work of providing stimuli for the ruined economy with a programme of reform there seemed ground for hope. But then the country was subjected to renewed unrest from without – the rightwing Contras, supported by the USA, continued the armed opposition to the Sandinistas from bases in Honduras.

The hanging of a trade embargo against Nicaragua by the United States in 1985 then disrupted the economy of the Central American state completely.

The tobacco and cigar industry was naturally also disrupted. The area stretching along the border with Honduras was the main scene of fighting between the Contras and the Sandinistas. This is also the region in which tobacco is cultivated and cigars manufactured, and during the struggle many a plantation was devastated and many a tobacco shed served as a hideout for a bomb squad.

The regressive politics of the United States administration succeeded in sealing off a second source of high quality cigars for its *aficionados,* after Cuba. "Damned power politics!" thought not a few cigar fans in Alabama and Arizona, in Minnesota and Montana, in Nebraska and Nevada, and elsewhere.

In the meantime, everything looks very rosy once more for our friends in the States. Since a more moderate government came to power in 1990, the reconstruction of Nicaragua is in progress, albeit somewhat sluggishly here and there, with the occasional setback,

Evilio "Jipio" Oviedo, a Nicaraguan cigar legend, is considered one of Central America's best torquedores.

and a general slow but steady upward trend is recognisable.

The upward trend in the cigar industry is more rapid, since each new harvest brings a considerable improvement in the quality of cigars from the land between the Caribbean and the Pacific Ocean.

Meanwhile not only is the number of premium cigars from Nicaragua increasing, but a growing number of *puros* are also being produced.

Costa Rica

This Central American country of only 50,000 square kilometres, lying between Nicaragua to the north and Panama to the southwest, has only played a secondary role in the field of tobacco cultivation and cigar manufacture.

The amount of cigar tobacco grown here is relatively small and is mainly used as filler tobacco. The Gold and the Trinidad series from Bahia, as well as the Flor Real and the Mythos Solitude, are the few cigar brands that should be mentioned.

Panama

Anyone who believes that Panama has relatively little to offer apart from the canal of the same name is greatly mistaken, not least in respect of the cultivation of high quality cigar tobacco. A tobacco is grown in the Chiriquí province, situated in the northwest of this country in which an artificial waterway connects the Pacific Ocean with the Caribbean, which is more than suited for the production of cigars and which

need not shy from comparison with tobaccos from other sources.

Of the two factors which effectively enhance the quality of Panama tobaccos, apart from the warm, moist sea climate, the main is the rich nutritious soils found in the province of Chiriquí.

It is by no means an overstatement to call the Caribbean the "very heart of premium cigars". This is true in regard to cultivation as well as production – for it was on the eastern part of the island of Hispaniola (i.e. the current territory of the Dominican Republic) that the first tobacco plantations were created, and anyone who calls Cuba the "motherland of the cigar" will surely not be contradicted.

Cuba

As this book deals with the largest of the islands of the Greater Antilles on almost every other page in some or other respect, here it should suffice to discuss the individual areas of cultivation briefly.

The Oriente region in effect extends over three areas of cultivation, of which two lie on the extreme east of the island near Santiago de Cuba, the former capital, while the third stretches to the north of Ciego de Ávila in the centre of the island – if one can talk of a centre at all in respect of this elongated island.

The Remedios region borders the latter of these growing areas to the west. There then follows the Partidos region which begins to the southwest of the capital, Havana, and has San Antonio de los Baños as its centre.

The Caribbean

The Vuelta Abajo region lies practically in the extreme west of the country in the province of Pinar del Río. Just before this region, i.e. to the east, towards Havana, is found the region of Semi Vuelta.

Of all the regions with their many hectares of cultivation, only one, strictly speaking, satisfies the demands made of plants later to be turned into completely hand-made long filler – into Havanas. That is – *nota bene* – the region of Vuelta Abajo.

The Vuelta Abajo appears to be blessed with a soil that cannot be matched anywhere in the whole world as far as tobacco cultivation is concerned. This is accompanied by a climate which also appears to be specially created for this evergreen, softly undulating, hilly landscape, broken here and there by small rock formations also covered by greenery. When the

copious rainfall enters an unintentional symbiosis with the tropical heat, wafts of mist rise over the many small valleys, lingering briefly – as if the veils of mist were only there as a protective layer to prevent this part of the earth from being dried-out by the sun. Both soil and climate ensure the best conditions and give the tobacco plants the chance to develop to their full potential. It now "only" depends on the expertise and skill of all the *tabacaleros* …

Finally, a (vexatious) explanatory note – the Vuelta Arriba region has been increasing recently. This is not a region at all in the true sense, but the name given by the Cubans for some years now to the areas of tobacco cultivation to the east of the capital.

Because the cigar industry is set on further growth (the state is in urgent need of foreign currency), it is forced to resort to tobaccos from these areas, tobaccos that were previously not used for products destined for export. That is in itself no bad thing, for the tobaccos grown in Cuba are, as a whole, good.

Nevertheless, the term, Vuelta Arriba, is annoying. The attempt here to draw a veil over the precise origin of certain tobaccos for certain exports is too blatant. A classic example of the ostrich …

Jamaica

Each wave of emigration in the history of Cuba has brought a number émigrés to settle in Jamaica. Included among these were, of course, cigar makers – and so the most southerly of the Great Antilles islands can show a tradition of over a hundred years of manufacturing cigars and growing tobacco (which is mainly used for filler).

"Even the most pointless and unfortunate of days seems well spent when looked back upon through the blue fragrant smoke of a Havana."

*Evelyn Waugh,
English author*

The First European Cigar Smoker

The Genoese seafarer Christopher Columbus set anchor on his first expedition in the services of Spain on the 12th of October 1492 near one of the Bahama Islands. He had reached Guanahaní, which he named "San Salvador" and had discovered, albeit by accident, the Americas. 15 days later, on the 27th of October, he sailed his ships, La Santa Mária, La Pinta, and La Niña into the protecting waters of the Bahía de Gibara of the island of Colba, as the indigenous peoples called the largest of the islands there. Columbus believed himself to have reached Zipangu, the legendary land of Japan, which was supposed to lie before the empire of the great Khan described by Marco Polo. But he had not come across Japan, but, as already mentioned, Colba, modern day Cuba.

The two sailors that the Argonaut of the Atlantic sent on land for a first reconnoitre of the Island, Rodrigo de Jerez and Luis de Torres, came across people who made strange staffs from dried leaves which they then proceeded to "set alight" on one side in order to inhale the resulting smoke from the other. Rodrigo de Jerez and Luis de Torres were thus the first Europeans to experience the smoking of tobacco and – when only in a most remote sense – to get to know cigars.

Today, a round dozen premium brands are still produced in Jamaica, although the tendency in this field is falling slightly, not least because several well-known brands such as the Temple Hall and the Macanudo have left Jamaica and found a new home in the Dominican Republic.

Dominican Republic

The Dominican Republic, independent under the name of República Dominicana since 1865, is one of the two states that share the island of Hispaniola. The other state, Haiti, is situated on the west of the island, while the Dominican Republic stretches over the rest – Haiti accounts for 36.4 percent of Hispaniola's total area, the Dominican Republic the respectable rest.

Although both states have populations of roughly the same size (over seven million), the gap between the levels economic development of each land has widened, if not drastically then noticeably, in the last few decades, to the detriment of Haiti.

Whereas the gross national product there in 1983 amounted to 320 US-dollars per head, in 1995 it was only just 250 US-dollars. During the same period of time, the gross national product of the average Dominican rose from 1,380 to 1,460 US-dollars.

This modest growth on the part of the Dominican Republic is principally the result of the respective political development of both states.

In the region of Central America, which in itself is characterised by a political instability that is almost inherent in its continuity, it has been Haiti that has figured predominantly in the international headlines of the last few years as this land has struggled with internal unrest and attempted to overcome a situation of almost civil war. In contrast, the political situation in the Dominican Republic has been more or less stable since the middle of the 1970s.

An early Illustration (1493) of reports of Christopher Columbus' voyages of discovery show indigenous people smoking cigars.

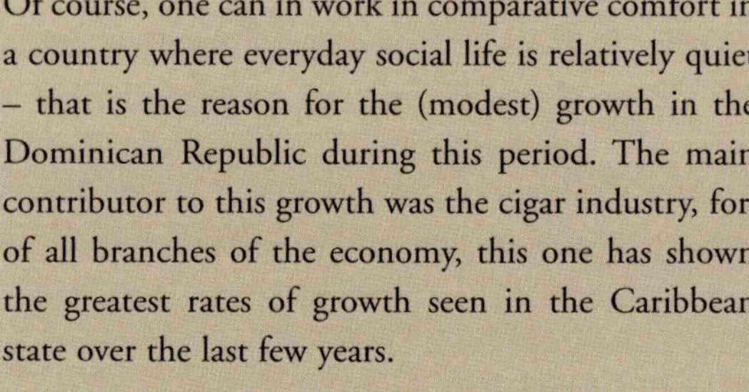

Of course, one can in work in comparative comfort in a country where everyday social life is relatively quiet – that is the reason for the (modest) growth in the Dominican Republic during this period. The main contributor to this growth was the cigar industry, for, of all branches of the economy, this one has shown the greatest rates of growth seen in the Caribbean state over the last few years.

If, in this context, the somewhat restrained phrase "rate of growth" is replaced by the word "boom", the enormous upsurge the Dominican Republic's tobacco industry (and most of all cigar manufacturing) has experienced over the past few decades becomes clearly apparent.

It is therefore not surprising that some visitors to the Caribbean island receive the impression that this boom has gripped the Dominicans in just the same way that the Americans who made their way westward from the east were gripped by that rush for a metal – gold.

Whereas, in those days it was "yellow gold" that fed the hopes of becoming rich, here it is "brown gold" that sustains the dream of prosperity. In short, the processing of this gold – i.e. the production of cigars – is by now one of the few trades in the Dominican Republic that are regarded as lucrative.

Since the United States insists on maintaining its embargo against Cuba, and the demand for premium cigars is unbroken in the land of unlimited possibilities, it is principally cigars from the non-Cuban Caribbean that are in demand in the USA – cigars of the highest quality that conform to the premium standard and awaken memories of the good old Havana. This is principally a challenge for the producers in the Dominican Republic, the country in which most premium brands are produced and which exports most premium cigars.

Since this demand is not decreasing – Europe is another important market in addition to North America – factories producing "premium cigars" can be found in almost every backyard of every region of the Dominican Republic where either tobacco is grown or cigar manufacturing is a dominant factor.

This is obviously disproportionate, but it just goes to show the upsurge there has been in the Dominican Republic's cigar industry – and explains why not every premium brand on offer actually meets the criteria for a premium cigar.

However, the exporters and producers – North American and European alike – can quickly differentiate between good and poor quality, and therefore as a rule only premium cigars that merit the title, and which are the basis of the Dominican reputation for cigars, actually make it to the cigar shops of both the Old and the New World.

Dominican Republic: top quality cigars are brought into shape – torcedoras and torcedores in one of the Davidoff cigar factories.

And yet Dominican production of cigars cannot look back on all that long a tradition. Although tobacco perfectly suitable for cigar making has been grown here for an eternity, it is only since the beginning of the last century that cigar production itself also began in the Caribbean state. The production of premium cigars that justify the name commenced, by contrast, somewhat later.

It was first and foremost Cuban exiles who left the fields of their homeland at the turn of the last century and in greater numbers after Castro's rise to power, that sought to build an existence for themselves elsewhere. Usually only after several intermediate stops along the way, did they at last reach the Dominican Republic, finally settle down and begin to do what they had always done – make cigars.

It was people such as Fuente, García, Menéndez, Quesada and Toraño who found here the ideal prerequisites for producing really good cigars, since one of the world's best filler tobaccos, the (relatively mild) *Dominican Olor* or *Olor Dominicano,* grew, in a manner of speaking, just around the corner. It was soon accompanied by the (somewhat stronger) *Piloto Cubano,* and after a while by the more aromatic *San Vincente* – tobaccos grown from Cuban seeds that the immigrants had brought with them as they left their home island.

By contrast, the other leaves were for export. Initially, tobaccos from Brazil, Ecuador, Honduras and Mexico were used for the binder before indigenous tobacco was also drawn upon for this purpose, while Connecticut and Cameroon tobaccos were trusted for the wrapper leaves since these combined wonderfully with the indigenous filler tobaccos. Stronger emphasis has been placed of late on wrapper leaves from

Ecuador which are in no way inferior to those from Connecticut. In the meantime, the Fuentes and, even more so, Hendrik Kelner, of Tabadom and Davidoff have succeeded in developing wrapper leaves to satisfy the highest demands.

Attempts to develop high-quality wrapper leaves have been going on for quite some time, since Hispaniola enjoys climatic conditions comparable to those on the large neighbouring island of Cuba. Whereas the Windward Passage separates the extreme east of the largest island of Antilles from the northwest of the second largest by only a little more than 40 kilometres, Cuba lies to the north of the 20° northern parallel, while Hispaniola stretches to the south of this degree of latitude.

Soil cannot be imported. Neither can wind and other climatic influences, and so it is merely possible to compare different areas of cultivation with each other – regardless of whether bananas or pineapples, wine or tobacco thrive there – in order to come to a conclusion about where, to what degree and in what quality, what crops grow.

In regard to tobacco cultivation one can say that the soil of the Cuban region of Vuelta Abajo – for many experts the most ideal in this respect – is unique, but each of the numerous growing fields of the Dominican Republic is just as unique. Furthermore, it can be said in this respect that even tobaccos grown in a very closely defined area, but harvested from separate fields, differ from one another, albeit sometimes only in nuance.

It is therefore pointless to talk of better or worse tobaccos, they are simply different. It is a matter of taste or preference of each individual Connoisseur, whether, for example, one prefers a Riesling from the Moselle or one from the Rhine area. In such a case it can only be stated that a Riesling from the Moselle usually presents more acidity. Whether that is to your taste or not is another matter.

Suffice it to say that the numerous fields of the Dominican Republic in which tobacco intended for the production of Premium cigars is grown, are among the best to be found anywhere in the world.

These fields lie primarily in the Valle del Cibao, as the fertile area along the banks of the River Yaque del Norte in the northwest of the Dominican Republic is called. Significant growing areas are also to be found a little further to the west, in the area around Moca, as well as to the south of Moca, around La Vega and Bonao.

Not only cigar tobacco intended for filler is grown in these areas, plants that provide binder and wrapper leaves also thrive here. And several large *fábricas,* in which, year for year, millions of premium cigars leave

As is the case with a good wine, a good cigar requires the necessary repose to mature. An aging room of the Davidoff factory in the Dominican Republic.

the *torcedores'* tables, can also be found here. However, cigar production is centred in the region around the provincial capital of Santiago de los Caballeros, in the city itself and in La Romana, which lies in the south-west of the island.

As already stated, the Dominican Republic is the greatest producer of premium cigars worldwide. Over 400 brands from this Caribbean state may bear the title that ennobles a cigar (although "only" between 100 and 120 can be regarded as truly top brands).

Dominican cigars are, as a rule, mild to medium-strong in flavour and very aromatic. There have been more and more strong exceptions to this rule recently.

And there is another factor that should also not be overlooked. Dominican cigars (the top 100–120 brands) are excellently well-made and thereby promise to provide unsullied smoking pleasure. They are also a pleasure for the cigar smoking novice who is generally well served by a mild Dominicano.

"A good cigar from overseas locks the door on the spitefulness of this world."

Franz Liszt, Hungarian composer

Anyone who thinks of the southern part of the double continent of America in relation to tobacco and cigars thinks first of Brazil, which can look back on a long tradition in this field. Other countries, however, also have something to offer in this respect, sometimes coming as quite a surprise.

Columbia

Columbia, situated in the north of South America, with its coast subject to the tides of the Pacific Ocean in the west and the waters of the Caribbean in north, plays a rather low-level role in the cultivation of tobacco.

It is only in El Carmen, a region in the northwest of Columbia, where a tobacco *(Cubita)* is grown that satisfies the requirements for use (usually for the filler) in a premium cigar.

Ecuador

Tobacco plants bearing first-class wrapper leaves for cigars largely to be found in the premium range have been grown in this South American country between Columbia and Peru for quite some time.

With the two Andean giants of Chimborazo and Cotopaxi forming its roof, this land offers the ideal prerequisites for the cultivation of tobacco with its rainforest in the lowlands, the mountain and cloud forests of the Cordilleras rising to a height of 3,500 metres and its predominantly tropical climate. Thus, some years ago, the cultivation of plants, especially chosen from Connecticut and Sumatra seeds intended to provide wrapper leaves of good quality, began.

The results are more than worthy of presentation. While the Sumatra seeds yielded a very satisfactory quality, the wrapper leaves resulting from the Connecticut seeds were even more rewarding.

Wrapper leaves from Ecuador, which virtually grow under a natural "veil of shade" owing to the constantly overcast sky, are in great demand, and need not shy from comparison with the "originals" (at least those from Connecticut) in respect of quality.

It is principally cigar manufacturers of the Dominican Republic that draw upon this product of the República del Ecuador – not least because it is comparatively cheap.

Now a word about the natural "veil of shade". The produce of this Andean country is sometimes called *Sun Grown,* or even *Virgin Sun Grown* tobacco. This is meant to signify that the tobacco plants are subjected to almost no direct sun despite their not being covered by cloths as is the case in the cultivation of *Connecticut Shade.*

Peru

Although this South American country cannot refer to any manifest tobacco tradition, scientists have no doubt that *Nicotiana tabacum* has its genetic origin in the highlands of the Peruvian and Bolivian Andes.

Following the start made by Davidoff in 2003 by acknowledging Peruvian tobacco in the filler for both new Zino series, this cigar tobacco has gradually become the object of other renowned cigar manufacturers' attention.

Hand precision – forming the cap on the head of a cigar demonstrates a torcedor's skill.

Peruvian tobacco is currently grown predominantly in the north of the country, on the eastern foothills of the Andes. It presents a respectable medium strength and possesses quite complex aromas. This tobacco has good burning properties and is, as already mentioned, very suitable for filler mixtures, but can by all means also be used as a binder.

Brazil

Tobacco cultivation in Brazil can look back on a tradition stretching over centuries. The first official building for selling tobacco opened its gates as early as the 1660s in this country which, with its eight and a half million square kilometres, encompasses almost half the total area of South America. The main cigar growing areas appear tiny by comparison.

Both lie in the northeast of the República Federativa do Brasil, and are found in the region of Arapiraca in the state of Alogoa, and in the region of Recôncavo, 500 kilometres further south in the state of Bahia. It is especially the latter region with its areas of Mata Sul, Mata Norte, and above all Mata Fina, the heart

of Brazilian tobacco cultivation, which many cigar smokers will recognize solely by the descriptions Bahia and Mata Fina found in many brand names.

In Recôncavo, home to the "tobacco capital" of Cruz das Almas, beans, maize, tapioca and most of all tobacco are cultivated, in contrast to in the Caribbean countries, by thousands of independent planters who each year, towards the end of July, begin to harvest the best Bahia tobacco from their parcels of land, known as *sitios*.

The process of harvesting is also different from that practised in Central America. There the leaves are plucked individually, while here the whole stalks of the plant are plucked and dried. This harvesting process guarantees a continuing supply of important nutrients to the leaves after cutting, whereby the development of the aromas of the later aromatic tasting tobacco is effectively enhanced.

The fermentation process beginning after the harvest also makes its contribution. It stretches over six

"Daydreams travel on the aromatic clouds of a noble cigar."

Geraldo Dannemann, German-Brazilian cigar pioneer

months, during which the tobacco is heated to 50 °C–55 °C in stacks of up to 11/2 tons to break down the nicotine, water and sugar.

Despite all the care both before and after the harvest, the efforts of the tobacco farmers would yield little success if the Recôncavo were not one of the most fertile regions of Brazil. Here, a tropical climate dominates with an average annual temperature of 25 °C, and copious heavy rainfall.

Due to both climate and the proximity to the Bay of Bahia, the Recôncavo enjoys a lightly sandy soil – and this is ideal for growing tobacco.

Similar conditions are to be found in the Arapiraca region further to the north. While clay dominates the soil of the hills, it is also lightly sandy and porous in the lowlands where tobacco is grown.

Unlike in Bahia, the plucking of individual leaves is practised in Alagoas. Drying is also done leaf for leaf. This in turn leads to top results in respect of wrapper leaf production.

The following generalisation can be made when comparing the tobaccos of these two regions – whereas the tobacco from Recôncavo is quite aromatic and the leaves display a clear structure, the *Arapiraca* leaves possess less aroma but have a finer structure.

A large proportion of Brazilian cigar tobacco is exported, as is the case in Indonesia. This means that, as a percentage, far fewer cigars are actually manufactured in the country for export than in the countries of the Caribbean.

Although internationally acknowledged Premium brands are also manufactured in Brazil, it remains to be said that a high proportion of Brazilian cigar tobacco is currently, as has been the case in the past, sent overseas as a coveted raw material.

*"In the end,
every cigar goes
up in smoke."*

Brazilian proverb

BALMORAL
Davidoff

Brands and Companies

LA AURORA
Fábrica de Cigarros
HECHOS A MANO DESDE 1903

As suggested in the introduction, this book does not pretend to be an encyclopaedia. It would be impossible to present here all the premium cigar produced worldwide. Even without Havanas, there are still some 1,000 brands of cigar bearing the label "premium". To list all these brands, in addition to the good Dutch brands plus those worthy of mention from other European countries, would go far beyond the scope of this book. A courageous exclusion policy was therefore in order. This was made easier if insufficient information was available about a certain brand. If not for that, almost every premium brand would have been worth listing here.

One thinks immediately of the Alonso Menéndez, the Balmoral, the Goya and the José Martí, of brands such as La Casa de Nicaragua, La Flor Dominicana, La Meridiana, La Paz and Las Cabrillas, and others such as Petrus, Pimentel, Quisquea, Regalia Fina, Royal Jamaica, Temple Hall, Thomas Hinds, Vargas, Vasco da Gama, Villa Dominicana and Wallstreet – to name just a few of the many that would have merited further consideration.

Abbreviations Found in the Tables

Ar	*Arapiraca*	*Cu*	*Cuba*	*Ni*	*Nicaragua*
B	*Binder*	*CuSe*	*Cuba Seed*	*NiSe*	*Nicaragua Seed*
Ba	*Bahia*	*DoOlor*	*Dominican Olor*	*Ph*	*Philippines*
Brazil	*Brazil*	*Dom.*	*Dominican*	*PiCu*	*Piloto Cubano*
Ca	*Cameroon*	*Rep.*	*Republic*	*SaVi*	*San Vicente*
Co	*Corojo*	*Ec*	*Ecuador*	*Sf*	*Short filler*
CoBr	*Connecticut Broadleaf*	*F*	*Filler*	*Su*	*Sumatra*
		Ha2000	*Havana 2000*	*SuDe*	*Sumatra Deli*
CoCuSe	*Connecticut Cuba Seed*	*Ho*	*Honduras*	*SuGr*	*Sun Grown*
		In	*Indonesia*	*SuSa*	*Sumatra Sandleaf*
Col	*Columbia*	*Ja*	*Java*		
Conn	*Connecticut*	*JaBe*	*Java Besuki*	*SuSe*	*Sumatra Seed*
CoRi	*Costa Rica*	*Lf*	*Long filler*	*Ts*	*Table Scrape*
CoSe	*Connecticut Seed*	*Ma*	*Maduro*	*ViSe*	*Vicente Seed*
		MaFi	*Mata Fina*	*ViSuGr*	*Virgin Sun Grown*
CoSh	*Connecticut Shade*	*Me*	*Mexico*		
		MeSe	*Mexico Seed*	*Vola*	*Vorstenlanden*
Cr	*Criollo*	*Mf*	*Medium filler*	*W*	*Wrapper*

All brands and series listed in the tables are made from 100 percent tobacco.
Strength from 1 to 6: 1 = very mild, 6 = very strong.

Altadis

This is the trading name of the fusion of the two state owned tobacco companies, Seita (France) and Tabacalera (Spain), which, in 1999, took a 50 percent holding in the Cuban state owned company, Habanos S.A. The holding is reputed to have cost the new business 500 million US-dollars.

Arnold André

1835 is the year in which the Gebrüder André tobacco factory was officially founded. In fact, it had all begun earlier, in 1817, for in that year the André brothers commenced tobacco manufacturing in Osnabrück. The business must have developed quickly. For only 16 years after the official founding, i.e.

1851, it opened a branch in Bünde in the east of Westphalia. Finally, the Arnold André Zigarrenfabrik company was founded in 1866. The name of the business has remained unchanged ever since. What has changed, however, is the location – the company moved into its present head office in Bünde in 1905.

If Arnold André was at that time one of the better known companies in the trade, today it is one of the largest. Arnold André is the absolute market leader in Germany in the field of economically priced cigars and cigarillos. The cigars of the Clubmaster brand, introduced in 1972, and produced in the Osterholz-Scharmbeck works near Bremen, are the best selling cigarillo brand in Germany, while the well-known Handelsgold brand, first produced in 1935 and for decades the best known cigar brand in Germany, should not go unmentioned either.

Over time, new brands: Tropenschatz (a Brazil), Garves (also a Brazil), El Bacco (a Sumatran, as is Bach-schmidt), were added – all cigars or cigarillos to be found in the lower priced segment of the market and all serving an established loyal public. For example, Tropenschatz is the most frequently sold cigar brand in Germany. Over the last few years, Arnold André has greatly increased its efforts to import high quality premium brands from overseas, and has now gained a good reputation in this field. Brands such C.A.O., El Crédito, and La Aurora definitely raise the pulse of many an *aficionado*.

Arturo Fuente

Their roots are in Spain and Cuba, traces of them can be found in the United States, Puerto Rico, Nicaragua and Honduras, and (in the literal sense of the word) their seed has been flourishing in the Dominican Republic for some considerable time. We are talking about the Fuente family, who have been making cigars for three generations.

Arturo Fuente and his family emigrated to the United States from Cuba towards the end of the 19th century. Over the following years, he deployed his mastery of the skill of cigar making in various factories in his new country.

Arturo Fuente

After Don Arturo set up his first factory (a slew of others was to follow) in Tampa, Florida, it was not long before Clear Havanas bearing the name of Fuente were on the market. His first workforce consisted of no more than seven employees, and this small troop would quite often work late into the

night to satisfy the enormous demand the Fuente products soon enjoyed. Time and again, events beyond their control forced the family to decamp and try their luck in another country. Whereas a fire completely destroyed the factory in Tampa, forcing Don Arturo to start afresh elsewhere, it was political troubles in Puerto Rico – as in Honduras and Nicaragua – which led to abandonment of the respective arrangements in each country, leading the passionate cigar makers to mull over precisely which location would best provide the necessary conditions for their vocation. In the Dominican

province of Santiago, they finally found somewhere that came very close to meeting their vision for the cultivation, reproduction and processing of high quality types of tobacco.

When patriarch Don Arturo died aged 85 – the number combination of his flagship cigar, the Flor Fina 8-5-8 (his erstwhile favourite), is a reference to his age at death – he had long initiated Carlos, his son, into the secrets of cigar manufacturing. Carlos, in turn, passed on his knowledge to his children, Carlos jr. and Cynthia, both of whom are also currently active in the family concern. They succeeded in something that even renowned experts had not considered possible to this degree. When they bought the El Caribe plantation from the Olivas at the beginning of the 1990s, and declared their intention of cultivating select wrapper leaf tobacco there, they harvested at the time only the astonished incredulity of the professional world. The Fuentes' plan to grow really good wrapper leaves certainly met with widespread scepticism. However, in the meantime, this scepticism has turned to respect for the Fuentes' achievements. Their great cigar-making skill is seen most notably in the formats of their Opus X series, which bear only wrapper leaves grown on the plantation they have renamed, Château de la Fuente. At all events, this series has enjoyed an excellent reputation among enthusiasts ever

since. Still to be mentioned is that the Fuentes also run a third factory, in Tampa. Here, a range of machine formed – but hand rolled – cigars are produced for the United States market.

Cigars are currently being produced in the north of the Dominican Republic that are among the best hand-made cigars available on the market. As mentioned above, the Fuentes finally settled here following a veritable odyssey. In 1980, they set up their first cigar factory in the provincial capital of Santiago de los Caballeros, before launching, in 1990, a second in Moca, about 20 kilometres to the southeast. The Fuentes have now advanced to become the largest Dominican producer of premium cigars, employing a workforce of about 800, of which 600 work in Santiago alone. More than 20 million cigars leave their factories annually. The Fuentes prove on a daily basis that quantity and quality are not mutually exclusive.

Ashton

Just over one-and-a-half decades on the market, the Ashton has established

itself firmly in the premium cigar sector. This may be due, at least in part, to the name of the producer, which has for some time had a good ring in *connoisseur* circles – Fuente.

As with other outstanding cigar makers, the Fuentes are masters of the skill of creating harmonious tobacco mixtures and compositions, as clearly demonstrated in the individual formats of the Ashton. Much of the harmony of individual cigars depends on the tobacco for the various series maturing over a long period. While the tobaccos for the standard series (Classic Line) are stored for maturing for three or four years, those intended for the Cabinets and the tobaccos for the Virgin Sun Grown series are four to five years old before they reach fermentation and are finally processed further.

One last remark – the name, Ashton, is a reference to the famous English pipe maker, William Ashton Taylor.

August Schuster

August Schuster Cigarrenfabrik (to be precise) is the full name of this medium-sized business. The origins of this firm, the last family-owned German cigar manufacturer, lie in the 19th century when the Gebrüder Schuster Cigarren-Fabriken in east Westphalian Bünde was proud to offer fine handmade makes as a speciality, and, what is more, advertised a "guarantee of pure overseas tobacco".

In 1909, August Schuster left the above company to set up his own manufacturing business under the name of Cigarren-Fabriken Aug. Schuster. There were soon three Schuster factories in the cigar town of Bünde, for Hermann Schuster, his brother, also set up shop. In the 1920s, the Cigarren-Fabriken Aug. Schuster alone could boast of four production plants, had at its disposal a postal cheque account, a bank account, and a bank giro account, not to mention a telephone. It was the heyday of German cigar manufacturing. Today, only one plant remains, the August Schuster Cigarrenfabrik, which is again managed by (two) brothers, Manfred und Philipp. The wheel has come full circle.

Whereas the company employed about 1,000 people at the peak of its success, the number today is a little more than 40. Nevertheless, their work is excellent, for they aspire to producing quality cigars – that only quality will finally prevail is the philosophy of the Schusters. The large proportion of work done by hand in the factory contributes to this quality. Although there are machines, they largely date back to (or before) the 1960s.

The Schusters use only choice Brazilian, Javanese, Havana and Sumatran

tobaccos, and emphasis is laid not only on the careful choice of wrapper leaves, but also on the composition of the filler. All cigars are traditional short filler, produced by machine, but always 100 percent tobacco.

Nevertheless, long filler are also to be found in the range offered by the cigar factory from Bünde. These are, however, imported cigars from Central America and the Caribbean. Nonetheless, these brands also bear the Schuster hallmark, since, before the two brothers import a brand, they take care to influence the production of the cigars using their wealth of experience of the smoking preferences prevalent over here. This primarily impacts the choice and mixture of tobacco. The brands Camacho, Casa de Torres and Maria Mancini should be mentioned especially here – to name only three of around ten import brands.

But to return to the firm's own production: apart from the top C. Mendoza brand, the Lepanto and Partageño y Cia should be mentioned in particular. The latter was first produced in 1906 and is therefore considered the traditional Schuster brand. The Brazil Trüllerie, first presented in 2004, could also become such a brand, for, with it, the Schusters have provided the friends of well-made Brazils with finely balanced cigars. The carefully composed mixture of tobacco and the great skill evident in the workmanship, clearly display the Bünders' love of a fine Brazil in each cigar.

Austria-Tabak

Cigars and tobacco in Austria are mainly in the hands of Austria Tabak, the large commercial company that manufactures its cigar products in Fürstenfeld, distributing them – and its imported tobacco products – in the Alpine Republic through its daughter company Tobaccoland. The last cigar factory of the many that existed in the former Austro-Hungarian state can therefore be found in Fürstenfeld, a small city situated near to where the borders of Austria, Slovenia and Hungary meet. Today, about 30 million cigars and cigarillos are produced in this factory, which has been in existence since 1694. These include other brands produced under licence. No reference to Fürstenfeld is complete without mention of Austria's "national cigar". This is the Virginier, which has been produced since 1846 using a recipe that has never been changed. These cigars are composed mainly of what the Austrians call "smoked" Virginia tobaccos. Always serving as wrapper leaves, they are also used in the filler of the Virginier Spezial Regie, together with tobaccos from Malawi and Zaire.

Avo

As if the exotic tobaccos of these two African countries were not enough, tobaccos from Tanzania and Uganda form another filler, that of the Regie Virginier. All these tobaccos are "dark fired"– that is, smoked. Only the Jubiläums-Virginier, available on the market since 1984, has a filler with more familiar contents – Brazil, Havana and Java.

A characteristic of the Virginier, apart from the mouthpiece, is a straw (for which a particular exotic grass is used). This straw is removed from the cigar before smoking, thus creating an air channel to facilitate drawing. And the formats? They are always the same. All Virginiers are 205 millimetres long with a diameter of 10 1/2 millimetres. And what is the name of this format? Quite simply – Virginier!

Although the Dominican Republic's Avos were not obtainable in parts of Europe for a long time, these excellently made premium cigars became more widely available to *aficionados* at the beginning of 1999.

They were created by the multitalented Avo Uvezian – a successful businessman as well as a gifted composer and (jazz) musician. The son of Armenian parents, he was born in 1926, and can look back on a life full of change. As a teenager, he travelled around the Middle East with his own jazz trio, before achieving at the age of 21 the fist climax of his career by being engaged by Shah Reza Pahlavi as a piano player at his court in Tehran. It was thanks to the Shah's advice and support that Avo went to study at the famous Julliard School of Music in New York few years later.

Another great passion – the smoking of noble cigars – led in the early 1980s to the creation of the cigars that bear his name. And in this, the international talent was also successful.

Shortly after its introduction, the Avo was considered one of the absolute premium brands. Finally, as Davidoff became aware of Avo and decided to take a financial and logistic stake in the Avo Cigar Company, Avo's success was assured. Whereas only several thousand Avos were produced in the first year, currently more than five million of these premium cigars leave the Dominican Republic each year.

Produced in the production halls of Davidoff (formerly Tabacos Dominicanos – or Tabadom for short) under the management of Hendrik Kelner (someone with an excellent understanding of his trade), all the series present a mixture with a persuasive balance between the effective strength and the development of the aromas. The XO series is recommended for the fairly advanced smoker since its cigars are generally a little milder than the other long filler series.

Brand/Series	Origin	Filler	Binder	Wrapper	Strength
1881 (Lf)	Philippines	Philippines + Brazil	Philippines	Indonesia (JaBe)	3
Acid (Lf)	Nicaragua	Nicaragua	Nicaragua	Ca/Conn/In	3–4
Alameda (Lf)	Dominican Republic	Dom. Rep. (PiCu + DoOlor)	Dom. Rep. (DoOlor)	CoSh	1–2
Alhambra (Lf)	Philippines	Philippines	Philippines	Indonesia (JaBe)	1–2
Alonso Menéndez (Lf)	Brazil	Puros: all tobaccos grown in Brazil (W: MaFi)			3–4
Ambiente (Lf)	Dominican Republic	Dom. Rep.	Dom. Rep.	Connecticut	2–3
Aromas de San Andrés (Lf)	Mexico	Puros: all tobaccos grown in the Mexican valley of San Andreas			3–4
A(rturo) Fuente					
• *Château (Lf)*	Dominican Republic	Dom. Rep. + Br + Me + Ni	Dom. Rep.	CoSh/Ca	3
• *Classic Line (Lf)*	Dominican Republic	Dom. Rep. + Br + Me + Ni	Dom. Rep.	CoSh/Ca	4–5
• *Gran Reserva (Lf)*	Dominican Republic	Dom. Rep. + Br + Me + Ni	Mexico	Cameroon	3–4
• *Opus X (Lf)*	Dominican Republic	Puros: all tobaccos grown in Dominican Republic			3–4
Ashton					
• *Cabinet Selection (Lf)*	Dominican Republic	Dominican Republic	Dom. Rep.	CoSh	3–5
• *Classic Line (Lf)*	Dominican Republic	Dom. Rep.	Dom. Rep.	CoSh	3–4
• *Virgin Sun Grown (Lf)*	Dominican Republic	Dom. Rep.	Dom. Rep.	Ecuador (CoSe)	4–5
Avo					
• *Domaine (Lf)*	Dominican Republic	Dom. Rep. (SaVi + PiCu + DoOlor)	Dom. Rep. (SaVi)	Ecuador (CoCuSe)	4–5
• *Puritos Classic (Sf)*	Dominican Republic	Dom. Rep.	Ecuador	Ecuador (CoCuSe)	3
• *Puritos Domaine (Sf)*	Dominican Republic	Dom. Rep.	Ecuador	Ecuador (CoCuSe)	4
• *Signature (Lf)*	Dominican Republic	Dom. Rep. (PiCu + SaVi)	Dom. Rep. (SaVi)	Ecuador (CoCuSe)	5
• *XO (Lf)*	Dominican Republic	Dom. Rep. (SaVi + DoOlor)	Dom. Rep. (SaVi)	Connecticut	3–4

Darier & Cleef
BALBOA
11 robusto cigars

Balboa

The Balboa is the only brand from Panama worth mentioning, apart from the José Llopis.

Strictly speaking, it would be more accurate to say "Panamanian origin" since the Balboas – named after Panama's discoverer, the Spanish seafarer Vasco Núñez de Balboa – are actually made in Nicaragua. They were first produced in 1881, admittedly in Panama, when a Frenchman called Alfons Darier and a Belgian nobleman Jean van Cleef set up the first cigar factory, the Tabacalera Darier & Cleef, in this narrow country between the Pacific and the Caribbean.

Production stopped in 1904, and it was a long time before the brand was awakened from its deep slumber in the year 2000.

The tobacco for this hand-made Nicaraguan long filler with its heavy, tangy aroma comes, as in the past, from Panama, where it is grown according to ecological principles on small, widely scattered tobacco farms in the province of Chiriqui. And there is something else worth mentioning. The tobacco for the filler matures over at least four years, while the storage of the binder and wrapper tobaccos can last up to six years – a precondition for a good balance between the individual components (which in turn has a positive effect on the drawing and burning properties of the cigars).

Bauza

First produced in Cuba, references to pre-revolutionary Havana can still be found on Bauza cigar boxes, although the production facilities of these really well made cigars have been situated in the Dominican Republic for years.

Although these cigars promise a pleasant smoking experience with a medium-heavy aroma, one important comment should be made.

Belinda

The Presidente with its filler – a combination of short and long leaf – does not quite reach the quality of the other formats. Otherwise, these hand-made Bauzas are not only to be recommended, but are also quite economically priced considering their quality.

The heyday of the Belinda, first produced towards the end of the 19th century in Cuba and therefore considered one of the old Havana brands, was in the days between the World Wars. The Belinda was, for example, the first choice of Groucho Marx, Hollywood's chaotic comic-actor and director.

Unfortunately, they are quite difficult to find nowadays because their production has been curtailed in the last few years. This is a pity, for several of the five (machine-produced) formats of this popular brand are particularly well suited for beginners as they are very mild. A small comfort and tip for the determined – try asking in a *Casa del Habanos,* you are more likely to find Belinda there.

Bock y Ca.

Since appearing on the market in the middle of 1998, the Bocks y Ca. have found a respectable following that appreciates these mild to medium-strong premium cigars from the Dominican Republic. Produced in Santiago de los Caballeros by experienced *torcedores,* the appeal of the "Bocks" is due to their combination of different tobaccos. The name of this brand is reminiscent of Gustav Bock of the lower Rhine – the lower Rhine

because it is a point of dispute whether the inventor of the cigar ring was of German or Dutch origin. Perhaps the term, of lower Rhine origin, is acceptable to all since it is well-known that the Rhine leaves Germany near Emmerich to flow into the Netherlands, where it later forms a wide delta. Be that as it may, the memory of one of the great figures of the cigar world during the final years of the 19th century, who soon after emigrating to Cuba called himself Gustavo, is kept alive by these pleasant-to-smoke cigars.

Bolívar

They are among the best (and strongest) Havanas – the cigars of the

Bolívar brand. The name is in memory of the leader of the Latin American independence movement, Simón Bolívar (1783–1830).

The descendant of a Basque Hidalgo-family that had emigrated to South America during the 16th century was a member of the Junta that rose against Spanish domination in 1810. Proclaimed *Libertador* (Liberator) in 1813, he was elected president of Venezuela in 1819 after the Spanish had been defeated, thereby losing their dominance over the country. Under the Bolívar's leadership, large parts of the northwest of the South America continent could be successively liberated, but the greatest wish of this fighter for the freedom of Latin America – to unite all these parts in a single union – was not granted.

Whether or not the Bolívar does justice to South America's greatest son (commemorated today with numerous memorials) is of no relevance in this context, but the full body which develops a markedly strong aroma is by all accounts something for the fighter, that is, for the experienced cigar smoker who loves the penetrating power of a Havana. This strength is most pronounced in the larger formats. In this, the strong, intensive even earthy tasting Bolívars belong to the last of classical Havanas.

The hand-made cigars, with their dark wrapper leaves, and cigar rings and *vistas* still bearing the portrait of Bolívar, owe their strong aroma principally to the filler mixture, which contains more *seco* than *volado*. First introduced in 1901 by the Havana-based José F. Rocha company, the brand gained its still excellent reputation in the 1950s when the brothers Rafael and Ramón Cifuentes took over production.

As already mentioned, the cigars of this traditional brand are something for the lover of a strong Havana – who should refrain from buying cigars when the stamp *Totalmente a mano* is missing from the cigar box, however, for there are also machine-produced formats of this brand that are of less good quality.

Bossner

Truly international – and versatile as well. Konstantin Loskutinov, born in the Soviet Union, emigrated to the West at the end of 1991 after the break up of the multi-ethnic state. On his arrival in Berlin he first sold Russian products before finally setting up a

chocolate factory. Cigars were added not long afterwards.

The Russian was not born a cigar manufacturer. He worked in Siberia in the 1970s as a turner and mechanic before going to Leningrad, at the start of the 1980s, to matriculate at the university there and to begin studying as an engineer. In 1989 he opened a jeans factory in that city (which by this time had regained its former name of St. Petersburg) employing about 300 employees before literally changing horses once again to become a horse breeder and organiser of art auctions.

Konstantin Loskutnikov

One day, Loskutnikov, the driven businessman, was holding an old family photograph in his hand when he suddenly remembered his grandmother saying that her father was never to be found without a cigar in his mouth.

It was soon clear to Loskutnikov, a cigar smoker of many years, that he should create his own cigar brand. After many attempts, he found the right partner in the Dominican Republic, which for him meant (and still means) the ability to influence the composition of the individual cigars. Thus, very well made cigars have been available for some years now under the Bossner label, augmented in the meantime by a series produced in Nicaragua.

It only remains to be explained how the name came about. In this respect, the cosmopolitan businessman remembers a female ancestor, for this was the name of the great grandmother whose husband, as mentioned above, was never to be found without a cigar.

Brazil Trüllerie

The latest series produced by the August Schuster company comes up with seven formats, all awaiting their buyers in gorgeous nostalgic boxes, the interior lids of which are adorned with artistic prints go back to the French painter Jean-Baptiste-Camille Corot (1796–1875). The most pleasing thing is that the presentation and content correspond to one another. The Trülleries are indeed first-class short filler that will impress every friend of a good Brazil.

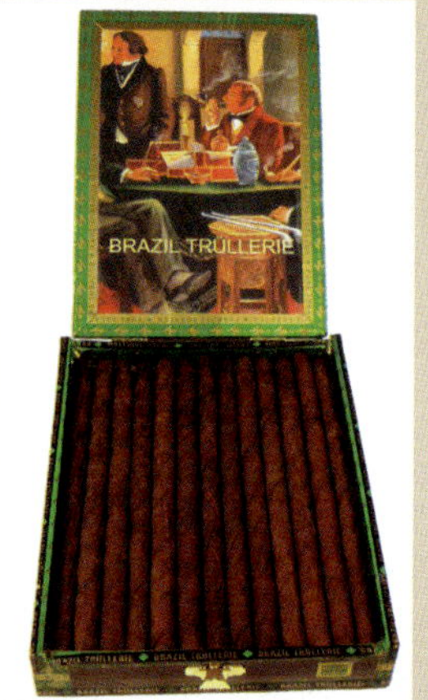

Burger

The company's full name is "Burger Söhne AG", but anyone who mentions the word "Burger" in the cigar world will very seldom be met by an inquisitive glance, as this public limited company is one of the leading European businesses in the tobacco product trade. In the meantime, Dannemann – among others – has also found its way under the roof of this Swiss company. This fourth-generation business dates back to the founding of a cigar factory by Rudolf Burger-Fröhlich. That was in 1864. At the time, this was a fairly ordinary step as cigar factories were springing up like mushrooms all over the north of Switzerland during the beginning of the 1860s – the region was soon known, somewhat disrespectfully as "cheroot country". Burger cheroots were soon well-known among cigar smokers. Cheroots (machine-made cigars with a somewhat compact appearance) are still popular today. The Burger company would not like to do without these traditional cigars, either. Their cheroots, in which tobacco imported from Brazil, Indonesia and Cuba are used, are produced under the name of "Rössli", and have a firm a following as ever.

Brand/Series	Origin	Filler	Binder	Wrapper	Strength
Backgammon (Sf)	Germany	various origins	Indonesia (JaBe)	Indonesia (Sumatra)	3–4
Bahia					
• Blue (Lf)	Nicaragua	Pures: all tobaccos grown in Nicaragua			3
• Gold (Lf)	Costa Rica	Dom. Rep.	Dom. Rep.	Ecuador (CoSe)	3–4

Brand/Series	Origin	Filler	Binder	Wrapper	Strength
• Trinidad (Lf)	Costa Rica	Nicaragua (CuSe)	Ecuador (SuSe)	Ecuador (SuSe)	4–5
Bahianos (Sf)	Switzerland	Brazil (Ba) + Cuba + Dom. Rep.	Indonesia (Java)	Brazil (Ba)	4–5
Balboa (Lf)	Panama	Pure Panama: all tobaccos of Panaman production			2–4
Balmoral					
• Dominican Selection (Lf)	Dominican Republic	Dom. Rep. + Brazil + Cuba	Dom. Rep.	Ecuador (CoSe)	2–3
• Rich & Light (Sf)	Netherlands	Cuba + Brazil + Indonesia (Java)	Indonesia (Java)	Cuba	2
• Royal Selection (Lf)	Dominican Republic	Dom. Rep. (DoOlor + PiCu) + Br (Ba)	Dom. Rep. (DoOlor)	Ecuador (CoSe)	2–4
• Royal Selection Maduro (Lf)	Dominican Republic	Dom. Rep. + Brazil (Ba)	Dom. Rep.	Brazil (Ba)	2–3
• Sumatra Selection (Sf)	Netherlands	Cuba + Brazil + Indonesia (Java)	Indonesia (Java)	Indonesia (Sumatra)	3
Bandera (Mf)	Nicaragua	Puros: all tobaccos grown in Nicaragua			3–4
Bauza (Lf)	Dominican Republic	Dom. Rep. + Nicaragua	Mexico	Ecuador (CoSe)	3–4
Belinda (Sf)	Cuba	Puros: all tobaccos grown in Cuba			2–4
Bering (Lf)	Honduras	Dom. Rep. + Mexico + Honduras	Honduras	CoSh/Ho/Me/Ni	2–3
Bermudez (Lf)	Dominican Republic	Dom. Rep. (PiCu)	Indonesia	Ecuador (CoSe)	3–4
Bock y Ca. (Lf)	Dominican Republic	Dom. Rep. (PiCu) + Nicaragua (CuSe)	Indonesia	Ecuador (CoSe)	2–4
Bolívar (Lf + Sf)	Cuba	Puros: all tobaccos grown in Cuba			3–6
Bossner					
• Dominican Selection	Dominican Republic	Dom. Rep.	Dom. Rep.	Connecticut	2–3
• Nicaraguan Selection	Nicaragua	Nicaragua	Nicaragua	Ecuador (CoBr)	3–4
• Rolando	Dominican Republic	Dom. Rep. (PiCu)	Dom. Rep. (DoOlor)	CoBr	2–3
Braniff					
• Gran Panetela Brasil (Sf)	Germany	various origins	Indonesia (JaBe)	Mexico	3
• Gran Panetela Sumatra (Sf)	Germany	various origins	Indonesia (JaBe)	Indonesia (Sumatra)	3
Brazil Trüllerie (Sf)	Germany	Brazil + Cuba	company secret	Brazil (MaFi)	2–3
Buena Cosecha (Lf)	Nicaragua	Puros: all tobaccos grown in Cuba			3–4
Bundles (Lf)	Dominican Republic	Dom. Rep. + Brazil	Nicaragua (CuSe)	Nicaragua	2–3
Bundles Best Buy (Lf)	Dominican Republic	Nicaragua (CuSe)	Indonesia	Ecuador (CoSe)	2–4

Camacho

The Camacho has been an internationally respected cigar for some
years – and justifiably so (particularly
in relation to the two main series).

The Camacho *Corojo* is the result of
decades of work on tobacco cultivation. The authentic old Cuban *Corojo*
seed was cultivated in Honduras for
almost 30 years before cigars could be
offered that are very reminiscent of
Cuban cigar tradition, full and aromatic in flavour.

The cigars of the Camacho Criollo
series are much lighter in comparison
to the *Corojos*. The tobacco for the
filler of the individual formats is also
grown on plantations in Honduras.
This time, however, it is grown from

old *Criollo* seeds originally from Cuba and combined with *Corojo* tobaccos to produce cigars that are aromatic, but not as dominant and complex as their counterparts. *Criollo,* by the way, is a typical regional tobacco that is cultivated in various forms in all Caribbean countries.

The fathers of these products are the members of the Eiroa family who are considered to be among the best tobacco growers and processors in Honduras. In their work, the Cuban exiles rely on their wealth of experience in successfully growing *Corojo* from seed formerly gained on the family's Cuban plantations prior to their exile.

C.A.O.

C.A.O. – these three letters have a better than good ring to them for numerous *aficionados.* Behind them lies the name Cano A. Ozgener.

Born in Turkey, Ozgener later studied in the United States. A meerschaum pipe developed by him provided the foundation of this passionate smoker's employ, and, since his model was soon much in demand from prominent politicians and actors, he set up a company in 1968 to import the pipes from his homeland. About 30 years later he made a great leap forward. Together with Cuban exiles Carlos Toraño and

Néstor Plasencia he created top-class long filler under the C.A.O label.

The Black was the first cigar that C.A.O. put on the market – it was an immediate success as a result of his absolute determination to achieve perfection. When the devastating El Niño storms of 1996 caused bottlenecks with this exquisite tobacco, Ozgener reaped the consequences as far as quality was concerned and temporarily stopped production.

The Black finally returned to the market in 2002, and was, with its tangy soft aromas, of even higher quality than before. In relation to their burning properties and the workmanship they display, the cigars of the other series (BraziIia, Cameroon, Criollo) impress through their balanced compositions and fine balance between bunch and wrapper leaf – witnesses to the striving for perfect harmony displayed by Cano A. Ozgener and

expected of his employees and partners.

Carlos Toraño

This striving for perfection is also seen
in the forms of packaging in which the
C.A.O.s are presented to the cigar
enthusiast. The desire for an ambitious
design and love of detail, whether it is
the various cigar boxes or the tissue
paper in which certain formats are
rolled, serve to awaken connoisseurs'
anticipation of the pleasure to be

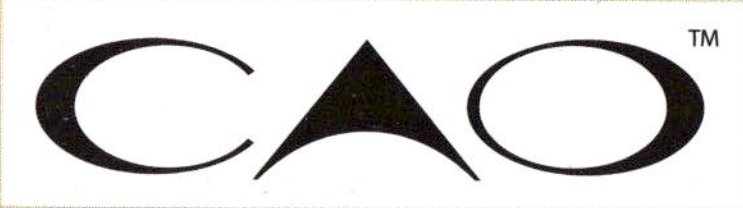

gained from smoking a C.A.O. (and
this anticipation will not be disappointed).

The Ozgeners and the Toraño family
set up the first of their own production
plants in Nicaragua and Honduras in
January 2003 – a family affair in the
worldwide competition for exquisite
long filler. Perhaps that's the reason
why the term, premium, is so appropriate in the context of C.A.O.s. The
Toraños, on the European market for
about a decade, have gained with time
a reputation and impressed many cigar
lovers. These long filler produced in the
Dominican Republic, Honduras and
Nicaragua impress with the workman-

ship they display. They have on the one
hand (Honduras) a light to medium-
strong aroma, on the other hand
(Nicaragua) a somewhat stronger one,
while the Signature Collection series
produced in the Dominican Republic
has formats available for those smokers
who prefer quite strong cigars.

Casa de Torres

The Casa de Torres presents very well
worked, hand-made, long filler cigars

that provide a good smoke.
The brown beauties are
rolled, leaf for leaf, from
Piloto Cubano, a first-class
Havana tobacco that has
been cultivated in Nicaragua
for a long time. They are
enclosed in wrapper leaves
of *Connecticut Shade*
tobacco that contribute to
the pleasantly mild flavour
characteristic of these cigars.
Casa de Torres are especially
well suited for the cigar
novice, for whom the rea-
sonable price is certainly no
drawback to choosing this
brand.

Cervantes

Fist produced in Honduras, the
Dominican Republic has been the

home of Cervantes for years now. The body of this hand-made long filler has also changed. Whereas it was previously termed a medium-strong cigar, it is now considered (relatively) mild – an aspect that appeals especially to the *aficionado* who has already gained his first experience of cigar smoking.

Should he choose a well-made Cervantes, he will hardly be disappointed, for, despite the mildness, they reveal interesting aromas while possessing a soft rounded flavour.

Chambrair

Climatic cabinets were first used for wine, not cigars. Since wine and cigars are well suited to entering a very eventful symbiosis of flavour, it was almost inevitable that it should happen.

Arne Butenschön, today one of the managers of Chambrair, brought with him cigars from Santo Domingo when he returned from one of his trips as Chief Steward onboard a luxury sailing ship. Butenschön secured for himself

the sales and distribution rights to the hand-made long filler produced in the factories of an experienced exiled Cuban cigar maker, and has made Gourmet Cigare de Chambrair available, since the beginning of the 1990s, exclusively to gastronomes in a number of formats.

Chambrairs have also been generally available since the end of 1996 – albeit not the same ones available to the catering trade. The *aficionado* can choose from four Cigare de Chambrair Privée formats. The mild to medium-

Hardy Rodenstock

strong aroma of the excellently made long filler makes it suitable for the *aficionado* who has preferred smoking cigars for some time.

Then, in 1998, the wine collector and cigar lover, Hardy Rodenstock, got together with Chambrair to create a Churchill and a Robusto under the name of HR.

Charles Fairmorn

The filler and wrapper of these relatively mild and yet aromatic long filler are composed of three various Santa Domingo tobaccos which are matured over at least seven years, thus promising unmitigated smoking pleasure. Charles Fairmorn offers quite a few cigar brands from the Caribbean and Central America, as well as the Netherlands, that are readily available in Germany. But the company also produces its own brands which are mostly to be found in the middle and upmarket price ranges. These cigars are well worth the money, regardless of whether they are Dutch-type cigars or whether tobaccos from the Caribbean and Central America have left their stamp on the format concerned.

The Charles Fairmorn business can look back on more than 25 years experience in the tobacco business. Founded in the Hanseatic city of Hamburg in 1978, the trading company transferred its seat of business to Dingelstädt in Thuringia in 1996 – not without reason, for cigars have been produced in the Tobacco House Dingelstädt since 1912.

The Charles Fairmorn Colorado and Charles Fairmorn Maduro series should be mentioned here, as well as the two long-time flagships of the business, the Charles Fairmorn Belmore and Charles Fairmorn Tradition series (the latter can be divided into the Honduras Wrapper and *Puros Finos*). All the formats of each series are excellent long filler cigars. In the meantime, the Belmores have also been expanded. One example is the Charles Fairmorn Belmore E.R.P. Selection, first smoked to celebrate the firm's silver anniversary – and it has already found numerous devotees due to its medium-strong aroma and fine flavour – another is the youngest child, the Charles Fairmorn Belmore Cameroon Selection, which presents a rather stronger body due to its excellent Cameroon wrapper.

But, as suggested above, it is not only Caribbean cigar makers who are busy for Charles Fairmorn. There are also those in Germany – or more accurately those in Dingelstädt – where production is predominantly of classical short filler.

A brand that was a part of the company's range for years but is no longer available should be mentioned at this point. The Erhard was not, as may well be assumed, a homage to the former German minister for economic affairs and Federal Chancellor, but rather alluded to a namesake of that "father of the economic miracle". His name was Hans Erhard, and he was responsible for the line that bore his name. Both Erhards were connected by their love of cigars, but while Ludwig Erhard from Fürth merely smoked them, Hans Erhard from Heidelberg produced them (and smoked them too, naturally) – and that for over three quarters of a century, for Hans Erhard died at the impressive age of 99, and had been occupied with the daily production of cigars right up to shortly before his death.

To conclude, there is also another series that must be mentioned – the Charles Fairmorn Puros de Nicaragua. These are not, as the name may well suggest, cigars made from tobaccos exclusively of Nicaraguan origin. In Spanish, *puros* means nothing more than "cigar". Be that as it may, full-bodied and flavourful, this hand-made long filler sets free a medium-strong aroma similar to that of many *puros* from the Central American country.

In all, Charles Fairmorn offers a wide range of long and short filler in the premium sector, and every well stocked specialist keeps several of these brands (at least) ready for sale to the *aficionado*.

Cifuentes

The name Cifuentes has had a good ring to it in the cigar world for more than a century. The reputation of the dynasty's founding father is legendary. Don Ramón first entered the Partagás factory in the heart of Havana at the beginning of the second half of the 19th century, and was to manage the production of Partagás cigars from the 1870s well into the 20th century.

The first Cifuentes came on the market in 1876, launched by (Don) Jaime Partagás the founder of the time-honoured brand that bears his name.

Within a short time the Cifuentes became one of the Havanas most constantly in demand from the *aficionados* of the time.

Ramón's son, also called Ramón, continued his father's work at Partagás.

C. Mendoza

His role model was his father, who was considered to one of the absolutely best cigar rollers of his time. The son also soon earned himself an excellent reputation as a cigar maker. And when the elder Ramón at last retired the younger Ramón was ready to continue the work of his father and uphold the great tradition of the Cifuentes.

On taking power, Castro asked the younger Ramón to take on the responsibility for the cigar production of the entire country, but the man, who first and foremost identified himself with the production of first-class Havanas, could not come to terms with the new social situation in Cuba and therefore left his homeland for the Dominican Republic. Here, he still oversees the Dominican Partagás marketed by the General Cigar Company of the United States, who (at the beginning of the 1970s) had bought the rights to them – in addition to the Cifuentes and Ramón Allones brand names – from him.

In contrast, Cuban Cifuentes are no longer produced. This is both a pity and a shame, for this formerly great brand was highly popular, especially with the lovers of classical Havanas.

The "C" stands for Cardenal, the "Mendoza" for itself – and behind the name, C. Mendoza (an excellently produced short filler), stands the top brand from the house of August Schuster in the east Westphalian town of Bünde.

Cohiba

This is the Havana par excellence, and accordingly also the brand that many experts consider to be the best from the Caribbean island state's cigar production.

Whether or not the Cohiba really is the best is a matter of the taste – and preferences – of the individual *aficionado*. Nevertheless this cigar brand is undoubtedly surrounded by an aura normally granted only to individual formats of other Havana brands.

Despite being created only about 40 years ago, the Cohiba has since achieved true cult status. Proof of this are the numerous stories hawked around many cigar enthusiast circles concerning its creation – for example, that Che Guevara played a part in it.

Whoever really created the first Cohiba will probably always remain a secret, although no less a person than Fidel Castro gave some information about its origins during the gala event celebrating the 30th anniversary of this model of Cuban cigars. At least, the *Máximo Líder* tried to shed light on the matter when he said the following about the history of the Cohiba's creation: "I will now explain something about the Cohiba. Once, I noticed that one of my bodyguards always smoked a very pleasantly aromatic cigar. He explained to me that it was a special brand – he had them from a friend who made cigars and always gave him some. I tried the cigar and found it so good that I said, 'Let's go visit your friend'. We met him and asked how he made these cigars (at the time we were founding a workshop in El Laguito) and he explained his mixture to us. He gave us details of which leaves he used, from which plantation, which wrapper leaf, etc. We then sought a few cigar makers, gave them the necessary material, and so the production began … I also wanted to create jobs for women, and that's why the factory is mainly run by them. The Cohiba is now world famous … That was 30 years ago."

Was this friend of the bodyguard none other than Eduardo Ribera, until then a little-known cigar maker who, immediately on being discovered, produced the three formats of Laguito No. 1, Laguito No. 2, and Laguito No. 3, that were reserved for Castro's personal use? Emília Tamayo, who ran El Laguito from 1994 to 2003, is convinced it was. This Fábrica del Tabaco is near Miramar, a suburb of Havana where many buildings are to be found in the colonial style that evokes a time when

counts and princes, bohemians and adventurers met, night after night, under the haze of fragrant wafts of smoke to indulge in their favourite pastimes – gambling and women.

The recorded explanation of the *Comandante* certainly contains a lot of truth, but as truth is a matter of subjectivity for all who experience it, there are several unanswered questions remaining in this case. Avelino Lara, a cigar-making legend during his own lifetime and revered in cigar enthusiast circles worldwide as the father of the Siglo series as well as other Cohiba formats, said modestly of himself during

Compay Segundo, Fidel Castro

the same event: "I was there and made my contribution as the Cohiba was created – that is more than enough."

Six hundred personalities from the cigar world came to the gala event that

took place on the 28th of February 1997 in Havana's world famous Cabaret Tropicana. Many more had been invited, but the expected guests from the United states, most prominent among them Arnold Schwarzenegger and Robert De Niro, decided to cancel their previously-booked flights to Havana when the government in Washington, mindful of the Cuba embargo, threatened sanctions on any US citizen who dared to follow the invitation and tread the soil of the communist country … A regrettable chauvinism. Those forced to stay at home missed a lot, for example the auction of a luxury casket signed personally by the state's president among others. The casket, together with contents and signatures, changed hands for 130,000 US-dollars. What proportion of this amount resulted from the value of the contents themselves – 90 Cohibas – is not known.

And now, back to the brand itself. For more than 20 years, there were only the three above-mentioned formats, to the *vitolas de galera* of which were soon added the *vitolas de salida* of Corona Especial (No. 2), Lancero (No. 1) and Panetela (No. 3). Although the term *vitola de salida* means nothing more than "trade name", it took more than 15 years before Cohibas could also be bought – and of course smoked – by the average mortal. Previously, only state guests had been able to experience these exquisite examples of Cuban cigar making skill – apart, that is, from Castro himself.

The dream of many *aficionados* finally came true at the beginning of the 1980s when they, too, could buy and smoke Cohibas – and that at any time, for those responsible have ensured that the numbers produced since the prime Cuban brand first appeared on the market have been held at a constantly high level. The *aficionados'* hearts took a further leap when, towards the end of that decade, even more Cohibas became available. For one thing, the Espléndido, Exquisito and Robusto formats appeared on the market, for another, Fidel Castro gave up smoking on the advice of his doctors. Later, the Corona followed, completing the range of the Clásica series which covers the standard formats.

Why the Cohiba – the name is borrowed from the language of the indigenous inhabitants of Cuba, the Taino Indians, and according to the latest conclusions of renowned linguistic researchers means quite simply "cigar" – is so highly praised by cigar experts may lie in the special choice of tobacco leaves and their further processing. Avelino Lara who was in charge of the El Laguito factory from 1968 to 1994 once gave away the most important preconditions to be strictly adhered to by all concerned when producing Cohibas.

Firstly, only the leaves of the ten best plantations *(vegas)* of the Vuelta Abajo are considered for Cohibas. At the appropriate time, the plants of these *vegas* are most carefully scrutinised to decide which growing area is best suited for which type of leaf. Finally, the *vegueros* harvest only wrapper leaves from the first two plantations, only binder leaves from the next two and from each following pair of plantations only *ligero*, *seco* and *volado* leaves respectively. Apart from this, the *ligero* and *seco* leaves are subjected to a third

consisting of five formats. The series is called Linea 1492, each format is a Siglo. In this scheme, both names refer to the discovery of the Americas – and of cigars – by Christopher Columbus. Siglo means nothing more than "century", thus each of the five formats stands for a century, taking us right back to the year 1492. The Cohibas of Linea 1492 received their international baptism a year later when they were officially presented at a gala event at Claridge's Hotel in London. Where the tanginess and pronounced aroma of Clásica series cigars are evocative of the traditional Cuban style of classical Havanas, the mixture of this recent series produces cigars with an even more voluminous body – as a result of which more than a few experts consider the newest creation, the Siglo VI, to be the absolute flagship of the Cohiba brand.

fermentation, which enhances the balance of the tobacco even more than the usual two conversion processes do.

Condal

Finally, only Cuba's best *torcedores* and *torcedoras* are allowed to give the Cohibas their ultimate form. In El Laguito this is mainly done by women, while in the H. Upmann and Partagás factories that also produced Cohibas, this honour is predominantly awarded to men.

In 1992, the prime Cuban brand was further expanded, this time in the form of a series

In contrast, two formats contest this title among the Clásicas – the Esplendido and the Robusto. The former *vitola* holds a sad record, it is the most forged format worldwide, and that to such an extent that there are said to be more forgeries produced and available for sale than originals. That is why, when purchasing Havanas in Cuba, care should be taken to buy only from the *Casas del*

Habano or in state authorised shops, and never from a street peddler. This goes for the entire Central American region, not Cuba alone.

In contrast, should an *aficionado* come across a box of Cohibas during a stay in the United States, he will most certainly – assuming that the cigars in question are legal goods – have found those produced in the Dominican Republic by the General Cigar Company. The company from the United States registered the trade name Cohiba in the USA in 1980, and has since supplied its home market with cigars bearing the same name as the original, but with a totally different taste.

Although the Cohibas from the Dominican Republic are also made by hand, whoever is faced with the choice between a Havana or a Dominican should waste no time in pondering over the quandary but plump immediately for the product of the ten best *vegas* of the Vuelta Abajo. These long filler are also long sellers, for the Condals from the Canary Islands with their range of about ten formats have enjoyed a consistent following over the years. That may result from their unusual tobacco mixtures – anyhow, *Connecticut Shade* wrappers, Mexico binders and Brazil, Havana and Santo-Domingo tobaccos in the filler all release their interesting aromas.

Cuaba

Presented in 1996, roughly 30 years after the appearance of the Cohiba, the

Cuaba is only the second Havana brand to be created under Castro. To underline that the Cuabas bear witness to the Cuban *torcedores* great skill, London was again chosen as the fitting venue for another such gala event as the international presentation of the Cohiba series Linea 1492, to introduce Cuabas to the international *aficionado* world. As if that wasn't enough, the new brand was also given a name from the Language of the Taino Indians, the indigenous inhabitants of Cuba. The word, Cuaba, refers to a bush that grows on the island, whose wood has excellent burning properties. According to oral tradition, the Taino used it to light their Cohiba – the Taino word for cigar.

The Cuabas are all *figurados* – or more accurately *perfectos*. This does not mean the Cuban *perfecto* format, but the form of the format. The *perfectos* of the

Cuaba are cigars with a cylindrical body that tapers at both the pointed burning end and at the more rounded head, where the burning end is open and the head is capped.

The Cuabas are a reminiscence of the time at the turn of the 19th century when such *perfectos* belonged to the most popular formats. These *figurados* were less and less to be found on the shelves during the early 1930s as the demand for them constantly fell.

Cuesta-Rey

Their home may be Santiago de los Caballeros, but their birthplace is Tampa in Florida, the Tampa of the end of the 19th century, a time when products were being manufactured in the southeast of the United States that were held in high regard by cigar enthusiasts – Clear Havanas.

First produced in 1884, the Cuesta-Rey were also endorsed with this (invisible) stamp of quality, because the man who created them, Ángel LaMadrid Cuesta, ran a cigar factory together with his partner Peregrino Rey that produced only Clear Havanas.

The Dominican Republic is now the home of the Cuesta-Rey, or more accurately since 1990, for in that year the

production was transferred from Ybor City to the land of numerous cigar manufacturers, to a factory run by the Fuentes.

The name Fuente is in itself a synonym for workmanship of quality, as can be seen at once from the carefully rolled cigars, despite fact that the production of the Cuesta-Reys is remittance work.

The rights to the brand lie with M & N Cigars of the United States, one of the last big cigar houses in Tampa. This family concern, which was founded in 1895 and can therefore point to a 100-year-old tradition, obtained the brand rights to the Cuesta-Rey from Cuesta's son, Carl, towards the end of the 1950s, and continued producing the cigars itself until the production was transferred to the Fuentes at the end of the 1980s.

In total, there are four Cuesta-Rey series. Besides the standard series that is still produced (by machine) in Florida, there are also the Cabinet Selection, Centenario Colección and the No. 95 series, where the latter's name is a reference to the founding year of the Newman cigar factory (precursor of the M & N Cigars company). This series is mainly intended for the US market while the other two long filler series are marketed worldwide. Only the Centenarios are available here, but *aficionados* are more than satisfied by this situation, for these cigars are of excellent quality and promise a perfect smoke.

Cumpay

"I am sure that the Cumpay … will surprise you with its candour and strength." This comment is from the creator of the Cumpay, María-Pía Selva. This impressive woman, who commutes back and forth between her main city of residence, Paris, and Central America, had already more than positively surprised the cigar world with her first brand, the Flor de Selva. When this graceful person has a fixed idea, she appears to launch her agenda with complete commitment and the necessary single-mindedness.

This was also the case with the production of the Cumpay. The results of her efforts are predominantly strong tasting formats with full aromas; devotees of such cigars should definitely give them a try.

Brand/Series	Origin	Filler	Binder	Wrapper	Strength
Cabañas H-2000 (Lf)	Dominican Republic	Dom. Rep.	Dom. Rep.	Nicaragua (Ha2000)	3–4
Cabita (Lf)	Dominican Republic	Dom. Rep. (PiCu)	Dom. Rep. (DoOlor)	CoSh	1–3
Camacho					
• Corojo (Lf)	Honduras	Puros: all tobaccos grown in Honduras from Corojo seed			3–6
• Criollo (Lf)	Honduras	Puros: all tobaccos grown in Honduras from Corojo seed (F: also Co)			2–5
Cameroon Legend (Lf)	Dominican Republic	Dom. Rep.	Dom. Rep.	Cameroon	3–4
C.A.O.					
• Black Line (Lf)	Honduras	Nicaragua + Honduras + Mexico (CuSe)	Nicaragua (CuSe)	Ecuador (SuSe)	4
• Brazilia Line (Lf)	Honduras	Nicaragua	Nicaragua	Brazil (Ar)	3
• Cameroon (Lf)	Nicaragua	Nicaragua	Nicaragua	Cameroon	3–4
• Criollo Line (Lf)	Nicaragua	Nicaragua (Cr '98)	Nicaragua (CuSe)	Nicaragua (CuSe)	4
Capadoro (Lf)	Dominican Republic	Dom. Rep. (DoOlor + PiCu) + Brazil	Dom. Rep.	Ecuador (CoSe)	2–3
Carlos Toraño					
• Nicaraguan Selection (Lf)	Nicaragua	Nicaragua	Nicaragua	Honduras/CoSh	3–4
• Reserva Selecta (Lf)	Honduras	Dom. Rep. + Honduras + Nicaragua	Indonesia	CoSh/Costa Rica	2–4
• Signature Collection (Lf)	Dominican Republic	Dom. Rep. (PiCu) + Nicaragua	CoBr	Brazil	3–5
Carmen					
• Brasil (Sf)	Austria	Indonesia (Java) + Cuba + Brazil	Indonesia (Java)	Brazil	3–4
• Sumatra (Sf)	Austria	Indonesia (Java) + Cuba + Brazil	Indonesia (Java)	Indonesia (Sumatra)	3–4
Casa de Torres (Lf)	Nicaragua	Nicaragua (PiCu)	Nicaragua (PiCu)	CoSh	1–3
Cerdan (Lf)	Dominican Republic	Puros: all tobaccos grown in the Dom. Rep. from Piloto-Cubano seed			4–5
Cervantes (Lf)	Dominican Republic	Dom. Rep. (PiCu + DoOlor)	Dom. Rep.	CoSh	2–3
Charatan (Lf)	Nicaragua	Nicaragua (CuSe)	Indonesia (JaBe)	Indonesia (Java)	3–4
Charles Fairmorn					
• Belmore Cameroon Selection (Lf)	Dominican Republic	Dom. Rep. (PiCu)	Dom. Rep. (PiCu)	Cameroon	4
• Belmore Classic Line (Lf)	Dominican Republic	Dom. Rep. (DoOlor + PiCu) + Ni	Dom. Rep. (DoOlor)	CoSh	3–4
• Belmore E.R.P. Selection (Lf)	Dominican Republic	Dom. Rep. (PiCu + DoOlor)	Dom. Rep. (DoOlor)	Ecuador (CoSh)	3–4
• Colorado (Lf)	Dominican Republic	Dom. Rep. (DoOlor) + Nicaragua	Dom. Rep. (DoOlor)	Nicaragua (Cr '98)	4–5

Brand/Series	Origin	Filler	Binder	Wrapper	Strength
• Maduro (Lf)	Dominican Republic	Dom. Rep. (PiCu)	Indonesia (Java)	CoBr	3
• Puros de Nicaragua (Lf)	Nicaragua	Nicaragua (CuSe)	Dom. Rep. (DoOlor)	Ecuador (CoSe)	3–4
• Tradition Honduras Wrapper (Lf)	Honduras	Honduras + Nicaragua	Ecuador	Honduras (Ha2000)	4–5
• Tradition Puros Finos (Lf)	Honduras	Nicaragua + Honduras	Honduras (CuSe)	Ecuador (CoSe)	3–4
Chinchalero (Lf)	Nicaragua	Nicaragua + Honduras	Honduras	CoSh	1–2
Churchill (Lf)	Nicaragua	Nicaragua	Nicaragua	Indonesia (Sumatra)	2–3
Cibao (Lf)	Dominican Republic	Dom. Rep. + Cuba	Dom. Rep.	CoBr	3–5
Cigare de Chambrair Privée (Lf)	Dominican Republic	Dom. Rep.	Dom. Rep.	CoSh	3–4
Cimero Exactos (Lf)	Dominican Republic	Dom. Rep.	Dom. Rep.	Connecticut	2–3
Club Galerie Edition (Lf)	Indonesia	In (Java) + Dom. Rep. + Br	Indonesia (JaBe)	Indonesia (JaBe)	2
C. Mendoza					
• Brasil (Sf)	Germany	Dom. Rep. + Br + Cu + In (Ja)	Indonesia (Java)	Brazil (MaFi)	2–3
• Sumatra (Sf)	Germany	Dom. Rep. + Br + Cu + In (Ja)	Indonesia (Java)	Indonesia (Sumatra)	2–3
Cohiba					
• Clásica (Lf)	Cuba	Puros: all tobaccos grown in Cuba			3–5
• Linea 1492 (Lf)	Cuba	Puros: all tobaccos grown in Cuba			4–5
Condal (Lf)	Canaries	Cuba + Dom. Rep. + Brazil	Mexico	CoSh	3–4
Corazón del Tabaco (Lf)	Nicaragua	Puros: all tobaccos grown in Nicaragua from various seed (W: CuSe)			2–3
Corps Diplomatiqué (Sf)	Belgium	Brazil + Cuba + Indonesia (Java)	Indonesia (Java)	Indonesia (Sumatra)	1–3
Cuaba (Lf)	Cuba	Puros: all tobaccos grown in Cuba			2–3
Cuesta-Rey					
• Classic Line (Lf)	Dominican Republic	Dom. Rep.	Dom. Rep.	Cameroon/Connecticut	2–3
• Centenario Colección (Lf)	Dominican Republic	Dom. Rep.	Dom. Rep.	CoSh	5
Culebras					
• Brasil (Sf)	Switzerland	Brazil (Ba) + Cuba + Dom. Rep.	Indonesia (Java)	Brazil (Ba)	4
• Havana (Sf)	Switzerland	Cu + Dom. Rep. + In (Su)	Indonesia (Java)	Cuba	2–3
Cumpay (Lf)	Nicaragua	Puros: all tobaccos grown in Nicaragua			3–5
Cupido (Lf)	Nicaragua	Nicaragua	Nicaragua	Indonesia	3

Dannemann

Born in Bremen in 1851, he was baptised under the name Gerhard, a name he kept until he emigrated to Brazil in 1872. From then on, he was known as Geraldo. He nevertheless still bore his surname with pride – Dannemann

He set up his first cigar factory in São Félix, situated on the Río Paraguaçu in northeast Brazil's Recôncavo region, just a year after his arrival in the largest South American country. Here, in the state of Cidade Bahia, not for from the former Brazilian capital of Salvador – the full name of which, São Salvador da Bahia de Todos os Santos, awakens thoughts of Samba music and coffee-brown dancers – the émigré found what he had been seeking, a fertile soil with a high sand content, a climate simply made for growing tobacco and, not least, the above mentioned city of Salvador with a harbour also frequented by ships which traversed the Atlantic, for over there lay the Old World, and, more importantly, Europe, which at the time was experiencing a cigar boom. This first cigar factory employed a total workforce of six women when it began production – and yet this was the very source of the tobacco empire that Geraldo Dannemann bequeathed to his successors on his death in 1921. But much water was to flow down the Río Paraguaçu before then.

Dannemann grew up in Bremen in at a time of strong economic growth. This was at least partly due to the lifting in 1848 of a ban on smoking that had been in force until that year. The city on the Weser soon became a trans-shipment centre for tobacco from all over the world (and still is so for Europe) including Cuba and Sumatra but, most of all, from Brazil.

Hardly a week passed in those years without a cigar factory opening in Bremen – in the end, they numbered in the hundreds. One in ten citizens of the Hanseatic city lived from the tobacco trade and cigar manufacturing at this time. Gerhard Dannemann was wounded in the Franco-German War of 1870–71, and lived for a time in Freiburg im Breisgau following his convalescence. Here, he was soon concerning himself with the raw material that had so fascinated him in Bremen – tobacco. Although he widened his knowledge of cigar production in Freiburg, then a centre of tobacco growing in Germany, he soon realised something very important that would

become a basic principle and key to his professional advancement. Only a constantly high quality is a guarantee of success, and only the person who is operating on location can achieve the quality aspired to – and, above all, guarantee it.

Geraldo Dannemann organised his work from the very beginning according to this maxim. Soon, the six women employed by him had grown to 60, and then 600 – the Dannemann concern grew steadily. He experienced the first recognition of his work in 1893, when the then Emperor of Brazil, Dom Pedro II, visited São Félix and bestowed upon it the title of Imperial Cigar Factory Dannemann.

In the years that followed, the Imperial Cigar Factory Dannemann experienced growth of almost explosive proportions. Manufacturing plants, warehouses and branch offices bearing the name of the company owner from Bremen stretched all over the Recôncavo region.

Roughly 20 years after setting up his first cigar factory, Geraldo Dannemann was considered the most important businessman in the State of Bahia. This is shown by a few statistics. In the year 1895, the four large and about 300 small businesses produced 70 million cigars for the Brazilian market alone. When one considers that 90 percent of the production was exported solely to the Old World – and even disregarding the other sales markets – it is easy to imagine the gigantic production figures the Dannemann manufacturing plants achieved, year by year, during this period. At any rate, the Dannemann cigars were the first Brazilian trade brands to take hold on the European market. This success was in no small degree the result of the contacts in Europe that the Bremen-born businessman, and his later managers, had nurtured from the very beginning and thereafter continually extended.

Behind all this stood the hard work, not only of Geraldo and his partner (the tobacco merchant Ludwig Kruder, who had supported the business's founder since 1885), nor only the members of management, but also the numerous tobacco planters and many employees in the pay of Dannemann.

Geraldo Dannemann possessed something that characterised more than a few large-scale businessmen in the Old World – social responsibility. Like the industrial barons in the Ruhr region, and the textile businessmen of the Lower Rhine, Dannemann championed public causes – a rarity in the Brazil of the time. He had buildings erected that were accessible to the public, cared for social facilities, fostered the infrastructure of the region by having streets paved and pressing ahead with canalisation, and was even responsible for the first street lighting and the first telephone in São Félix.

His commitment had begun with the building of the railway bridge that still crosses the Río Paraguaçu, connecting the two towns of São Félix and Cachoeira, over which traffic could cross from 1885 thanks to his initiative.

All this took place – in the Old World as well as in many colonial states – during the later 19th century, and it was the entrepreneurs, the industrial barons, who were particularly concerned not only with increasing their own prosperity, but who also shouldered their social responsibility by making the welfare of the region in which they operated a matter for their attention. The high esteem in which Geraldo Dannemann was held was demonstrated in 1889, when he was elected as São Félix's first Mayor, following the declaration of Brazil as a republic. This one-time market town had in the meantime grown to a respectable community and had been granted a city charter – also on the initiative of Geraldo Dannemann – before the mayoral elections.

Despite all this social commitment, the industrial baron did not lose sight of his empire's future. Since none of his children – his wife had borne him 13 – showed any great interest in sharing their father's passion to the degree he would have wished, Adolf Jonas joined the business shortly before the end of the 19th century. This tobacco expert identified himself completely with the founder's philosophy, which was still orientated around that previously defined first principle of quality. In the full knowledge that the future of his business was secured, Geraldo Dannemann returned at last to Germany. That was shortly before the outbreak of the First World War.

He only returned to Brazil after the guns had once again fallen silent. By this time almost 70 years old, he noticed that strong competition had grown in the previous years, but also soon realised that the export of tobacco rather than cigars promised the best rate of growth. Geraldo Dannemann then made his last great commercial decision that would set the future course of the business. He instituted an increase in capital after agreeing to found a joint stock company with Stender & Co. Finally, the Companhia de Charutos Dannemann, even today the mother concern of the Dannemann group, was set up in 1922 – one year after the death of the man who like no other had helped to shape the cigar world, and most of all the aromatic-mild Brazil so very popular in Germany.

The current Dannemann seat of business is the small town of Lübecke, situated to the west of Osnabrück on the northern edge of the Wiehen Hills. Owned by the Swiss Burger Söhne

AG, Dannemann is still closely bound to Brazil by companies of its own, is also present in Indonesia, runs cigar factories in Treffurt in Thuringia and Veendaal in the Netherlands – and markets in numerous countries of the world a wide range of brands, the packaging of which shows the portrait of the business' founder.

As far as packaging is concerned, it was also Dannemann that introduced a climatic packaging made from aluminium paper, called Humidorpack. This paper encases each individual cigar, not only preserving the aroma of the fresh tropical tobacco until opened, but also protecting the cigar from damage and environmental influences.

Dannemann's wide range is characterised, among other things, by its many cigarillo brands. The Moods, aromatised cigarillos which became the undisputed market leader in this sector within a very short time, should be mentioned here. However, normal cigars come from Lübecke too. For example the Dannemann Tubes, which are available either with a finely aromatic Brazil wrapper or a light Sumatra leaf, or as a Havana short filler – all in classical Corona format and 100 percent tobacco.

Then there are also the Dannemann long filler, made by hand both in Brazil, as Artist Line Mata Fina, and in Estelí in Nicaragua under the name Artist Line HBPR. A method of production is used in the manufacture of these premium cigars that had been heard of, but not practiced for a long time, and therefore considered to have been buried. This is namely the HBPR method, whereby the abbreviation stands for "hand bunched pressed rolled". This method dispenses with the press stock usually used in the production of long filler. Instead, specially trained *torcedores* make the cigars of the Dannemann Artist Line. These two series have gained a well established place among numerous *aficionados* – and rightly so, for the larger format cigars in particular (although the smaller formats should not be scorned, either) are very pleasant to smoke and move the smoker with their good burning properties and interesting unfolding of Aromas.

It would take up too much space to list all the brands produced and marketed under the Dannemann aegis, but it is really remarkable how a company founded more than a hundred years ago in a small town in today's Brazilian state of Bahia does not rest on its (well-earned) laurels, but constantly seeks new paths to tread. A wise man once said, "a standstill is a step backwards" – the axiom could have come from the lips of Geraldo Dannemann himself.

Davidoff

Geneva has, since its establishment on the shores of the lake named after it, always drawn people wishing to realise their ideas and beliefs here – Jean Cauvin, for instance, who as Johannes (John) Calvin began in 1536 to make Geneva a stronghold of the reformation, or, for example, those numerous émigrés who from the middle of the 19th century increasingly chose the city as their goal. This was partly due to the liberal attitude generally prevailing here on the one hand, to its geographical position on the other, and, later, to the generous asylum rights granted by Switzerland right up to the beginning of the 1940s.

In any case, more than a few people sought asylum in the Alpine Republic because of persecution by the authorities of their homeland, but others did so because they considered their livelihoods endangered or their futures blighted by war or political disorder. Among them, was a certain Hillel Davidoff who, as a Jew, had left his native Kiev in 1911 to escape the pogroms of the Tsar. A difficult three-month odyssey led the native Ukrainian and his family finally to Geneva. Here, he opened a business near the Boulevards des Philosophes to continue doing what he had been doing in Kiev.

His work, and that of the whole family, had consisted of choosing, cutting and mixing high-grade tobaccos of choice oriental origins, and then to work the tobacco compositions into cigarettes. So he began creating tobacco mixtures here, too, but for pipes instead of cigarettes. Hillel Davidoff soon also began to teach his son, Zino, who had reached only five

years old on their arrival in Geneva, how to combine special mixtures.

In 1924, after finishing his schooling, the young Zino Davidoff was drawn to the large tobacco-producing and cigar-manufacturing countries of Latin America. He reached the Mata Fina, the heart of Brazilian tobacco cultivation, via Argentina, and finally took a look around Cuba, the Motherland of the Cigar.

During the five years he spent abroad, Zino Davidoff not only learnt about the secrets of tobacco from the basics upward by studying the whole alphabet of cultivating, drying, fermenting, mixing and tasting of tobacco, he also learnt about the great skill involved in cigar making by looking over the shoulders of the *torcedores* at their work – predominantly in the Hoyo de Monterrey factory.

On his return to Switzerland in 1929, he first opened a tobacconist's shop in Lucerne before settling three years later in Geneva. A special cigar department was the focus of the business, with a humidified cellar for the correct storage of the cigars. It was the first of its kind anywhere in the world.

Zino Davidoff maintained a lively contact with Cuba from the day of his return, and it was not long before the young businessman began importing Havanas. The closer this contact became over the following years the higher the numbers imported. When, following the outbreak of the Second World War, innumerable Havanas awaited their fate in a French duty-free warehouse, it was the on-the-ball Ukrainian who was asked by Cuba to take over the marketing of these coveted products of the high art of cigar rolling. And so it came about that, from the beginning of 1940, the Davidoff shop in the Rue du Marché was the only one, worldwide, to stock Havanas until the end of the Second World War.

It was not long before the city in the shadow of Mont-Blanc became a Mecca for cigar enthusiasts from around the world. And when in 1946, this cosmopolitan of Ukrainian origin created, in the style of the Cabinet series of his beloved Hoyos de Monterrey, the Château cigar series for the traditional Cuban brand – whose formats he named after the most coveted Grand Crus of the Bordeaux – the name of Davidoff, which had until then been known only among *aficionados,* became well-known in other circles too.

Many older Havana enthusiasts still mourn Château series, whose formats, with the additional appellations, Haut Brion, Lafite, Latour, Margaux, and Yquem, or the later Château Mouton-

Rothschild, constitute the very best to leave Cuban sites of cigar manufacturing. Many *aficionados* become restive and roll their eyes in delight at the mere mention of these names – much more should they be able to light one up. The Dom Pérignon, a Double Corona, for whose production choice tobacco leaves from six different harvest times were annually used, was later added – in the opinion of many cigar experts this was the best cigar ever available (and, not only for that reason, it is still a legend today).

In 1968, more than 20 years after the birth of this great series, Cubatabaco, the state owned company responsible for the whole Cuban tobacco industry since 1966, proposed to the native Ukrainian that he should found a Havana brand under his own name.

Davidoff was considered at the time not only the world's greatest Havana dealer, but also the cigar *connoisseur* par excellence. Such an extraordinary proposal implies both acknowledgment and gratitude, for Zino Davidoff had always remained loyal to the Cubans and over the years devoted himself entirely to the cause of the Havana – especially during the time when the production and sales figures of the Queen of Cigars steadily declined. Castro's announcement that, apart from the Siboney, he would in future produce only one brand had sent the remaining *abacaleros* in Cuba into shock, which then turned to trauma.

Fortunately, this trauma did not last for long because Davidoff's advice at the time – to retain the old brands and to make use of their aura, of their magic (attributes associated with names such as Romeo y Julieta, Partagás and Hoyo de Monterrey) – caused a gradual change of heart in those responsible. The Siboney file was closed in the end; the trauma receded, and hope grew – the *tabacaleros* could once again hope for a better future.

Whether such gratitude was behind the offer mentioned above cannot be said with certainty today. Nor is it of much importance. What is significant

Zino Davidoff

is that the offer was made, and the fact that Zino Davidoff accepted it.

The degree of influence the great *connoisseur* gained at this time over the selection of the leaves, their fermentation and further processing, including the compilation of each mixture, or even continuous quality control, has been much debated. According to the one theory, Davidoff influenced every step along the way, according to another he was made suggestions but that was all. It is pointless to delve further into this aspect, for what is of real importance is the product born of this marriage between the communist comrades and the epicure capitalist.

The Havanas that soon came on the market under the name of Davidoff – made, by the way, in the famous El Laguito factory – had no need to fear scrutiny. Firstly, there were the two Davidoff No. 1 and Davidoff No. 2 formats, and then there was the Ambassadrice, a cigarillo that caused a sensation, all accompanied by the formats of the Thousand series. The enthusiast of Havana cigars who at this point had not heard of Davidoff was beyond help, especially after Davidoff began opening branches in the world's cities from his headquarters in the Rue de Rive, Geneva.

This expansion was mainly due to the work of one man – Dr. Ernst Schneider.

Dr. Ernst Schneider

This long-time friend and confidante of Zino Davidoff (then manager of the Oettinger-Gruppe – as he still is today) took over the Geneva Davidoff business in 1970.

The wedding of these two *aficionados* made an ideal partnership, as the meteoric success of the Davidoff products impressively underlines.

Oettinger could, at this time, look back on an almost 100-year tradition in the tobacco business. Founded in Basle by Max Oettinger in 1875, the firm – which still has its city headquarters in that triangle where Switzerland, France and Germany meet – at first concentrated on the import, marketing and sale (in its own stores, too) of cigars, cigarillos, cigarettes and tobacco for smoking and snuff, while also purveying smoking accessories such as pipes and lighters.

As suggested above, this business marriage ushered in an era for the house of Davidoff that was not only new but also most successful.

The Davidoff name, already a synonym for first class Havana cigars, soon came to stand for luxury articles in the area of cosmetics and fashion as well (to name but two fields in which the Swiss were active). All this was not only available in the main store in Geneva, but, in time, also in the other branches that opened their doors under the direction of Dr. Ernst Schneider – in Amsterdam, Berlin, London and Moscow, as well as in Hong Kong, New York, Singapore, Tokyo and even Beijing – to provide an exclusive public with exclusive products.

Their love of cigars did not, however, suffer as a result. The Zino brand first saw the light of day in 1977 (see also Zino). These cigars, produced in Honduras, were created with the United States market in mind for, as a result of the disastrous US embargo against Cuban products, no Havana cigars could be sold in US stores nor any with the name Davidoff on the cigar ring.

Today, however, all the Davidoffs available in Europe and elsewhere in the world are also available in the United States. This has nothing to do with an interim or partial lifting of the US embargo against a particular group of Cuban products, for that economic sanction (a relict of the Cold War) is still in force – no, it has another simple, almost banal reason. No Davidoffs are now made in Havana.

The final break between Cubatabaco and Davidoff occurred in 1988, when the contract between the two was not extended but cancelled by Davidoff in September. Of course both parties blamed the other for ending their cooperation. It would be a waste of time to go into the reasons for this separation merely to come to a conclusion about which side bore the greater share of blame.

Zino Davidoff himself remained very diplomatic about this less than pleasant news for dyed-in-the-wool Havana supporters. He answered questions

about the reason for the break with the wisdom of a man who has withstood more than one storm in his life: "I had a good marriage with Cuba. It lasted for many years. But now it is time for a change. I've found a younger, slimmer lady – so I've married again."

Back to the facts, to the discernible, to something not built on sand. Fact number one in this case: 1991 saw the worldwide introduction of a new generation of cigars bearing the name Davidoff, made in the Dominican Republic under the expert supervision of Hendrik Kelner, the manager of Tabacos Dominicanos S.A. (or Tabadom for short).

Fact number 2: Dominican Davidoffs were not, and are not, comparable to those produced in Havana. Since the Santo-Domingo tobaccos – from which the Davidoffs bunch is formed – are on average significantly milder that the Cuban, the cigars made from

them do not display the strength characteristic of the majority of Havanas.

It is therefore extremely difficult to conclude a divergence in quality. Cigars from Cuba are quite simply different than those from the Dominican Republic, or from Honduras and Nicaragua. No one would think of comparing a lively, fruity Riesling from the mid-Moselle with a full-bodied Ruländer with little acidity from Baden.

Fact number 3: Dominican Davidoffs are among the very best cigars available on the market in respect to their quality. This is particularly well expressed by their excellent burning and drawing properties – indicative of flawless work by the *torcedores* – as well as the development of the subtly fragrant aromas released during smoking. And that in turn is indicative of the careful cultivation and selection of the tobacco leaves

beforehand, as well as the combination made from various leaves. For ultimately, no matter how excellent a *torcedor* may be, the results of his work will hardly be worthy of a place in the premium sector when the material used is of inferior quality.

It is particularly this select quality that is characteristic of Davidoffs, a quality that is – perhaps more importantly – always constant. A fairly early comment by someone in charge at Tabadom seems to highlight the high standard of Davidoff quality control: "I think Davidoff is probably the only firm that rejects more cigars than it accepts."

As previously mentioned, the Dominican cigars that Davidoff put on the market in 1991 were different – cigars that many who had previously smoked Davidoffs, that is, Havanas, first had to get used to. In contrast, however, several of the "new" cigars' formats were familiar. The Davidoff No. 1, the Davidoff No. 2, and the Ambassadrice retained their previous sizes and titles, and were augmented by the Davidoff No. 3 and the Tubos. The Châteaux also remained, albeit mutating to Grand Crus, while the formats of the Mille series, known until 1977 under the name of Thousand, also retained their measurements.

In time, the Aniversario, Exquisitos and Special series were added – this last is a reference to La Belle Époque, a time when the Torpedo was en vogue.

The Special range is rounded off by, among others, the Special C, a Culebra, which, as generally known, consists of three Panatellas twisted together. With the Millennium Blends – which certainly give off the strongest aroma, and are therefore extremely interesting for *aficionados* who prefer strong cigars – the latest series in Davidoff range is provisionally complete.

Zino Davidoff would not have been Zino Davidoff had he not had a major say at the time in the selection of the growing areas in the Dominican Republic. The tobacco plants for the Davidoffs are still grown on these areas, and the tabaqueros still store the harvested and fermented leaves for three to seven years before the pro-

duce of different harvests are drawn upon and appraised for the individual composition of each series of cigars produced. All this guarantees a consistent aroma and flavour as well as the optimal burning properties of Davidoffs.

Today, the Davidoff people not only have a major say in the whole production process in the Dominican Republic, they are actually responsible for it, since the former Tabadom has become a part of the Oettinger Davidoff Group. Thus, thanks to its vertical structure, Davidoff is the only producer in the world able to control the progress of a cigar from the cultivation of the tobacco to the sale of the finished product, and to influence all the decisive phases.

The range of aroma covered by Davidoffs ranges from mild to strong, with the cigars of the standard series as the mildest, followed by the somewhat stronger Mille and Aniversario series. The fuller Grand Crus release a wealth of flavours and aromas, as do the formats of the most recent series, the Millennium Blend. The Specials, for their part, are made from tobacco mixtures based on the compositions of the Grand Cru series.

What began in the backroom of a small shop in Geneva with the mixing of cigarette and pipe tobaccos, has now developed into an internationally active business with more than 25 branches and over 50 Flagship Stores worldwide. It employs a workforce of more than 2,700 (of which about 1,100 work in the Dominican Republic alone) and sells its products in about 500 outlets.

The product range is not restricted to the premium cigars so praised for their quality by experts and connoisseurs alike, but also includes other articles such as cognac, ties and the appropriate accessories; products such as reading-glasses, various cosmetic articles and even a leather collection; and all these products are raised to the level of exclusivity by the Davidoff label.

That is quite in line with the wishes of Zino Davidoff, who died in 1994, aged 88 and who constantly preached *savoir-vivre,* that (sophisticated) art of living which he himself embodied, as no other could.

And so the wheel turns full circle in his second home of Geneva. It was in that city that Calvin in his day shaped an epoch, building a system of city government completely shaped by the Reformation, and influencing the development of new, more democratic structures through his activities, teachings and writings, a development that has reached through the centuries to the present.

Zino Davidoff

Zino Davidoff also played a decisive part in preparing the way for a new era – that of the enjoyment of life, of elegance, of luxury.

One may greet this development, to which Zino Davidoff made a significant contribution, one may consider it to be corruptive, one may prefer to simply ignore it – but one thing one cannot do is ignore it.

For many a connoisseur, a Davidoff cigar is still a synonym for a noble lifestyle. For them, the enjoyment of a Double R, for example, crowns a sumptuous meal – and why shouldn't someone who lights up a Davidoff be allowed such a pleasure, even if we do seem to be far from an age of tolerance?

De Heeren van Ruysdael

The cigars of the De Heeren van Ruysdael brand are in the best Dutch tradition. These 100 % tobacco short filler have an excellent composition and offer the *aficionado* medium-flavoured cigars with a well-rounded aroma.

De Olifant

These would be at home in the Kamper Tobacco Museum, for that is the name of this brand's second series. But the word "museum" should not put anyone off because the cigars of the De Olfant brand are produced on a daily basis.

Production, however, may seem slow and antiquated, as much of the work – such as rolling the wrapper leaves over individual formats – has to be done by hand before these *sigars* can be approved for their primary purpose and placed in the appealing wooden boxes which catch the attention with their logos of a trumpeting elephant.

All this takes place in the Tabaksfabriek De Olifant. It is to be found in the small Dutch city of Kampen which lies on an eastern arm of the Ijssel Sea. The gabled brick buildings of the old quarter encapsulate the old-fashioned

Diplomáticos

These Havanas, with a medium to full body that develops a pronounced aroma, are bound to appeal to all *aficionados* set on the traditional Cuban style.

Two pleasing aspects of the Diplomáticos are, on the one hand, that all formats, without exception, are produced by hand, and on the other, that this brand is one of the more economically priced Havanas.

Don Diego

One of the best-known brands of the Consolidated Cigar Corporation of the United States in Europe is the Don Diego.

The father of these cigars is none other than Pepe García, who, as one of the best and most famous Cuban cigar makers, was also one of the first of this select guild to leave their homeland following Castro's rise to power.

That is why these relatively mild, very aromatic Dominican cigars have been available since the mid-1960s. A brand that has been on the market so long can hardly be thought inferior, while the latest series, Aniversario, is somewhat stronger (and just as worthy of recommendation).

charm typical of these structures. The factory itself and its shop area are just as charming – making the name "Kamper Tabacco Museum" quite appropriate.

Only select tobaccos from widely dispersed origins are considered for the "Elephants". Sumatra provides the binder and wrapper leaves, while top quality tobacco from Brazil, Java and Cuba are combined into a range of mixtures for the various fillers, to guarantee the unmitigated smoking pleasure that arises from great style.

A further Don Diego brand – Playboy by Don Diego – has been available since late 1996. Homage to a particular zeitgeist – or more likely the Playboy-makers' interpretation of it – is suggested by this lifestyle name. Whether it refers to the cigar or the magazine, is a point we will leave for the individual to decide.

In any case, the mildly aromatic Playboys are well worth trying.

Don Stefano

Although everything began in 1994, the roots go back to end of the 19th century. Around this time, Steffen Rinn's grandfather, born in 1870, began an apprenticeship as cigar specialist in a small place near Gießen – Stefano stands for Steffen, of course. Having completed his training, he was sure he knew so much about the tobacco business and cigars that he could not only feed himself and his family by manufacturing cigars, but also secure a life of relative prosperity. He was also eager to ty his hand at designing cigars on his own account. But he needed capital to set up a small business. He received this from a wealthy commercial counsellor who was willing to provide the necessary financial means as a partner, while otherwise giving Ludwig Rinn (now a businessman) a free hand. As the com-

mercial counsellor's name was Cloos, it was not long before they had decided upon the name of the firm – Rinn & Cloos. That was in 1895.

The fledgling business soon made a name for itself. This was primarily due to the high quality cigars that were produced in Wettenberg. At any rate, the firm was so prosperous that Ludwig Rinn was able to buy out his partner in the early 1920s. Rinn & Cloos was also able to maintain its position after the Second World War as one of Germany's leading cigar businesses.

Two figures are proof of this. At the end of the 1950s the cigar manufacturer employed a workforce of about 6,000 employees, while its carpentry department produced 200,000 cigar boxes – a month! By this time the founder's son, Hans Rinns had already been active in the company for about 30 years (he took over the management in 1958). His son, Steffen, joined him in 1967. Together with his brother, Klaus, he took on more and more responsibility, until both finally rose to the Board of Directors of the (now public) company in 1972. While Klaus led the marketing side of the business, Steffen Rinn was responsible for raw tobacco purchasing in addition to his job as production manager.

He still holds this position today – not with Rinn & Cloos, however, but with Don Stefano. He founded this cigar factory in 1994 following the closure of Rinn & Cloos at the beginning of 1991. The business had belonged to the Swiss Burger-Gruppe, for some time – since 1975, in fact. 250 people were still employed by Rinn & Cloos when it was closed, a considerable number for the period.

Don Stefano, with its roughly 20 employees is one of the few privately-owned businesses in the tobacco processing field to maintain the production of classical short filler. Only high quality raw materials are used and, regardless which product from the house of Don Stefano a cigar enthusi-ast chooses, each cigar is characterised by a well balanced composition.

Dos Hermanos

The name Indonesia usually conjures up thoughts from cigar smokers of Sumatra, Java, and even Vorstenland – and the excellent tobaccos that grow everywhere there and then find their way to many of the world's countries as filler and binder tobaccos, and are quite often used for the wrapper. That this does not have to be the case is shown by the well-made cigars of the Dos Hermanos brand, which are made by hand in Indonesia itself. There, the makers only use tobacco from outside the world's largest island state in the filler – thus ensuring the aromatic balance of the cigar.

Dunhill

The name Dunhill stands par excellence for smoking. Whether it is accessories, pipe tobacco, cigarettes, cigars or cigarillos – Dunhill has significantly shaped cultural experience of the blue haze. That is, of course, also true of the cigar world. Although Alfred H. Dunhill was already offering cigars for sale at the end of the 19th century, the actual upsurge in this field only began in 1907, when he set up his cigar shop in Duke Street, London. There were no walk-in humidors on the premises, instead, rooms lined with cedar wood awaited the cigars, which came primarily from Cuba and could, following their arrival from abroad, mature there for about a year before being offered for sale. This tobacco *connoisseur* realised that quality was the best basis for a business intended to serve a select clientele. This maxim also impressed Winston Churchill, who soon became the most renowned customer of the Dunhill store in Duke Street.

Since Alfred Dunhill had been ordering the coveted Havanas in ever greater numbers from the beginning of the century onwards, it came as no surprise when the Cuban state-owned tobacco company Cubatabaco also offered to produce Havanas under his name, several weeks after making Zino Davidoff the same offer. The Englishman reacted to the offer as positively as the Swiss, and as a result, the first Havanas with the name Dunhill on their cigar rings could be bought in 1968, the majority of which were produced in the Romeo y Julieta factory.

The marriage between the Cubans and the two Europeans, whose names had long become synonymous with sophisticated smoking, functioned for good 20 years. Then another duplicity of events occurred. The relationship between Cubatabaco and Davidoff on the one hand, and Cubatabaco and Dunhill on the other, deteriorated almost simultaneously, and both business liaisons were ended at almost the same time. Dunhill then also removed the Havana assortment from its range.

That a business such as Dunhill should be without cigars bearing the name of the worldwide active brand on their cigar rings is simply inconceivable. So cigars can still be bought bearing the name Dunhill, as before. Three series have long existed – Dunhill Aged Cigars, from the Dominican Republic; Dunhill Honduran Selection, which are also produced in the country between Guatemala, Nicaragua and El Salvador; and finally Dunhill Mild from the Netherlands, classic short filler in the best Dutch tradition. The filler of the Aged Cigars is quite interesting. Although the *Pilato Cubano* and *Olor Dominicano* tobaccos are quite often grown in the Dominican Republic, a rather rare Brazilian tobacco (also cultivated on the eastern part of Hispaniola) is used as the third component. Exceeding even the most exacting standards, this is the basis for cigars that give off a mild to medium aroma.

Once the Dunhill Aged Cigars have been rolled, they are stored in dark rooms panelled with cedar wood, and left to mature for at least 90 days. The cedar wood contributes to creating a subtle harmony between an agreeable humidity, a fragrance-rich aroma and a mature flavour, which has a pleasant effect upon smoking.

The cigars of the Dunhill Honduran Selection also display good workmanship, and appeal to the smoker who prefers something a little stronger. This series has been produced for several years in Estelí, Honduras, where Dunhill Tobacco of London has built a tobacco production plant. As previously mentioned, these cigars, with their balanced flavour endowed with an aromatic note, have more appeal for the somewhat more experienced *aficionado*.

The most recent series from the noble London establishment has been on the market since the beginning of 2005. The Dunhill Signed Range Cigars are comparable in strength to the Aged Cigars and are persuasive in their excellent workmanship as well as their harmonious composition. What is interesting here is that every cigar box bears the signature of the respective cigar roller and controller so as to enable any complaints to be traced back to whoever has failed to do their job 100 percent correctly. This is more an encouragement to the workforce than a burden.

Finally, the *Cubita* – one of the three filler tobaccos that ensure the cigars' mild flavour – is also interesting. Although this tobacco is primarily to be found in South America, the plant itself is cultivated from seeds that originally came from Cuba. The Signed Range depends on a *Cubita* that grows in El Carmen, in the northwest of Columbia.

Brand/Series	Origin	Filler	Binder	Wrapper	Strength
Dannemann					
• Artist Line HBPR (Lf)	Nicaragua	Puros: all tobaccos grown in Nicaragua			3–4
• Artist Line Mata Fina (Lf)	Brazil	Puros: all tobaccos grown in the Bahia region			4
• Espada Brasil (Sf)	Switzerland	Brazil (Ba) + Indonesia (Java)	Indonesia (Java)	Brazil (Ba)	4
• Espada Sumatra (Sf)	Switzerland	Br (Ba) + In (Ja) + Cu	Indonesia (Java)	Indonesia	3
• Tubes Brasil (Sf)	Germany	Br (Ba) + Dom. Rep. + In (Ja)	Indonesia (Java)	Brazil (Ba)	4
• Tubes Havanna (Sf)	Germany	Cuba	Cuba	Indonesia (Sumatra)	5
• Tubes Sumatra (Sf)	Germany	Br (Ba) + Dom. Rep. + In (Ja)	Indonesia (Java)	Indonesia	3
Davidoff					
• Aniversario (Lf)	Dominican Republic	Dom. Rep. (SaVi + PiCu + DoOlor)	Dom. Rep. (SaVi)	Connecticut	4–5
• Classic (Lf)	Dominican Republic	Dom. Rep. (SaVi + PiCu + DoOlor)	Dom. Rep. (SaVi)	Ecuador (CoSe)	2–3
• Exquisitos (Lf)	Dominican Republic	Dom. Rep. (SaVi)	Dom. Rep. (DoOlor)	Ecuador (CoCuSe)	3
• Grand Cru (Lf)	Dominican Republic	Dom. Rep. (SaVi + PiCu + DoOlor)	Dom. Rep. (SaVi)	Ecuador (CoSe)	4
• Mille (Lf)	Dominican Republic	Dom. Rep. (SaVi + PiCu + DoOlor)	Dom. Rep. (SaVi)	Connecticut	3–4
• Millennium Blend (Lf)	Dominican Republic	Dom. Rep. (PiCu + SaVi + DoOlor)	Dom. Rep. (SaVi)	Ecuador (CoCuSe)	5
• Special (Lf)	Dominican Republic	Dom. Rep. (PiCu + SaVi + DoOlor)	Dom. Rep. (SaVi)	Connecticut	4
De Heeren van Ruysdael (Sf)	Netherlands	Indonesia + Brazil + Cuba	Indonesia (JaBe)	Indonesia (SuSa)	3–4
De Huifkar (Sf)	Netherlands	Indonesia (Java) + Brazil + Cuba	Indonesia (Java)	Indonesia (Sumatra)	2
Delgados					
• Brasil (Sf)	Germany	Cu + Dom. Rep. + In (Ja) + Br	Indonesia (Java)	Brazil	3–4
• Sumatra (Sf)	Germany	Cu + Dom. Rep. + In (Ja) + Br	Indonesia (Java)	Indonesia (Sumatra)	3–4
De Olifant (Sf)	Netherlands	Indonesia (Java) + Brazil + Cuba	Indonesia (Sumatra)	Indonesia (Sumatra)	3–4
Diamond Crown (Lf)	Dominican Republic	Dom. Rep. (PiCu)	Dom. Rep. (PiCu)	Connecticut	3–4
Diplomáticos (Lf)	Cuba	Puros: all tobaccos grown in Cuba			3–5
Dominican					
• Classic Line (Lf)	Dominican Republic	Dom. Rep.	Brazil	Connecticut	2–3
• Santiago Selection (Lf)	Dominican Republic	Dom. Rep. (DoOlor + PiCu) + Ni	Dom. Rep. (PiCu)	Ecuador (CoSe)	3
Dominico (Lf)	Dominican Republic	Dom. Rep. (PiCu)	Indonesia	Ecuador (CoSe)	3–4

Brand/Series	Origin	Filler	Binder	Wrapper	Strength
Don Antonio					
• Brasil (Sf)	Dominican Republic	various origins	Indonesia (Java)	Brazil	1–3
• Havanna (Sf)	Dominican Republic	Cuba	Dom. Rep. (DoOlor)	Cuba	1–3
• Long filler	Dominican Republic	Br + Dom. Rep. + Cu + In (Ja)	Indonesia (Java)	Connecticut	2–3
• Sumatra (Sf)	Dominican Republic	various origins	Indonesia (Java)	Indonesia (Sumatra)	1–3
Don Diego					
• Aniversario (Lf)	Dominican Republic	Dom. Rep.	Dom. Rep.	CoSh	3–4
• Classic Line (Lf)	Dominican Republic	Dom. Rep.	Dom. Rep. (CuSe)	CoSh	2–4
Don Juan Urquijo (Lf)	Philippines	Dom. Rep. + Brazil (MaFi)	Dom. Rep.	CoSh	3–4
Don Lino					
• Colorado (Lf)	Dominican Republic	Dom. Rep. (CuSe)	Dom. Rep.	Indonesia (Sumatra)	2–4
• Havanna Reserva (Lf)	Dominican Republic	Dom. Rep. (CuSe)	Dom. Rep.	CoSh	2–3
• Oro (Lf)	Dominican Republic	Puros: all tobaccos grown in the Dom. Rep. from Corojo seed			5
Don Sancho (Lf)	Canaries	Brazil + Dom. Rep.	Dom. Rep.	CoSh	3–4
Don Sebastian (Lf)	Dominican Republic	Dom. Rep. + Mexico	Mexico	CoSh	1–2
Don Stefano					
• Corona Grande (Lf)	Dominican Republic	Dom. Rep. + Nicaragua	Dom. Rep.	CoSh	2
• Honduras Long filler	Honduras	Nicaragua + Honduras + Dom. Rep.	Honduras	CoSh	3
Dos Hermanos (Lf)	Indonesia	In (JaBe + Vola) + Dom. Rep. + Br	Indonesia (JaBe)	Indonesia (SuDe)	2
Dos Rios (Lf)	Nicaragua	Nicaragua + Dom. Rep.	Nicaragua	Ecuador (NiSe)	3–4
Dunhill					
• Aged Cigars (Lf)	Dominican Republic	Dom. Rep. (PiCu + DoOlor) + Brazil	Dom. Rep.	CoSh	2–4
• Honduran Selection (Lf)	Honduras	Dom. Rep. (PiCu) + Mexico + Brazil	Mexico	Indonesia	3–5
• Mild Cigars (Sf)	Netherlands	Brazil (Ba) + Indonesia (Java)	Indonesia (Java)	Indonesia (Sumatra)	2
• Signed Range Cigars (Lf)	Dominican Republic	Dom. Rep. (PiCu) + Columbia	CoBr	Ecuador (Connecticut)	2–3

El Credito

Although the cigar maker Ernesto Pérez-Carrillo has been responsible for the quality of this premium brand in Santiago de los Caballeros, Domini-can Republic, since the early 1990s, this was preceded by a long and moving story associated with these cigars, behind which is concealed a traditional Cuban brand (among other things).

It all began with the family of Ernesto Pérez-Carrillo, which had already been closely connected with tobacco in Cuba at the start of the last century, as both father and grandfather had traded in tobacco since 1907. In common with many other Cubans, the family left the country following the Castro revolution, taking with them the rights to and recipe for the famous La Gloria Cubana brand, to finally settle in nearby Florida. In 1968, the father then set up the El Credito cigar factory

Ernesto Pérez-Carrillo

in Miami, and in 1972, brought La Gloria Cubana onto the US market.

At first, Ernesto Pérez-Carrillo went his own way, mostly indulging his great hobby, the drums, playing successfully in several bands but never losing contact with his family. When his father's health failed, he engaged himself in the parental firm, got to know

the secrets of the cigar maker's skill, and then, in 1980, on the death of his father, took over the factory. He appears to have done a good job, for in the early 1990s La Gloria Cubana enjoyed a meteoric rise in the United States (and is still one of the country's absolute top brands). As a result, a second factory was set up in the Dominican Republic.

His Glorias Cubana still impress smokers, now including those in

Europe, where they are marketed for legal reasons under the name of El Credito instead of La Glorias Cubana (see also Duplicates). Ernesto Pérez-Carrillo has said the following about the characteristics of El Credito: "It is a cigar from the medium to strong range. We use tobaccos from Nicaragua and the Dominican Republic for the filler. The wrapper comes from Ecuador, and is grown from Sumatran seed. The El Credito is a cigar with a complex flavour, much aroma and a soft bouquet. In blending, I have taken care to approximate the aroma of Cuban tobaccos – always with the proviso that we utilise leaves from various growing areas and lands of origin. Our El Credito is just right for anyone who is fond of Cuban tobaccos and also open to something new." There is no more to be said.

El Rey del Mundo

Cigar makers are on the whole modest beings. They know the skill they possess, and that's enough for them. Of course, there is an exception to every rule. One such exception was the naming of this Havana.

Those in charge of the Antonio Allones company were absolutely convinced of the quality of the cigar they brought on the market in 1882, and so, displaying no modesty whatsoever, they named it King of the World. And indeed, the El Rey del Mundo soon became one of the most coveted Havanas of the late 19th century.

Day by day, around 7,000 and sometimes as many as 8,000 Kings of the World left the factory that soon bore

the name of the brand of cigars it predominantly produced – Fábrica de Tabacos Rey del Mundo Cigar.

Today? As in the past, the El Rey del Mundo, with their quite oily wrapper leaves, are among the lighter representatives of their species, which makes them especially well-suited for smokers who are just beginning to explore the world of the Havana.

Ermuri

Behind this name lies a purchasing association which orders cigars and smoking accessories from the respective producers, and then offers these products, partly under other names, to the public through its contractual partners in the retail tobacco trade.

The Detmold-based association stocks the most varied range of products in its assortment, for example, the Ambiente, Comendador and Firmeza cigar brands – products that, as a rule, need not shy from comparison with similar products in their price category.

Brand/Series	Origin	Filler	Binder	Wrapper	Strength
El Credito (Lf)	Dominican Republic	Dom. Rep. + Nicaragua	Nicaragua	Ecuador (SuSe)	4-6
El Prado (Sf)	Switzerland	Dom. Rep. + In (Su) + Br + Cu	Indonesia (Java)	Indonesia (Sumatra)	2-3
El Rey del Mundo (Lf)	Cuba	Puros: all tobaccos grown in Cuba			1-3
Excalibur (Lf)	Honduras	Honduras + Nicaragua + Dom. Rep.	CoBr	CoSh	3-4

Flor de Copán

The name alone of this Honduran brand and the cigar factory of the same name that produces the Flor de Copán, leads us to conclude that these cigars are of good quality. Apart from other premium cigars, the Flor de Copán factory also produces those of the Zino brand, which, as is well-known, opened up the US market for Davidoff. Apart from the seasoned standard series, the *Puros Finos* are also worthy of further attention. These cigars made fropm tobaccos all grown in a single country, which first appeared on the market in 2004, satisfy smokers'

demands with their very good work-manship and flavoursome aromas.

Their flavour is owed to the tobaccos grown from Cuban seed that are partly used for their mixture. Seeds had already found their way, in 1962, from the Vuelta Abajo to the regions around El Paraiso, Santa Rosa de Copán and Santa Bárbara – cool hilly landscapes near the border with Guatemala and Salvador (where the Mayans have also grown tobacco for centuries).

The tobaccos used for these cigars are of the best Cuban species of the Vuelta Abajo, from the seeds introduced to

Honduras in 1962, and grown in the regions mentioned above.

There is something else also worth mentioning – the Flores de Copán are agreeably economically priced, which is (unfortunately) only seldom the case with excellent premium cigars.

Flor de Juan López

This time-honoured Havana brand markets only a few formats, and in - limited numbers. Nevertheless, the Flowers of Juan López can be found in good specialist shops. Here,

the interested buyer will find medium-strong cigars, the majority of which display a wrapper leaf usually of the *Colorado Maduro* category.

Anyone who loves the unmistakeable fragrance of a Havana and prefers a medium-strong cigar can do no wrong with Flor de Juan López.

Flor de Rafael González

This Havana, created in 1928 especially for the British market by George Samuel and Frank Warwick, is still produced today – and is mostly popular with cigar smokers who have just entered the Havana world due to its pleasantly light aroma and balanced flavour.

Although the Flowers of Rafael González cannot look back on a tradition as long as that of the oldest Havanas, they have nevertheless made history. For it was no less a person than the Earl of Lonsdale who, ordering Rafael González by the case in the 1930s, insisted on a format that until then had not existed. As the

English nobleman was the *fábrica's* best customer, his wish became their command – and so, the Lonsdale format that is still very popular today, came into being.

The following recommendation could be found, even then, on every case of Rafael González to leave the harbour of Havana: These cigars should be either smoked within a month or allowed to mature for a year. It was reputedly an English importer who, in the 1930s, first wrote these lines by hand on a box of Rafael González cigars. This piece of well-founded advice can still be found on every box of this brand's cigars. As all Havanas are subject to further fermentation processes during storage, they secrete, usually in late summer, natural oils. For this reason, they should be smoked either straightaway or, indeed, a year after their production when they completed this further fermentation process.

Flor de Selva

On the market for quite some time now, the Flores de Selva has become a

Mária-Pía Selva

Fonseca

This Havana brand, named after its founder, was born in the early 1890s. Today, it consists of only a few formats, but they catch the eye immedi-

constant part of the sometimes incomprehensible cigar market. At any rate, there are many *aficionados* who keep one format or another of this premium brand in their humidors.

These cigars are produced under the direction of Nestor Plasencia, one of the great figures of the trade, in his Tabacos de Oriente factory, using selected tobaccos.

This brand was created by a woman — Señora María-Pía Selva. Her "flowers" have caused many a veteran cigar maker to redden with shame, for this native Honduran's Flores de Selva are among the best premium cigars exported by the Central American country.

ately. The reason for this is that every individual Fonseca is wrapped in a wafer-thin sheet of white tissue — a reminiscence of the love of detail most notably cultivated during *La Belle Époque.* Although increasingly to be found in northern Europe, the Fonsecas chiefly enjoy great popularity in Spain. There, especially in that European metropolis of cigar smoking, Barcelona, a considerable number of *aficionados* swear by the very mild-tasting Fonsecas.

Incidentally, the Fonseca boxes are decorated with illustrations of both Havana's Morro Castle and New York's

Statute of Liberty – and are thus a reminder of the time when relations between Cuba and the United States were not sullied by the disastrous US embargo.

Fundadores

These medium-strength long filler are produced in Jamaica, in a factory where the famous Macanudos were once also made.

Fundadores need not hide behind other brands, for the *tabaqueros* of Kingston understand their trade. These hand-made cigars with their somewhat dark Colorado wrapper leaves are definitely worth trying because of their interesting spicy note. One format attracts special attention, although it is the smallest – in length that is. This is the Petit Robusto, which although conforming to the common ring gauge for a Robusto, does not quite reach the normal minimum length – an invitation to a short, intensive smoke for spare moments.

Fürst Bismarck

Every now and then, products even remotely to do with food and drink have been named after the Iron Chancellor. And so, in addition to various mineral waters, there is also a spirit named after him, produced in a distillery by the name of *Fürstlich von Bismarck'sche Kornbrennerei Schönau Friedrichsruh*. Since the late 19th century, another stimulant has also borne the name of the Imperial Chancellor, the Fürst Bismarck cigar.

Whether Otto von Bismarck liked to drink mineral water or schnapps is not the point here, but he most certainly liked to smoke cigars. Perhaps it was in remembrance of this that Carl Eduard von Bismarck, the Prussian aristocrat's great-great-grandson and passionate cigar smoker, travelled many times with Michael Kohlhase, the tobacco and cigar importer from Hamburg who unfortunately died much too young, to the Dominican Republic to create, with the help of cigar makers who understand their trade, this cigar brand.

Bismarcks are still produced there, in La Romana, and are still rolled by hand – first-class long filler that stand out due to a gentle aromatic and yet harmonious mélange.

Brand/Series	Origin	Filler	Binder	Wrapper	Strength
Felipe Gregorio					
• Dominican Selection (Lf)	Dominican Republic	Nicaragua (CuSe)	Dom. Rep. (PiCu)	CoSh	4
• Honduran Selection (Lf)	Honduras	Puros: all tobaccos grown in Honduras from Cuban seed			3–4
Festividad	Dominican Republic	Dom. Rep.	Dom. Rep.	CoSh	1–2
Fire by Indian Tabac (Lf)	Honduras	Nicaragua + Honduras	Nicaragua	Honduras	3–5
Flor de Copán					
• Classic Line (Lf)	Honduras	Honduras + Nicaragua	Honduras	Ecuador (CoSe)	3–4
• Linea Puros (Lf)	Honduras	Puros: all tobaccos grown in Honduras			3–4
Flor de Juan López (Lf)	Cuba	Puros: all tobaccos grown in Cuba			3–4
Flor de Rafael Gonzáles (Lf + Sf)	Cuba	Puros: all tobaccos grown in Cuba			2–4
Flor de Selva (Lf)	Honduras	Honduras (CuSe)	Nicaragua/Honduras	CoSh	3–4
Flor Real (Lf)	Costa Rica	Pure Nicaragua: all tobaccos from Nicaraguan production			2–4
Fonseca (Lf + Sf)	Cuba	Puros: all tobaccos grown in Cuba			2–3
Fundadores (Lf)	Jamaica	Jamaica + Dom. Rep. + Mexico	Mexico	CoSh	2–4
Furore (Lf)	Dominican Republic	Dom. Rep. (DoOlor + PiCu)	Dom. Rep.	CoSh	2–3
Fürst Bismarck (Lf)	Dominican Republic	Dom. Rep. (CuSe) + Brazil + CoBr	Dom. Rep. (CuSe)	CoSh	2–4

G

Gebrüder Berens

Gebrüder Berens

Situated in Lennestadt, in Sauerland, this Tobacco and cigar factory that was founded in 1867 and which is now managed by the fifth generation has specialised both in shag tobacco, and the import of several high quality long filler, such as the Corazón del Tabaco from Nicaragua and the La Corona from the Dominican Republic.

Gispert

This classical old brand has its origins in the province of Pinar del Río, and was one of the Cuban cigars of the late 19th and early 20th century that made Havanas famous the world over. Today, the Gispert, hardly known in Europe, is only made in a machine-produced format (Standard), available under the *Vitola de salida* of Habaneros No. 2.

Guantanamera

Entering the international market in 2002, the most recent Cuban brand is intended for those cigar smokers who have just discovered the Browns, for these economically priced (machine-produced) Havanas are very mild.

GUANTANAMERA

Brand/Series	Origin	Filler	Binder	Wrapper	Strength
Gilberto Oliva (Lf)	Nicaragua	Nicaragua + Dom. Rep.	Ecuador	Ecuador (CoSe)	3–5
Gispert (Sf)	Cuba	Puros: all tobaccos grown in Cuba			2
Goya (Lf)	Canaries	Cuba	Cuba	Ecuador (CuSe)	4–5
Grenadier (Sf)	France	Dom. Rep.	Dom. Rep.	Cameroon/CoBr/CoSh	1–2
Guantanamera (Sf)	Cuba	Puros: all tobaccos grown in Cuba			1
Guaranteed Jamaica (Lf)	Jamaica	Jamaica + Dom. Rep. + Mexico	Mexico	Connecticut	2

Hacienda

That the long filler from the Canary Islands have regained their former good reputation after a considerable period of quiescence lies in the excellent quality of a number of brands – much to the joy of numerous *aficionados* who have come to appreciate cigars bearing the accreditation *Hecho a mano en las Islas Canarias*. Hacienda, an absolutely top product of Canary Island cigar makers produced by Tabacos Vargas in Santa Cruz on the island of La Palma, has also contributed to this development.

Although the hand-made Hacienda cigars are relatively mild in taste, they release a pleasant piquancy when smoked.

Hajenius

This is the "Cigar Temple" par excellence – worldwide. Built from German sandstone, its external appearance with rounded, crimson awnings that reach far into the street may well be imposing, but cannot hope to compete with impression the visitor gains on entering the store itself. Perhaps one should rather call it a hall of business, as the room is several metres high – providing plenty of space for the heavy, monumental chandeliers hanging from the ceiling and dating back to a time when Amsterdam was lit by gas (see photo on the left). The fittings of this imposing foyer have not changed since it opened in 1915 – everything is in the Art Deco style, and the materials used are those of that period, wood, leather and marble.

But Hajenius has existed significantly longer than the 90 years suggested by the 1915 date. P. G. C. Hajenius, to give the firm its full name, was founded in 1826 when Pantaleon Gerhard Coenraad Hajenius opened a cigar store on Vijgendam. This was a good choice of location, since he could not only serve a well-funded clientele, but about 30 small cigar manufacturers were also to be found in the area. It was the best of these small concerns that the young Hajenius – he was just 19 years old when he arrived in Amsterdam – chose to produce his cigars from first-class tobaccos.

Success was not long in coming – even royal houses were among his customers – and quite soon, the capacity of his business premises no longer sufficed. He moved to the Dam, one of the canal city's grand avenues.

Within time, this domicile also became too small, giving rise to the desire for larger premises. The plans resulted in the noble house on Rokin, itself a desirable address, where P. G. C. Hajenius can still be found.

There are still cigars that bear the name of the firm's founder. However, they are no longer produced in Amsterdam as the formerly blooming cigar industry of the Dutch cigar metropolis has long ceased to exist. But there are other production locations that enjoy a good reputation. Thus Hajenius still ensures first-class tobaccos are processed into cigars manufactured in the best Dutch tradition. And what is more, the firm from Amsterdam has even jumped over its own (traditional) shadow by offering excellent Nicaraguan long filler, completely rolled by hand using the HBPR method, under a name that is also a guarantee of quality – P. G. C. Hajenius.

Handelsgold

This is the best known German cigar brand – if not for the general public, then certainly for the generation over the age of fifty.

The heyday of the Handelsgold was in the 1950s and 1960s, when the traffic landscape of German cities was dominated by such cars as the BMW Isetta, the Borgward Isabella, the Mercedes 170, the Messerschmidt Kabinenroller, the Opel Kapitän and the rear window – more reminiscent of a porthole – of

Theodor Heuss

the Volkswagen Beetle, while small trucks made do with three wheels and bore the great names of Krupp and Magirus Deutz.

In the thick of it the Handelsgold logo with its globe of the world was almost ever present on trams, buses and railway station hoardings. It was the era of the economic miracle, and the Handelsgold was simply a part of it – both the father of this miracle, Ludwig Erhard, and President Theodor Heuss, puffed away at one or more of these cigars produced in the east Westphalian town of Bünde. The term premium cigar didn't even exist at that time, and while the knowledge of products of Caribbean origin was almost zero among the wide mass of cigar smokers, a Havana was considered pure luxury.

The Handelsgold is still available today – as in former days, still without the 100 percent tobacco guarantee seal – and many a producer would be more than glad to reach the sales figures that this downright anachronistic brand still achieves. Whereas a certain mood of nostalgia on the part of cigar smokers when they light up a brown legend plays a part in this, it is the extremely low price that persuades the many smokers in Eastern Europe (the main export market) who have discovered the Handelsgold to reach for the cigar of the economic miracle.

H. de Cabañas y Carbajal

Perhaps the name of the oldest existing Havana brand will awaken nostalgic memories in the foreseeable future, for the Cabañas are only produced in very small numbers which are available in only certain countries. Although the formats of this brand are exclusively produced by machine, they are nevertheless inviting for the confirmed Havana enthusiast, for these cigars evoke memories of the old Cuban style, and possess a predominantly strong body.

Henry Clay

This cigar brand with its moving history derives its name from the United

States politician of the same name (1777–1852), who was elected in 1811 as a Republican to the House of Representatives, where he served as speaker (with interruptions) for years, before crowning his political career by becoming United States Secretary of State.

The US Foreign Minister from 1825 to 1829 was a passionate cigar smoker, thus it came as no surprise when a cigar brand bearing the name Henry Clay was created during that century.

As was common in the Havana of the day – as elsewhere – the brand name and factory name were one and the same, that is, identical, and the Henry Clay factory was soon producing the Henry Clay brand which quickly established itself on the market and within a short time became one of the great Havanas.

Both the factory and the name took their leave of the Cuban capital in the 1930s when cigar production was transferred to the State of New Jersey in the USA. Today, though, the production location of the Henry Clay is no longer to be found in the United States, but in the Dominican Republic.

The Dominican Henry Clay cigars cannot, however, totally forget their origins, for their medium-strong to full aroma approximates the strength of many cigars of Cuban workmanship (most certainly the case with the H-2000 series) which contrasts with numerous other Dominican brands. And there is another reminder of their origin. On opening the cigar box, the observer is greeted on the inside of the lid by a *vista* depicting the former Henry Clay factory in Havana.

Hommage 1492

This brand name awakens associations, referring to Christopher Columbus and the year in which he accidentally discovered a new continent for the Spanish crown – America.

The Hommages have been on the market for some time, and many an *aficionado* has found them worthy of a place in his humidor. These well-made long filler, made by hand in the Dominican Republic, convince with their generally rounded flavour.

Hoyo de Monterrey

Hoyo means hollow, or pit, in English, while Monterrey refers to a location. So the correct translation of this tobacco brand, one of great Havanas, would be "Monterrey hollow". Behind this name is also one of Cuba's best known *vegas finca* – a plantation were

sun-grown types of tobacco are cultivated for absolutely first-class binder and wrapper leaves.

It all began around the middle of the 19th century, as shown by the following words: "Hoyo de Monterrey: José Gener. 1860." This inscription can be found on a wrought-iron gate, reached via a square in the village of San Juan y Martínez Monterrey – to give it its full name – in the Vuelta Abajo.

The reference to the location contained in the brand name is, however, of no great interest, for the Vuelta Abajo growing area, in the province of Pinar del Río, is more the rule than the exception for such outstanding Havana brands. Far more interesting is the "hollow", for fields with swales are most welcome for tobacco growers, as surplus water can drain into it naturally – and here there is rain galore, especially during the Cuban summer, which usually brings copious rainfall.

Here, in a provincial nest on the west of the largest Caribbean island, began the career of José Gener (whose name, by the way, is still to be found on every box of Cuban Hoyos de Monterrey). The horizons of this career stretched far beyond his fields, as José Gener's activities were not confined to those of a tobacco grower but also extended to the mercantile world, for in this he found an area of activity he considered to be more lucrative.

Señor Gener proceeded to build the La Escepcíon factory, in which his brand, created in 1865, was soon to be produced under his direction. Then, in 1867, he set up the José Gener y Miguel business with his uncle, Miguel

Hoyo de Monterrey

Jané y Gener, a native of Catalonia, before going on to found José Gener y Cia with his brothers, to be followed by José Gener y Batet which he managed alone.

On his death in 1900, the experienced cigar maker and successful business-man left behind him a well prospering business. It was sold to a consortium led by Señores Ramón Fernández and Fernando Palicio who used Gener's own factory as their headquarters, to which other production plants were then added.

Today, the Monterreys are produced predominantly in the Miguel Fernández Roig factory. Behind this name lies the time-honoured factory of La Corona, which was renamed years ago, like almost all of Havana's large cigar factories.

According to the experts, one format stands above all others, the Double

Corona, although the Epicure No.1 and Epicure No. 2, both bundle cigars, offered in bundles of 50 cigars without

cigar rings as a Cabinet Selection, should also meet the most exacting standards.

But back to our story. It was precisely these Cabinet Selection cigars that, long ago, inspired none other than Zino Davidoff to create his Chateaux. And they, in turn, served the cigar makers of La Corona in the 1970s as a model for the Le Hoyo series, the cigars of which display a more pronounced flavour and fuller aroma than the Standard series, and are a sensible supplement to the existing range. With its Standard and Le Hoyo series together, Hoyo de Monterrey today covers a wide range of formats, in which a large variation of flavours and strengths of aroma can be found.

One more backward glance – this time to the period after Cuban Revolution. Shortly after the US embargo against the island state came into force in 1960, hardly a single Hoyo de Monterrey was to be found in the cigar stores of the United States.

Initially, one might be inclined to see the economic sanctions against Cuba as the explanation for this, but the most important reason was something else. Cuba found itself in a phase of internal upheaval after Castro took power, and this upheaval also gripped the tobacco industry. All cigar factories were nationalised, and for a time, the

Comandante's idea of producing a single cigar brand in Cuba haunted the tobacco fields.

Such worrying thoughts about the future of a significant branch of the economy were hardly going to inspire the *vegueros* to tend their fields joyfully in this situation, nor were the *torcedores* taken by the idea of wasting all their cigar-making skills. Such thoughts paralyse. The result was that the post-revolutionary cigar industry was no longer the equal of the pre-revolutionary one.

The Hoyos de Monterrey and many other cigar brands were soon no longer available in the United States as the existing reserves – which could hardly be termed abundant anyway – were soon exhausted. The *aficionados* of the United States were first able to breathe a small sigh of relief in 1963, for in that year a new Hoyo de Monterrey enlivened their tobacco stores.

These cigars, made in Honduras, were of astonishing quality and somewhat fuller in aroma than their Cuban sisters. Until the early 1970s, they were even externally reminiscent of the good old Havana – *Made with real Havana leaf* could be read on the boxes of the Hon-duran Hoyos de Monterrey. This statement reflected the reality of the situation, for stupendous amounts of Cuban tobacco had been stockpiled in the United States long before the Cuban revolution, not to mention the embargo (the tobacco made its way from these warehouses to Honduras among other places).

But the above information is, of course, no longer to be found on the boxes of Honduran Hoyos de Monterrey since this tobacco has long been exhausted.

But that is not all there is to the Hoyos. Another brand also trades under this name, albeit with an addendum. This is the Excalibur, behind which name lies one of the best non-Cuban brands, according to many experts. The Excalibur was created towards the end of the 1970s and named after the famous sword of Arthurian legend.

One piece of information – whereas this cigar is obtainable in many parts of the world as Hoyo de Monterrey Excalibur, it is only available in Europe under a single designation, that is, Excalibur.

H. Upmann

Anyone who loves relatively mild cigars, but does not want to forego the typical flavour of a Havana is definitely well served by most formats of the H. Upmann brand.

The "H" of the brand name stands for Hermann, and the "Upmann" refers to a European banking dynasty. Hermann Upmann was an offshoot of this dynasty, and, as befitting the progeny of such a family, he began a career in banking. Whether or not he carried out his occupation with verve is not known, what is known is his consuming passion for good cigars.

When his bank's plans to open a branch in Havana took concrete form in 1840, our *connoisseur* knew exactly what he intended doing with his future. In that year, Hermann Upmann could be seen everyday at his desk in the new branch of his bank, and almost everyday he could be seen in cigar stores, or encountered on a tobacco plantation, or observed in discussion with people who shared his passion for smoking cigars.

And in all his activities this lover of good Havanas never forgot his cigar friends in his homeland: he continually supplied them with the best-tasting and most fragrant cigars he could obtain.

Once a train of affairs is set in motion, and the resulting spiral of events begins to turn ever quicker, the situation develops a momentum of its own. That is what happened in this case. What happened was exactly what simply had to happen – in 1884 the banker Upmann set up his own cigar factory, and soon the H. Upmanns were enjoying general popularity.

The creation of a cigar brand that can look back on a long tradition, as well as all the ups and downs of people and factories connected with such a brand, has always been the stuff of stories and legends.

That is also the case with the chequered history of the H. Upmann for it is by no means certain that the above story is true in all points. Nevertheless the story has been retold time and again. Of course, this doesn't make it any truer, but it is without doubt a good story.

There is another version which, while in agreement with certain details of the first, differs in one important point in relation to the founder. In this version it is a pair of German brothers who, during a long stay in Cuba, had nothing else to do than open a cigar shop in Havana, and shortly afterwards to create a cigar brand that naturally also needed a factory for its production – and so the factory was soon set up, too.

A year later, the brothers received the support of a new partner, a certain Enrique Claufsen, also a German. Cigar, shop and factory all naturally required a name. The brothers' family name was an obvious candidate for this – and the H. Upmann was born.

The "H" was not derived from the forename of one of the brothers, but was a part of the surname – Hupmann (and not Upmann). Augustin and Hermann Hupmann chose "H" for *Hermanos,* the Spanish word for brother, while waiving the "H" of the surname in the brand's name, as "H" is not pronounced in Spanish anyway.

Hermann Hupmann had two nephews, Alberto und Germán, who were successful bankers. When the two set up the Banco Comercial in Havana, the firm of H. Upmann officially took a holding in this financial institute. That will do for the origins of the brand's name and the connection of the Upmanns to the banking sector.

What then followed is more or less the same in both versions of the story. The businesses flourished, both the banking house and that the (by that time) three cigar factories. The tributes they received between 1855 and 1893 bear witness to the high esteem in which the H. Upmann brand was held. Seven gold medallions, of which six are still displayed today on the *vista* of the Upmann cigar box, presented in Paris (twice), London, Porto, Vienna and finally Chicago, prove the brand's prestige during this period (and, of course, the skill of its many fathers).

H. Upmann

This successful symbiosis of skill and commerce accompanied the H. Upmann into the early 1920s.

But then dark clouds gathered over Cuba with the beginning of an econ-

omic crisis. First the bank was forced to close in 1922, and shortly afterwards the factory, which found itself unable to pay the bank's debts, could no longer be considered to be capable of survival. It was the London company of Frankau & Co. (today Hunters & Frankau, the largest British importer of Havanas and cigars of Caribbean origin) which took over the factory.

The Britons, used to trading in cigars but not producing them, leased the business to a German-Spanish concern, which pressed ahead with the firm and upheld the brand that by now was one of the great names in the world of cigars. It was these leaseholders who introduced an innovation in the field of packaging – the aluminium tube lined with cedar wood.

Anyhow, this marriage lasted only 14 years, since the leaseholders lacked the necessary capital to guarantee a high level of production without trouble. Finally, Frankau & Co. terminated the existing leasing contract in 1936, and soon afterwards the firm Menéndez y García (formerly Menéndez y Cia) took over the company and the name.

Soon afterwards the H. Upmann factory began making a profit again. One of the most important reasons for this was the introduction of a new brand that really took off when it appeared on the market, and which today is still considered a great Havana – the Montecristo.

Then, in 1944, exactly 100 years after the business was founded by the Upmanns or Hupmanns, a new production plant bearing the H. Upmann name was opened in the old quarter of Havana (in the Calle Amistad to be precise) to keep up with the continually increasing demand for the various formats of the legendary brand.

The Upmanns are still produced there. Whereas about 50 *vitolas* left the factory a few years ago, today there are less than 20, of which the H. Upmann No. 2 and the Magnum 46 are the most outstanding.

Brand/Series	Origin	Filler	Binder	Wrapper	Strength
Hacienda (Lf)	Canaries	Canaries + Cuba + Indonesia (Java)	Indonesia (Java)	CoSh	2–3
Hajenius					
• Grand Finale Serie (Sf)	Netherlands	Indonesia (Su + Ja) + Brazil + Cuba	Indonesia (Java)	Indonesia (SuSa)	2–3
• HBPR (Lf)	Nicaragua	Puros: all tobaccos grown in Nicaragua			3–4
• Sumatra Serie (Sf)	Netherlands	Indonesia (Su + Ja) + Brazil + Cuba	Indonesia (Java)	Indonesia (SuSa)	1–4
Hardy Rodenstock (Lf)	Dominican Republic	Dom. Rep.	Dom. Rep.	CoSh	3–4
Harvill (Lf)	Jamaica	Jamaica + Dom. Rep.	Mexico	CoSh	3
Havana					
• Handrolled (Sf)	Switzerland	Cuba + Dom. Rep. + Indonesia (Su)	Indonesia (Java)	Cuba	2
• Seed (Sf)	Switzerland	Cuba + Dom. Rep. + Brazil	Indonesia (Java)	CoBr	3–4
H. de Cabañas y Carbajal (Sf)	Cuba	Puros: all tobaccos grown in Cuba			5–6
Henry Clay					
• Classic Line (Lf)	Dominican Republic	Dom. Rep.	Dom. Rep.	CoSh	3–4
• H-2000 (Lf)	Dominican Republic	Dom. Rep.	Dom. Rep.	Nicaragua (Ha2000)	4–5
Hommage 1492					
• Classic Line (Lf)	Dominican Republic	Dom. Rep. (DoOlor + PiCu)	Dom. Rep. (CuSe)	Indonesia (Vola)	3–4
• Vintage (Lf)	Dominican Republic	Peru + Dom. Rep.	Dom. Rep.	Honduras (Co)	2–4
Hoyo de la Romana	Dominican Republic	Dom. Rep.	Dom. Rep.	CoSh	2–3
Hoyo de Monterrey					
• Clásica (Lf)	Cuba	Puros: all tobaccos grown in Cuba			1–3
• Le Hoyo (Lf)	Cuba	Puros: all tobaccos grown in Cuba			3–5
H. Upmann (Lf + Sf)	Cuba	Puros: all tobaccos grown in Cuba			1–3
Hurricanos (Lf)	Honduras	Honduras	Honduras	Ecuador (SuGr)	5

John Aylesbury

In 1977, the year Germany won the World Cup for the second time, something very important happened in another area of German life which, like football, may not be exactly crucial to survival but is nevertheless a wonderful distraction – cigar smoking.

Eight retail traders representing seven tobacconist businesses got together. Their aim was to establish a loosely meshed network of tobacconists for which they intended to create joint platform of quality products. This platform was also to have a name which, on the one hand, should be distinctive and unmistakeable – in short, memorable – and at the same time should be a synonym for the product standards to which they aspired. The search for such a name proved more difficult than expected until, finally, a suggestion came from outside – John Aylesbury – and the name was found.

Also found were 30 retailers who could be enthused by the idea. Thus, what began over 30 years ago with a mere four sorts of pipe tobacco, offered under the name of a London suburb near Wimbledon added to the forename John, has now become firmly established. The first cigars were added to the range after a few years, and, apart from accessories and pipes, John Aylesbury currently offers for sale a very fine, if not wide, selection of cigars and cigarillos that are characterised by their moderate price range.

The initial 30 stores have now grown to about 50 – not a great many for John Aylesbury's 25 years. But that is all in accordance with the concern's philosophy, they only accept businesses enjoying and actively promoting a first-class reputation. Whether an application is finally accepted or not is decided by the members. A business must not only have a good reputation, it must also be run by the owner. Even when these and several other criteria are fulfilled, the application is pointless when there is already a business belonging to the John Aylesbury Werbegesellschaft in the city concerned. Only one vendor is accepted per city – that is the ultimate criterion required by exclusivity and claims of quality.

José Gener

This is the second brand created by José Gener, the first being the Hoyo de Monterrey. At one time the Geners were much in demand, under both the José Gener La Escepción and La Escepción product logos. Cigars of this brand are no longer produced – which is a comfort for the novice who would most certainly have (had) problems with this strong Havana.

José L. Piedra

The Piedras is one of the Havanas created towards the end of the 19th century. The creators were Spanish immigrants from the province of Asturias who settled in Santa Clara, a town in

the Remedios region in which tobacco has been grown since the 16th century.

The Josés L. Piedra are hand-made short filler that display a predominantly strong aroma.

Joya de Nicaragua

The Jewel of Nicaragua can look back on a history full of change, full of ups and downs, as so often is the case. Many Cubans turned their backs on their island following the US embargo and found a new home in Nicaragua. Tobacco planters found something more; something that was very helpful for their purpose in life (making

cigars) – a soil comparable to what they had given up in Cuba. The result was that the Joya de Nicaragua brand appeared on the market as early as 1965.

Subsequently, the cigars built up a strong number of regular customers, for the Joyas de Nicaragua were really good cigars. Their tobaccos were grown in the most fertile areas of Nicaragua; the filler was of native tobacco grown from Havana seed, Jalapa leaves were resorted to for the binder leaves, whereas the tobacco for the wrapper leaves was also grown in Nicaragua from Connecticut seed. The Joyas de Nicaragua could therefore be designated *puros*.

Then came 1978. The murder in January of the leading opposition politician, Chamorro, by supporters of the dictator, Somoza, at an election rally, soon led to this Central American country being rocked by a bloody civil war in which the leftist Sandinistas finally won the upper hand. There then followed the emigration of Somoza in 1979, the formation of the Sandinista Junta and the beginning of the armed resistance of the right-wing Contras in 1981.

The latter were supported by the USA, which in 1985 also imposed an embargo against Nicaragua, that would be lifted again only in 1990.

Calm was to return to the country in that year. It was desperately needed, for the political instability that had mainly been imported from outside the country had almost totally disrupted the economy.

This, of course, also affected the cigar industry – fields were devastated, factories bombarded, skilled workers killed. As with the other sectors of the economy, the tobacco industry recovered only gradually from the results of this bloody conflict that had lasted for a decade and had almost torn the country apart.

This is also why the Joya de Nicaragua that were produced after the civil war, when cigar-making had begun again and was gradually steering into calm waters, were of noticeably poorer quality than those from before the bloody conflict.

Today, these cigars have regained their former high standard, for they have been improving significantly, from harvest to harvest, over the last few years.

Juan Clemente

It is, of course, a cliché that only a fine line separates genius from madness, and sometimes one simply has to be mad, or a least mad about something, to astonish the world with one's showpiece.

The presentation took place in 1982, but it had all began significantly earlier. The well-travelled Frenchman, Jean Clement, a completely committed connoisseur, finished up – as could only be the case – in Latin America. For here were not only Caribbean beauties to be found, but also those Caribbean treasures that he – as a man of pleasure – treasured especially well.

He spent four years in the region between the two semi-continents before his love finally turned into his profession. In 1975, this energetic businessman set up a small cigar factory in the Dominican city of Santiago de los Caballeros, and, as mentioned above, in 1982 the first Clementes left its gates.

All the cigars of the current three series present excellent binder leaves *(Santo Domingo)* as well as *Colorado* wrappers from Connecticut. This is welcome but not unusual, for a whole range of other cigars also present these types of tobacco leaves – the unusual aspect is the cigar rings they bear. These cigar rings are not wrapped around the head of the cigars in the normal way but are found instead around the burning end – certainly a clever method of protecting this sensitive part of a cigar from its very birth.

Justus van Maurik

The art of making cigars has a long tradition in the Netherlands – reaching far back into the 18th century. One of the former colonial power's most renowned cigar brands is the Justus van Maurik – a cigar that can also look back on a long history. Named after an old aristocratic family, the Justus van Maurik appeared on the market during the second half of the 18th century (in 1794 to be exact) and is regarded as the figurehead of Dutch cigar-making skill, and not only because of its 200-year-old tradition.

Brand/Series	Origin	Filler	Binder	Wrapper	Strength
Impulso (Sf)	Switzerland	Indonesia (Su) + Dom. Rep. + Brazil	Indonesia (Java)	Indonesia (Sumatra)	2–3
Indian Tabac Cigar					
• *Cameroon Legend (Lf)*	Dominican Republic	Dom. Rep.	Dom. Rep.	Cameroon	3–5
• *Classic Line (Lf)*	Honduras	Nicaragua + Honduras + Costa Rica	Nicaragua (MeSe)	Nicaragua (CuSe)	4–5
• *Tubos (Lf)*	Honduras	Nicaragua + Honduras + Costa Rica	Nicaragua	Nicaragua	4–5
Industrial Press (Lf)	Nicaragua	Nicaragua	Nicaragua	Ecuador (ViSuGr)	4–5
José Benito (Lf)	Dominican Republic	Dom. Rep. + Ecuador + Honduras	Dom. Rep.	CoSh	2–3
José L. Piedra (Sf)	Cuba	Puros: all tobaccos grown in Cuba			3–5
José Llopis (Lf)	Panama	Dom. Rep. + Nicaragua	Dom. Rep.	Ecuador	4
José Martí (Lf)	Nicaragua	Nicaragua + Honduras + Dom. Rep.	Nicaragua	Ecuador (SuSe)	3–4
Joya de la Romana (Lf)	Dominican Republic	Dom. Rep.	Dom. Rep.	CoSh	2–3
Joya de Nicaragua (Lf)	Nicaragua	Puros: all tobaccos grown in Nicaragua (F: CuSe; B: CoSe; W: CuSe)			2–4
Juan Clemente					
• *Classic Line (Lf)*	Dominican Republic	Dom. Rep. + Brazil	Dom. Rep. (DoOlor)	CoSh	2–3
• *Club Selection (Lf)*	Dominican Republic	Dom. Rep. + Brazil	Dom. Rep. (DoOlor)	CoSh	2–3
• *Reserve (Lf)*	Dominican Republic	Dom. Rep. (PiCu + DoOlor)	Dom. Rep. (DoOlor)	CoSh	3–4
Justus van Maurik (Sf)	Netherlands	Br + Cu + In (Ja) + Ph	Indonesia (Vola)	Indonesia (SuSa)	4–5
Krumme Hunde					
• *Brasil (Sf)*	Switzerland	Brazil (Ba) + Cuba + Dom. Rep.	Indonesia (Java)	Brazil (Ba)	4
• *Havana (Sf)*	Switzerland	Cuba + Dom. Rep. + Indonesia (Su)	Indonesia (Java)	Cuba	2–3

La Aurora

Here, long filler from the oldest producer in the Dominican Republic present themselves. Although the quality of the classic Standard series' formats is beyond doubt, it is the Preferidos – an exclusive series made up of various lines – that should be mentioned in some depth here. Of much more recent date and nothing like as old as the Standard series, the Aurora Preferidos Editions nevertheless point to earlier times, as they rely on criteria set up by Eduardo León Jimenes in 1903 when Don Eduardo concentrated solely on the Perfecto (Torpedo) format. There are three further lines in this series in addition to the fairly well-established Preferidos Platinum – Corojo Gold, Maduro de Luxe and Sapphire.

The Preferidos are produced according to strictest quality guidelines. For example, only master rollers are allowed to produce these editions (which is why no more than 100 cigars are rolled per day), while the tobaccos used are subjected to a storage process that lasts many years before they mature for a year in oak barrels – only to pursue perfection in the aging-room for six more months after the production process. At the end of this period, the Preferidos are packed into splendid metal tubes. In all, the Preferidos are absolutely premium cigars to enthuse every *aficionado*. These perfectly worked long filler have their price, however – of which they are definitely worthy.

La Corona

The La Corona was born in 1845, and is therefore among the oldest Havana brands – or perhaps one should say *was* among them, since the production of the Cuban La Coronas was stopped for good in 1999. A pity, for this time-honoured brand embodied the traditional Cuban style.

The Crowns have been made in the Dominican Republic for many years and exported to numerous countries. They are, however, quite different cigars, in no way reminiscent of the strong Havanas treasured by so many *aficionados* throughout the world. Despite this, the mild to medium-strong *Dominicanos* can certainly be recommended, for they are characterised by good workmanship and subtle aromas, and are therefore suitable for smokers who have just made their first steps in the world of cigars.

La Flor de Cano

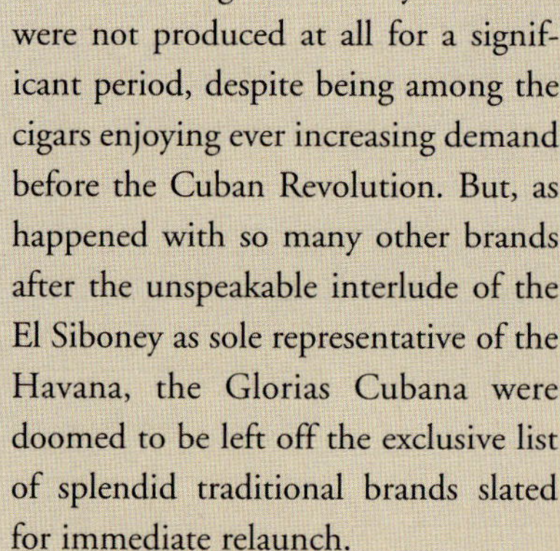

The Flowers of the Canos – this name refers to the José and Tomás Cano brothers, the creators of this brand. The filler for these cigars were granted special care before being finally allowed to tread the public arena in 1884.

Unfortunately only four formats of this brand are produced today – two by hand as short filler, and the other two by machine. However, all four have one thing in common – their medium-strong aroma.

La Fontana

The La Fontanas – in some countries available under the name La Fontana Vintage as vintage cigars – are especially well suited for the novice and for those smokers who have already gained their first experience of cigars. One could easily gain the impression by reading the trade name that this is a brand produced in Italy. This is not the case. The La Fontanas are manufactured in Danlí, in Honduras, and the *torcedores* who work in this factory run by the Eiroa family certainly know their job, for these cigars with a mild aroma are excellently made.

La Gloria Cubana

In a sense, the Havana brand, La Gloria Cubana, doesn't fit in with a Partagás factory product range that includes the Bolívar, the Partagás and the Ramón Allones – all definitely among the stronger Havanas available for purchase and smoking. The Glorias Cubana are in stark contrast to these brands, for they belong without doubt to the mildly aromatic Havanas.

Those who prefer a Havana with a mild aroma can count themselves lucky that the Glorias are still available at all. Or, more accurately put, are available again, for they were not produced at all for a significant period, despite being among the cigars enjoying ever increasing demand before the Cuban Revolution. But, as happened with so many other brands after the unspeakable interlude of the El Siboney as sole representative of the Havana, the Glorias Cubana were doomed to be left off the exclusive list of splendid traditional brands slated for immediate relaunch.

Nevertheless, the Glorias Cubana are now enjoying increasing support and have firmly established themselves

once again – luckily for those who wish to acquaint themselves with the world of the Havana, for the Glorias have that unmistakeable flavour almost all Havanas can call their own, despite their manifest mildness.

La Rica

The adjective *rico* means "well-off" and "rich" as well as "rich in content" and "delicious", which leads to the conclusion that the makers of this fairly young brand selected this name deliberately.

The La Ricas from Nicaragua are quite reticent in unfolding their aromas but display instead another positive attribute. They are particularly well suited to accompany spirits, because they form a pleasant union of flavours most notably with the various rums from the Caribbean and Central American region. There is also another positive attribute of the solidly made long filler that should be empha-sised – the relatively economic price.

Laura Chavin

The Laura Chavin brand was created and named after his daughter by Helmut Bührle, a long-time designer for large concerns and son of a Stuttgart mercantile family linked with tobacco for decades. He was assisted in this by the experts of Tabacalera de García, and it is there in the Dominican Republic that the Laura Chavins are still pro-duced by hand.

Smokers are mostly persuaded by the two Concours des meilleurs Connaisseurs and Pur Sang series. However, both product lines are to be found in the very high price category. We leave it to each prospective customer to decide whether the price accurately reflects the product.

León Jimenes

As with very many Dominican brands, León Jimenes cigars also present a medium-strength body, which is a result of what can be called a successful balance between the filler, binder and wrapper leaves.

The León Jimenes can, incidentally, look back on a long tradition. First produced in 1903, it is the oldest extant Dominican brand. However, it has not rested on the laurels it has gained over this long period, as its makers have continually striven to improve and refine the existing mixtures, and so it is no wonder that the León Jimenes can still count, as ever, on its firm supporters.

Los Statos de Luxe

The initial "S" of the Statos (or more precisely Los Statos de Luxe) could easily stand for "sad", as these Havanas are sadly not available everywhere, and, in addition, are only produced in a limited number. This is certainly sad because the Statos are cigars of the traditional Havana style – they are relatively strong in aroma and meet the penchant of a dyed-in-the-wool Havana enthusiast for a strong cigar very well.

Brand/Series	Origin	Filler	Binder	Wrapper	Strength
La Aurora					
• Classic Line (Lf)	Dominican Republic	Dom. Rep.	Dom. Rep. (PiCu)	Cameroon	3
• Preferidos Classic (Lf)	Dominican Republic	Dom. Rep.	Dom. Rep. (PiCu)	Cameroon	5
• Preferidos Gold (Lf)	Dominican Republic	Cameroon + Brazil + Dom. Rep.	Dom. Rep. (PiCu)	Dom. Rep. (Co)	4
• Preferidos Maduro de Luxe (Lf)	Dominican Republic	Dom. Rep.	Dom. Rep. (PiCu)	Brazil	3
• Preferidos Platinum (Lf)	Dominican Republic	Dom. Rep.	Dom. Rep. (PiCu)	Cameroon	3
• Preferidos Sapphire (Lf)	Dominican Republic	Dom. Rep.	Dom. Rep. (PiCu)	Connecticut	2
La Casa de Nicaragua (Lf)	Nicaragua	Puros: all tobaccos grown in Nicaragua			1–2
La Corona (Lf)	Dominican Republic	Dom. Rep.	Dom. Rep. (PiCu)	CoSh	2–3
La Diva (Lf)	Dominican Republic	Dom. Rep.	Dom. Rep.	CoSh	3
La Flor de Cano (Sf)	Cuba	Puros: all tobaccos grown in Cuba			2–3
La Flor de Ynclan (Lf)	Dominican Republic	Dom. Rep. (PiCu) + Nicaragua (CuSe)	Indonesia	Ecuador (CoSe)	2–4

Brand/Series	Origin	Filler	Binder	Wrapper	Strength
La Flor Dominicana					
• Classic Line (Lf)	Dominican Republic	Dom. Rep. (PiCu) + Nicaragua (CuSe)	Dom. Rep. (DoOlor)	CoSh	2–3
• Double Ligero (Lf)	Dominican Republic	Dom. Rep. (PiCu) + Nicaragua (CuSe)	Dom. Rep. (DoOlor)	CoSh	6
La Fontana (Lf)	Honduras	Honduras (CuSe)	Mexico	Honduras (CoSe)	2–3
La Gloria Cubana (Lf)	Cuba	Puros: all tobaccos grown in Cuba			2–3
La Hoja Tribal (Lf)	Honduras	Nicaragua + Dom. Rep.	Honduras	Ecuador	2–3
La Intimidad de A. Caruncho (Lf)	Honduras	Nicaragua (CuSe) + Honduras	Honduras (CoSe)	Indonesia	2–3
La Libertad (Lf)	Honduras	Honduras + Nicaragua	Honduras	Honduras (CuSe)	4–5
La Meridiana					
• Cameroon Selection (Lf)	Nicaragua	Nicaragua (CuSe)	Nicaragua (CuSe)	Cameroon	4–5
• Classic Line (Lf)	Nicaragua	Puros: all tobaccos grown in Nicaragua (F: CuSe; B: CoSe; W: CuSe)			3–5
La Paz					
• Corona (Sf)	Netherlands	Pure Indonesian: all tobaccos produced in Indonesia			5
• Wilde Brazil (Sf)	Netherlands	Brazil (MaFi)	Indonesia (JaBe)	Brazil (MaFi)	5
• Wilde Cigarros (Sf)	Netherlands	Pure Indonesian: all tobaccos produced in Indonesia			5
La Regenta (Lf)	Canaries	Cuba + Brazil (MaFi)	Dom. Rep.	CoSh	2–3
La Rica (Lf)	Nicaragua	Nicaragua	Indonesia (Java)	Ecuador (CoSe)	3
Las Cabrillas (Lf)	Honduras	Honduras + Nicaragua	Mexico	CoSh	3–4
La Única (Lf)	Dominican Republic	Dom. Rep.	Dom. Rep.	Connecticut	1–2
Laura Chavin					
• Classic Line (Lf)	Dominican Republic	Dom. Rep. (DoOlor + PiCu)	Mexico	CoSh	2–3
• Concours des meilleurs Connais. (Lf)	Dominican Republic	Dom. Rep.	No details	No details	4
• Pur Sang (Lf)	Dominican Republic	Dom. Rep.	No details	No details	3–4
La Vencedora (Lf)	Nicaragua	Nicaragua + Dom. Rep.	Ecuador	Ecuador (CoSe)	2–4
La Villa de Chavon (Lf)	Dominican Republic	Dom. Rep.	Dom. Rep.	CoSh	1
León Jimenes					
• Classic Line (Lf)	Dominican Republic	Dom. Rep.	Dom. Rep. (PiCu)	CoSh	2–4
• Maduro (Lf)	Dominican Republic	Dom. Rep.	Dom. Rep. (PiCu)	Brazil (MaFi)	2–3
Longchamp (Sf)	France	Pure Havana: all tobaccos from Cuban production			4
Los Statos de Luxe (Sf)	Cuba	Puros: all tobaccos grown in Cuba			4–5

Macanudo

The origins of this brand are to be found in Cuba, as are those of so many Caribbean cigars. In actual fact a format of the Punch, a Havana brand produced during the second half of the 19th century almost exclusively for the British market, the Macanudo gained its autonomy quite quickly when, in 1868, the first formats were rolled in a Cuban-owned factory in Jamaica. This

constellation was to last for more than 90 years.

Then came the Castro Revolution, and in the midst of the following confusion the Cuban owners of the Macanudo found themselves forced to give up the production plant of this famous cigar, and to sell the brand rights to a Jamaican concern which then continued producing the Macanudos under their own name. This situation came to end after only a few years when the Jamaicans, who had not been able to cope with the production and marketing as well as they had imagined, finally sold the rights. These were transferred to a concern in Tampa, before they were ultimately acquired a few years later by the General Cigar Company. General Cigar, one of the leading tobacco and cigar concerns in the USA, still produces the Macanudo, but now does so exclusively in the Dominican Republic.

Until a few years ago that was not the case. After the respected cigar maker Benjamín Menéndez had decamped from the Canary Islands, and at first taken on the responsibility for the production of the Partagás, another General Cigar brand, in the Dominican Republic, he began to devote himself increasingly to the production of the Macanudo from the mid-1980s onwards. In this he became something of an international wanderer for the cigars of this traditional brand were produced in roughly equal quantities in both Jamaica and the Dominican Republic.

The cigars sold in Europe came mostly from Jamaica and for a good reason. The Caribbean island-state and member of the British Commonwealth, operates an extremely modest tax policy whose benefits continue when the product is exported to the motherland, and since Great Britain is a member of the European Union, the export of Jamaican tobacco products to the Old World positively affects the balance sheet.

But regardless of the tax benefits, the Americans decided several years ago to transfer the whole responsibility for the Macuando to the *tabaqueros* of the Dominican Republic, which naturally simplified the logistics of production greatly. Whether the cost advantage gained in the area of logistics makes up for the resulting additional expenditure in taxation may be open to question, but the decision has not done any damage to the quality and workmanship of the Macunado.

This brand still belongs to the very best the international cigar market can offer – and that applies to all five series, with perhaps the possible exception of the Robusto. This last has not been able to assert itself as well as its makers may have hoped but is, nevertheless, to be regarded as belonging to the top quality sector. Without wishing to devalue the other series, two deserve special mention.

Firstly, there is the Vintage Cabinet Selection. These vintage cigars first appeared on the market in 1989 with a *Connecticut Shade* wrapper that had been harvested ten years previously whose extremely long storage had allowed it to mature accordingly. Following the Vintage 1979, the vintages 1984, 1988 and 1993 also appeared on the market, all bearing an additional cigar ring documenting the year of the vintage. All the quite mild Macanudo Vintages made under the experienced direction of Daniel Núñez present a balanced composition in which the individual tobaccos harmonise excellently with each other.

The same can be said of the Maduros. The novice would no doubt wince at the sight of these cigars, for the unambiguous *negros* wrapper leaves give the impression that these cigars have an extremely strong body.

The novice who overcomes this and actually lights up a Macanudo Maduro will be surprised by the mildness of this cigar which also releases a wealth of aromas. This is thanks, mainly, to the almost black *Connecticut Broadleaf* wrapper that has been subjected to the sun so long that it becomes quite oily, making it responsible for the strongly sweet aromas.

Maria Mancini

"And so he withdrew from its automobile-leather and silver monogrammed case an exemplar of the Maria Macini – a beautiful example of the very highest quality, slightly flattened on one side, of which he was particularly fond. He docked the tip with a small angular cutting instrument, which he carried on a watch chain, let his pocket lighter flare, and set the rather long blunt-ended cigar alight with several devoted puffs."

And again – "I don't understand how anyone could not smoke – he forsakes the best part of life and by all accounts a very eminent pleasure! When I wake up, I look forward to being allowed to smoke during the day; and when I eat, I look forward to it – yes, I can even say that I only eat so that I can smoke – although I'm exaggerating a little, of course. But a day without tobacco would be the height of vapidity, a completely bleak and boring day."

The author was Thomas Mann and the character speaking is Hans Castorp, the main figure of the novel, *Der Zauberberg,* (The Magic Mountain).

Although the Maria Mancini had long fallen into obscurity, it experienced a renaissance a few years ago and quite rightly so. And what is it that so characterises this Honduran long filler? The answer is provided by this 1929 winner of the Nobel Prize for Literature, since what he gave Hans Castorp to say still applies, by and large, to the Maria Mancini of today: "She is a medium-full mixture and very flavoursome, but light on the tongue. She prefers to have a long ash; I level it off only twice, at most. Of course, she has her little moods, but the production control must be especially thorough, for Maria has very reliable qualities and draws altogether evenly."

Montecristo

While many experts consider the Cohiba the most perfect Havana brand, plenty of others regard the Montecristo A as the Havana that merits crowning as the best cigar ever to leave the gates of a Cuban factory.

That's the trouble with expert opinion. To rely on it alone is to become one of the world's disappointed. We must all work out our own preferences, especially when the subject is one of taste. This applies to cigars, as it does to every other medium of pleasure. So there can be no "best cigar".

As the acknowledged staunch *connoisseur,* Zino Davidoff, has said, the best cigar is the one you prefer at any given moment.

But the Montecristo A is indisputably one of the best Havanas available on the market. It is also indisputable that this largest format produced under the Montecristo brand is also one of the most expensive cigars to be had anywhere in the world.

Moreover, of all the Havanas available in normal cigar stores (as opposed to the *Casas del Habano*) it is *the* most expensive. But the Montecristo brand is more than just the A. Its other formats have also helped make the Mon-

tecristo brand (along with the Cohiba) the most famous Cuban brand of all.

This is mainly owed to José Manuel González, who took over sole responsibility for Montecristo production when the Menéndez and García families – the brand's owners – emigrated soon after Castro's rise to power.

Held by many to be the best cigar maker ever, González is renowned for not permitting even the smallest mistake or the slightest lack of attention by the *torcedores* to pass, and it is he who is responsible for the impressive selection of leaves that make the Montecristo so distinctive on the one hand, and each format so unique on the other.

Even *aficionados* who love a strong Havana flavour are enthusiastic about the "Montecristo", for although kept not quite so strong, it is still rich in aromas.

The Montecristo's road to success could not have been foreseen, however, when it was created in 1935 by Alonzo Menéndez and Pepe García. It

was not intended as a brand, but rather as a format for a brand they had just acquired.

Nevertheless, it did not take long for the H. Upmann Montecristo Selection format to develop into autonomous Montecristo brand. Shortly afterwards it embarked upon its phenomenal road to success.

We no can longer be certain why the assistants to the birth christened it Montecristo. As with so much to do with cigars in Cuba, there are a number of quite extraordinary stories as to how this brand got its name.

The truth is usually less spectacular. It was most probably this: that the lector's reading of Alexandre Dumas' world-famous novel, *The Count of Montecristo,* had stuck in the mind of one of the fathers thus suggesting the name.

Brand/Series	Origin	Filler	Binder	Wrapper	Strength
Macanudo					
• *Café (Lf)*	Dominican Republic	Dom. Rep. + Mexico	Mexico	CoSh	1–2
• *Gold (Lf)*	Dominican Republic	Dom. Rep. + Mexico	Mexico	CoSh	1–2
• *Maduro (Lf)*	Dominican Republic	Dom. Rep. + Mexico	CoSh	CoBr	1–3
• *Robust (Lf)*	Dominican Republic	Dom. Rep. + Mexico	Dom. Rep. (CuSe)	CoSh	3–4
• *Vintage Cabinet Selection (Lf)*	Dominican Republic	Dom. Rep. + Mexico	Mexico	CoSh	1–2
Maria Mancini (Lf)	Honduras	Puros: all tobaccos grown in Honduras (F: CuSe; W: Ha2000)			1–3
Marqués					
• *de Coronas (Lf)*	Dominican Republic	Cuba	Cuba	CoSh	1–2
• *de Habana (Lf)*	Dominican Republic	Pure Havana: all tobaccos from Cuban production			5–6
• *de León (Lf)*	Dominican Republic	Dom. Rep. + Cuba + Nicaragua	Dom. Rep.	Indonesia	2–4
• *de Montego (Lf)*	Dominican Republic	Dom. Rep. + Cu + Br + Ni	Dom. Rep.	Indonesia	2–4
• *de Moran (Lf)*	Dominican Republic	Dom. Rep.	Dom. Rep.	Indonesia	1–2
Maxima Reserva (Lf)	Honduras	Brazil + Dom. Rep. + Nicaragua	Ecuador	Ecuador	3–5
Maya (Lf)	Honduras	Honduras (CuSe) + Nicaragua (CuSe)	Honduras (CuSe)	Honduras (CuSe)	2–4
Montecristo (Lf)	Cuba	Puros: all tobaccos grown in Cuba			3–6
Monte Palma (Lf)	Canaries	Indonesia (Java) + Canaries	Indonesia (Java)	Indonesia (Sumatra)	2–4
Montero					
• *Conn. Broadleaf Maduro (Lf)*	Dominican Republic	Dom. Rep. (SaVi + DoOlor + PiCu)	Dom. Rep. (PiCu)	CoBr	2
• *Ecuador Connecticut. Shade (Lf)*	Dominican Republic	Dom. Rep. (SaVi + DoOlor + PiCu)	Dom. Rep. (PiCu)	Ecuador (CoSe)	3–4
Montesino (Lf)	Dominican Republic	Dom. Rep.	Dom. Rep.	Ecuador/CoBr/CoSh	2–3
My own Blend (Lf)	Dominican Republic	Dom. Rep. (PiCu + DoOlor) + Brazil	Cameroon	Connecticut	1–2
Mythos Solitude (Lf)	Costa Rica	Pure Nicaragua: all tobaccos from Nicaraguan production			2–4

Nobel

The Danish firm founded in 1835 by Emilius Nobel is mentioned here briefly, although it mainly focuses on the production of cigarillos. However, in this sector, the E. Nobel company is one of the world's greats. Apart from this, the Danes were among the very first to produce their machine-made small formats 100 percent from tobacco (and thus found many imitators).

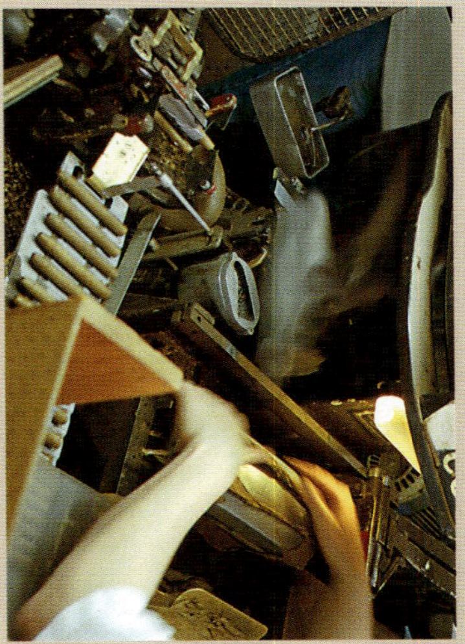

Oud Kampen

"Sumatra cum Laude" that is the embossed stamp to be read on every box of cigars of the Oud Kampen brand. This is a reference to the fine Sumatra wrapper presented by every cigar of this famous Dutch brand. What is more, other select tobaccos from the best cultivation areas are used for binder and filler of the Old Kampener, which are today produced under the supervision of the renowned Ritmeester company, a part of the Swiss Burger Söhne AG concern. These mild, 100 percent tobacco short filler are made in the traditional Dutch style and reveal their finely balanced mixture when smoked, while also giving rise to a wide development of aromas.

Brand/Series	Origin	Filler	Binder	Wrapper	Strength
Navegador (Lf)	Dominican Republic	Dom. Rep. + Cuba	Dom. Rep.	Indonesia	2–4
Nicaragua by Drew Estate (Lf)	Nicaragua	Bunch with up 12 various origins	Cameroon/ConnMe	2–4	
Nostalgia (Lf)	Honduras	Honduras + Mexico + Indonesia	Nicaragua (CuSe)	Honduras (CoSh)	2–3
Orient Express (Lf)	Dominican Republic	Dom. Rep. (PiCu)	Dom. Rep. (PiCu)	CoSh	3–4
Ortolan (Lf)	Honduras	Honduras + Nicaragua	Ecuador	CoSh	3–4
Oud Kampen (Sf)	Netherlands	Brazil + Caribbean + Indonesia	Indonesia (Java)	Indonesia (Sumatra)	2–3

Partagás

Partagás

First produced in 1845, this is one of the oldest Havana brands still in existence and enjoys great popularity, mainly with those *aficionados* who love the typically strong flavour of a Havana. It was created by Jaime Partagás (which explains the origin of the brand name) and produced in the *fabrica* of the same name, which also opened its gates in 1845 – another synchronicity of events.

The numerous formats of the Partagás are still produced, some by machine, within these time-honoured walls. However, the *fabrica* is now known under the name, Francisco Pérez Germán. Setting aside, briefly, the matter of its trading name, the Partagás factory is the oldest industrial production plant of Havanas still in use.

As mentioned, the Partagás are particularly strong, full-bodied cigars with striking earthy-tasting aromas. A whole range of cigars of a high quality of workmanship is made under the expert direction of experienced *tabacaleros* in the Calle de la Industria No. 520, opposite the *capitolio,* in the heart of the old city.

Peñamil

This cigar from the Canary Islands first came onto the market in 1939. It was created by a certain José Martin Lesmes, who took the Peñamil name after his wife's family. These handmade cigars became very popular relatively quickly, at first on the Canaries themselves, then on the Spanish mainland, and finally in Europe – only to be increasingly forgotten from the beginning of the 1970s. They experienced a new upsurge after a take over by the Cita-Tabacos de Canarias S. A. company in 1991, and today enjoy great popularity once more.

This is only right, as the tobaccos for the still relatively young Peñamil Oro series come from the Vuelta Abajo in Cuba, among other places, which lends the relatively mild, but aromatic cigars a certain flavour.

Incidentally, the Peñamils are no longer made on the island of La Palma, the actual centre of cigar production on the Canaries, but at Santa Cruz de Tenerife, under the direction of José Lorenzo Gonzáles, a Cuban exile.

P. J. Landfried

The headquarters of Germany's oldest existing (and producing) cigar factory, P. J. Landfried, can be found on the Bergheimer Straße, in close proximity to Heidelberg's central railway station.

Founded in 1810 by Philipp Jakob Landfried, the young company's volume of orders grew fairly rapidly and, with it, the workforce. Towards the end of the 19th century the business employed 2,000 employees and was thus one of the largest in the field.

Now managed by the sixth generation, the business' current 25 employees produce short filler in the best European tradition under the direction of Dieter Schinz.

Plasencia

Produced in Nicaraguan Estelí, the name of the brand alone guarantees that these cigars are excellent hand-made long filler, because Néstor Plasencia is one of the great cigar makers of the Caribbean region, continually bringing interestingly composed creations to the market.

Nestor Plasencia relies on native tobaccos for the bunch, while depending on *Colorado-Claro* leaves from Ecuador for the wrapper. In brief, these pleasing long filler are of medium strength and give off a rich variety of aromas.

Pléiades

Each Pléiades is certain to have made a long journey before arriving in the hand of an *aficionado*. These cigars are manufactured in La Romana in the Dominican Republic. On completion, they are then sent on the long journey to France to mature further there – or more precisely in Strasburg – for up to six months.

They are then subjected to a final check before being packed into their

cigar boxes with integrated humidifier and finally sent on their way.

First appearing on the market in the mid-1980s, the Pléiadesare among the first premium cigars – the date betrays this at once, and few top brands merit this distinction – to be produced in the Dominican Republic, thus preparing the way for the cigar boom that gripped the Caribbean state in the subsequent years.

The Pléiades are very well made, relatively mild hand-rolled long filler with a *Connecticut Shade* wrapper in *Colorado Claro* and a bunch composed of Dominican tobaccos with a persuasive balance and harmony.

Por Larrañaga

This is the oldest Havana brand still produced (apart from the Cabañas) and their history is full of change. At one time, the Por Larrañaga was also the most famous. That was at least partly due to the English storyteller and novelist, Rudyard Kipling, who wrote this oft-quoted line in one of his poems: *a woman is only a woman, but a good cigar is a smoke.*

Elsewhere in that book, the same comment has the word "smoke" replaced by the word "pleasure". This has led to boundless confusion on the part of those who have not read the book – not to mention those who do not smoke cigars – but it raises an interesting issue about the nature of cigar smoking.

For the cigar smoker, the concept of smoking is far richer than puffing on a wad of tobacco. That wad's power to soothe, to excite, to tantalise, to gratify, and to engender thoughts on life itself – to please, in short – is all encompassed in the single word "smoke". For many connoisseurs it is an experience to light up a cigar of an evening, and to review quietly the day's events. In this, a cigar demands attention. One has to occupy oneself with it in order to experience it. At the same time, the senses also come into play. A "smoke" is more than just the act of smoking a cigar.

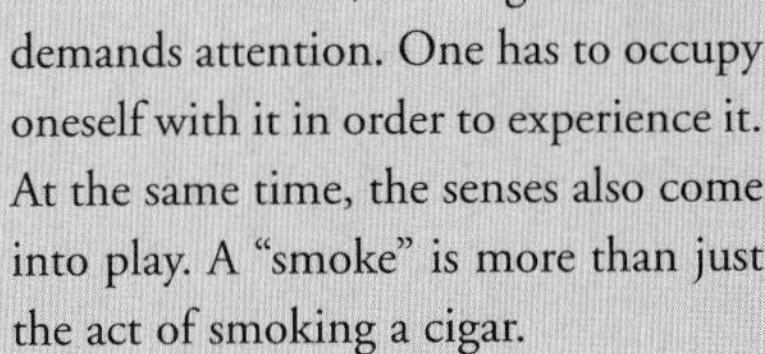

Quotes can sometime be misleading, especially when taken out of context. This is perhaps the case with the above quotation. Another interpretation is also possible: a cigar is only a cigar when insufficient attention is paid to it, and when one doesn't duly occupy oneself with it, just as a woman – or a man – remains a person like all the rest if one is not willing to get to know them better. This is why smoking should be an engaging experience.

Of the four formats of the Por Larrañaga still in production, it is the Montecarlo that promises the best smoking experience for *aficionados* of medium-strong Havanas, since this *vitola (de salida)* is the only one bearing the stamp *Totalmente a mano Tripa Larga*, denoting a long filler made completely by hand. The other three carry the label *Totalmente a mano Tripa Corta* (hand-made short filler) or *Mecanizado* (machine produced).

In addition, it may well prove a little difficult to obtain a Por Larrañaga as they are not produced in very large numbers, and are not available everywhere.

Private Stock

The Private Stock of the Oettinger Davidoff Group are among the premium cigars produced in the Dominican Republic that are worthy of recommendation.

Tobaccos from the Valle del Cibao are used for both the filler and the binder, and are largely responsible for their mild to medium-strong body. This harmonious bunch is ideally augmented by a medium-brown *Connecticut Shade* wrapper. All ten formats, ranging from the Cigarillo to the Churchill, are unselected and ungraded long filler, which means that the colour of the wrappers and ring gauge sometimes differ slightly from one another – an unmistakable feature of work done completely by hand.

As the task of colour sorting is saved and the consequent reduction in the otherwise normal costs is passed on to the customer, the interested purchaser obtains a first-class cigar at quite an economical price.

The standard formats have been augmented since 1999 by a series whose cigars constituted, then as now, a real innovation in the premium product area. This series bears the name Private Stock Medium Filler, whereby the operative word is the one following "Medium" (see also Medium Filler).

Like all Private Stocks, the cigars are produced in the Davidoff factory under the direction of the experienced Hendrik Kelner. Whereas top Dominican tobaccos are used for the filler, he trusts *Connecticut Shade* for the binder and *Connecticut Seed* for the wrapper, both grown in Ecuador. The result is a very mild, but rich in aroma, medium filler that appeals mainly to young smokers just beginning to smoke cigars.

Pro Cigar

This is the name of an association of Dominican cigar producers whose aim (essentially) is to publicise the country's products abroad. Hispaniola's most renowned cigar makers – such as Juan Clemente, Hendrik Kelner and Manuel Quesada, among others – belong to it as the representatives of their concerns.

General Cigar Dominicana, La Aurora, Tabacalera de García, and UST Industries International are four more businesses that belong to Pro Cigar.

Unfortunately, this association, that no doubt has much to report, works rather furtively by contrast with the more active Cubans with their Habanos S. A. Interested parties hardly ever see a joint public appearance of Pro Cigar.

Profesor Sila

The Profesor Sila is one of the Dominican brands whose cigars are among the mild to medium-strong representatives of their species.

At the same time, the Profesor Silas has only found a home on the island of Hispaniola since 1997. Their previous home was Las Palmas de Gran Canaria. They were produced there from1934 onwards, the year in which they first became available for purchase.

This was the leading brand of the Canary Island producers even long after the Second World War, and

Winston Churchill was only one of the prominent consumers who contributed to this brand's exclusivity. The exclusivity remained, but the sales figures fell back slowly, and when the tax incentives for the Canary Islands were withdrawn following Spain's accession to the European Community in 1986, the factory began fighting to survive.

The turnaround came in 1993 when Dr. Nader Bayzid, a Syrian businessman brought up in Lebanon, bought both the factory and the brand rights. He left the production of the Profesor Sila in the Canaries for a few years before transferring manufacturing to the capital of the Dominican Republic, Santo Domingo, in 1997.

For a long time, a veil of secrecy lay over the individual format's bunch composition, as previously had been the case on the Canaries. But the situation has changed in the meantime, as such customer information is an important selling criterion today.

Those responsible for Profesor Silas accepted the consequences of this several years ago.

Punch

A German is said to have created this popular brand in 1840 not, however, under the name that was later to denote one of the most famous Havanas. Nevertheless, if the Cabañas is discounted briefly, the Punch is, following the Por Larrañaga and the Ramón Allones, the oldest Havana brand still in production.

Because Cuban cigars were on the brink of a triumphal worldwide success, and especially because Britain was considered a lucrative market, a whole host of cigar makers focussed their attention on finding special features to make the Havana even more attractive to the British than before.

Those running the factory where the above cigars were being produced did the same. In the end, they were given unexpected help from the country they were eying most closely, from England itself. In 1841, a satirical weekly magazine was founded there under the name of *Punch,* which was also the name of its central character – a harlequin who was to be found, week on week, as a figure of fun with a profound sense of humour in the magazine's cartoons.

When the satirical magazine began to enjoy increasing popularity, the idea dawned on the cigar makers of using

its popularity by naming one of their anonymous brands after the magazine. And to make their product more palatable to the British, they soon decorated each box of Punch with a colourful lithograph in which the character smokes a cigar with great pleasure while a loyal canine companion lies at his feet. These two figures, beaming contentment, are framed by several scenes from the production of cigars.

This *cubierta* still decorates boxes of Punch, whose cigars, with their medium-strong aroma, still enjoy great popularity, not only in Great Britain but also world-wide. A further pointer to the changeful history of the Punch can be found on the cigars' rings. There, the name of Manuel López can be read.

The Punch were made under his direction by the Juan Valle y Cia company from the mid-1880s onwards, after the owner of the factory, his brother Fernando, had acquired the rights to the brand – which had already changed hands once before.

The worldwide presence of this brand is accompanied by a degree of confusion, for not all formats bear the same name in all countries. So when buying a Punch, one should rely on the knowledge of an experienced dealer in case irregularities emerge concerning the format.

Brand/Series	Origin	Filler	Binder	Wrapper	Strength
Padron					
• *1964 Aniversario (Lf)*	*Nicaragua*	*Puros: all tobaccos grown in Nicaragua*			*5*
• *Classic Line (Lf)*	*Nicaragua*	*Puros: all tobaccos grown in Nicaragua*			*3–5*
Palmar Arriba (Lf)	*Dominican Republic*	*Dom. Rep. (DoOlor + PiCu)*	*Dom. Rep.*	*CoSh*	*2–3*
Palmarito (Lf)	*Dominican Republic*	*Dom. Rep. (DoOlor + PiCu) + Ni*	*Dom. Rep.*	*CoSh*	*3–4*
Partagás (Lf + Sf)	*Cuba*	*Puros: all tobaccos grown in Cuba*			*4–6*

Brand/Series	Origin	Filler	Binder	Wrapper	Strength
Partageno y Cia					
• *Brasil (Sf)*	Germany	Dom. Rep. + Br + Cu + In (Ja)	Indonesia (Java)	Brazil (MaFi)	2
• *Sumatra (Sf)*	Germany	Dom. Rep. + Br + Cu + In (Ja)	Indonesia (Java)	Indonesia (Sumatra)	2
Particulares (Lf)	Dominican Republic	Dom. Rep. (PiCu) + Nicaragua (CuSe)	Dom. Rep. (PiCu)	Ecuador (CoSe)	3–4
Peñamil					
• *Clásico (Lf)*	Dominican Republic	Dom. Rep. + Brazil + Mexico	Indonesia (Java)	Connecticut	2–3
• *Oro (Lf)*	Canaries	Cuba + Brazil + Dom. Rep.	Mexico	CoSh	2–3
• *Plata (Lf)*	Canaries	Cuba + Brazil + Dom. Rep. + Mexico	Mexico	Indonesia	2–3
Perdomo the Cigar (Lf)	Nicaragua	Puros: all tobaccos grown in Nicaragua			3–4
Petrus					
• *Classic Line (Lf)*	Nicaragua	Puros: all tobaccos grown in Nicaragua (B: CoSeSuGr)			2–3
• *Special Selection (Lf)*	Honduras	Honduras	Honduras	Connecticut	2–3
Placeres (Lf)	Honduras	Puros: all tobaccos grown in Honduras from Cuban seed			2–4
Plasencia (Lf)	Nicaragua	Nicaragua	Nicaragua	Ecuador	3–4
Playboy by Don Diego (Lf)	Dominican Republic	Dom. Rep. (CuSe)	Dom. Rep.	CoSh	2–3
Pléiades (Lf)	Dominican Republic	Dom. Rep.	Dom. Rep.	CoSh	2–3
Por Larrañaga (Lf + Sf)	Cuba	Puros: all tobaccos grown in Cuba			2–4
Pride of Jamaica (Lf)	Jamaica	Jamaica + Dom. Rep. + Mexico	Mexico	Cameroon	4
Private Stock					
• *Long Filler*	Dominican Republic	Dom. Rep. (SaVi + DoOlor + PiCu)	CoSh	Ecuador (CoSe)	2–4
• *Medium filler*	Dominican Republic	Dom. Rep. (SaVi + DoOlorTs + PiCuTs)	CoSh	Connecticut	2
Profesor Sila (Lf)	Dominican Republic	Dom. Rep. + Cuba	Dom. Rep.	CoSh 2)	2–4
Punch (Lf + Sf)	Cuba	Puros: all tobaccos grown in Cuba			2–5
Puros Indios					
• *Classic Line (Lf)*	Honduras	Brazil + Dom. Rep. + Nicaragua	Ecuador	Ecuador	2–3
• *Máxima Reserva (Lf)*	Honduras	Nicaragua + Brazil + Dom. Rep.	Nicaragua	Ecuador	4–5
Puros Irene (Lf)	Mexico	Pure Honduran: all tobaccos grown in Honduras from Cuban seed			2–3

Quai d'Orsay

Quai d'Orsay

The name indicates that the Quai d'Orsay has at least something to do with France. This is quite true, as this still quite young Havana brand (it was developed in the 1970s) was originally only available from good tobacconists in France. In the meantime, these hand-made long filler Havanas – named after a famous Parisian road on the banks of the Seine – have become available outside *La Grande Nation,* although all four formats are not always available. That won't trouble the *aficionado* purist who, committed to the traditional Havana, prefers to smoke strong cigars – for the Quai d'Orsays are quite mild cigars. They are therefore ideal for the novice to the Havana world.

Quintero

The Quinteros present a body of medium strength and have over time become one of the most well known Havana brands. This at least partly because they are available worldwide and have thus gained firm supporters in many countries.

The Quinteros were not originally Havanas, and they were not produced in Havana but in Cienfuegos, a city on Cuba's southern coast, to the west of the Remedios area of cultivation.

There, in Cienfuegos, where he and his four brothers had previously scraped together a living, Agustín Quintero opened a small cigar factory in the mid-1920s. He must have made good cigars and run his business well, because in 1940 he was able to move to the capital and realise his dream of making first-class cigars.

With the aid of his eldest brother, Agustín set up the Quintero y Hno. cigar factory, and brought relatively mild cigars onto the market – cigars that contrasted with the generally strong-tasting products of the other manufacturers. They have remained committed to this line.

Thus, even though Quinteros are not still not classed as very strong cigars, they present that unmistakable character which differentiates Havanas from cigars of other origins. They are ideal cigars for the somewhat more advanced smoker who wants to come to grips with Cuban exports.

Brand/Series	Origin	Filler	Binder	Wrapper	Strength
Quai d'Orsay (Lf)	Cuba	Puros: all tobaccos grown in Cuba			2–3
Quevedo (Lf)	Ecuador	Puros: all tobaccos grown in Ecuador (F: SuSe + CuSe; B + W: SuSe)			3–4
Quintero (Sf)	Cuba	Puros: all tobaccos grown in Cuba			3–4
Quisquea					
• Bundle (Mf)	Dominican Republic	Dom. Rep. + Nicaragua (Fr + Ts)	Indonesia	CoSh	3
• Forte Bundle (Mf)	Dominican Republic	Dom. Rep. (PiCu Fr + Ts)	Dom. Rep. (DoOlor)	Ecuador (CoSe)	4–5
Quorum Toro (Lf)	Nicaragua	Puros: all tobaccos grown in Nicaragua			2–3

Ramón Allones

After the Por Larrañaga – and setting aside the Cabañas – the Ramón Allones is the oldest Havana brand still produced today. This takes place in the Partagás factory where it has been produced since the mid-1820s when the famous Cifuente cigar-making family took over the factory, and acquired the rights to the Ramón Allones at the same time. This was (and still is) the home of the Bolívar and Partagás brands, which provide excellent company for the Ramón Allones, since the Allones and the other two brands give off a strong aroma thanks to a quite high proportion of *ligero*.

RAMON ALLONES

That was already true in 1837 when Ramón Allones, a native of Galicia, created the brand he named after himself.

Allones was not only a good cigar maker; he also knew something about marketing, although the term was unknown at the time. Thus, he became the first producer to decorate his cigar boxes with colourful lithographic labels adorned with gold embossing. He also introduced the 8-9-8 packaging, pioneering the way for the round (see also the entry for 8-9-8).

Romeo y Julieta

This brand actually first began life in 1903 although it was born in 1850, more than half a century previously. For in that turn-of-the-century year Fernández Rodríguez – also called Pepín, and usually known by that name – acquired the rights to the Romeo y Julieta from the Álvarez y García company, which had owned the brand rights since 1875, and had also produced the cigars (albeit exclusively for the home market).

All that changed at a stroke when Pepín took the reins of Romeos y Julieta into his hands. This erstwhile manager of the Cabañas cigar factory – one of the largest in Cuba at the time – saw the takeover of that factory by American Sumatra Tobacco of the United States as a reason to leave and tread the business stage himself, because at exactly that moment he was given the opportunity to buy the Álvarez y García factory, including the rights to the Romeo y Julieta (the only cigars that factory manufactured).

What happened after that had never been seen before in the cigar world. As an expert, the energetic Pepín was convinced of the quality of the Romeos y Julieta, and he also realised the business possibilities presented by the world's most famous pair of lovers. There then followed a veritable firework display of marketing, including direct advertising, events, product advertising and promotion tours – in short, everything would belong in the repertoire of any respectable advertising and marketing agency 90 years

later on. After only a few years, the Romeos y Julieta were not only renowned beyond the shores of the island state, but were known in almost every corner of the world, gaining popularity comparable with that of the Shakespearian lovers themselves.

This was mainly due, it must be said, to Pepín's untiring commitment. He travelled the world constantly, beating the drum for his Romeos y Julieta. He named one of his racehorses Julieta, and she went on to race against the world's greatest mounts on the racecourses of Europe. He tried to buy the Casa Giulietta (Juliet's House), with its famous balcony in the Via Cappello 23 of Verona's old town (and the location for Shakespeare's play) from that north Italian city. He was turned down, but licensed to present one of his cigars to each and every visitor to this stone memorial of world literature (a practice which continued up until the end of the 1930s). He delivered Romeos y Julieta to the aristocracy, recipients of the royal lists, ministers and money-makers, playboys and prime ministers, kings and emperors – in short, both the pinnacles of society and those who considered themselves such – and each cigar bore a paper ring embellished with an illustration of the respective recipient. The orders for printing the *anillos* went into the thousands and more than a few printers in Havana who specialised in producing colourful lithographs were forced to work extra shifts.

Incidentally, one of these recipients was Winston Churchill – and, according to tradition, because the politician ordered cigars of a certain large format, this same format received the name "Churchill". The fact that there is no Cuban format bearing this name does not detract from this story.

It is also uncertain that Shakespeare actually wrote the play about the lovers from Verona. What is important is that this piece exists at all, for the world's literature would be poorer without it – and it is equally important for the *aficionado* to know about the Churchill format.

Extra shifts were also the order of the day for the managers and employees of the Romeo y Julieta factory, which was renamed after the brand name of the products it manufactured. When, owing to the immense demand for the best known Havanas of the time, the number of employees constantly increased and neared the 1500 mark, the workforce moved to a new factory.

There, the Romeos y Julieta continue to be produced – Havanas, that are still among the best known representatives of their species.

Brand/Series	Origin	Filler	Binder	Wrapper	Strength
Ramón Allones (Lf + Sf)	Cuba	Puros: all tobaccos grown in Cuba			4–5
Rattray's (Lf)	Nicaragua	Nicaragua	Nicaragua (CuSe)	Ecuador (CoSe)	1–2
R.C. Bundles (Lf)	Nicaragua	Nicaragua + Honduras	Nicaragua	Ecuador (SuSe)	2–3
Regalia Fina					
• Long filler	Brazil	Puros: all tobaccos grown in Brazil (W: MaFi)			2–4
• Short filler	Germany	Brazil + Cuba	Brazil	Brazil (MaFi)	2–4
Remedios (Lf)	Nicaragua	Nicaragua (CuSe) + Dom. Rep. (CuSe)	Nicaragua (CuSe)	CoSh	3–4
Rey de Reyes (Lf)	Dominican Republic	Dom. Rep. (CuSe)	Dom. Rep. (DoOlor)	Connecticut	4–5
Rocky Patel Vintage 1990 (Lf)	Honduras	Puros: all tobaccos grown in Honduras (W: Broadleaf)			3–5
Romeo y Julieta (Lf)	Cuba	Puros: all tobaccos grown in Cuba			1–6
Royal Barbados (Lf)	Barbados	Cuba	Cameroon	Ecuador	3–5
Royal Jamaica (Lf)	Jamaica	Jamaica + Dom. Rep.	Indonesia (Java)	Cameroon	2–3

Saint Luis Rey

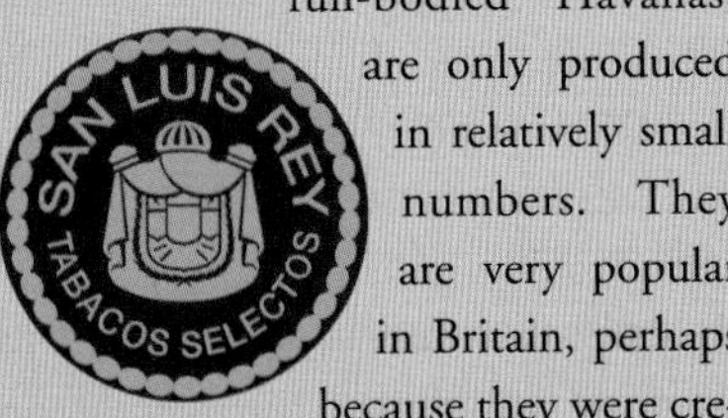

The Saints Luis Rey, among the best full-bodied Havanas, are only produced in relatively small numbers. They are very popular in Britain, perhaps because they were created in Cuba at the end of the 1930s to meet the wishes of two British importers, or perhaps because many *aficionados* of these islands love the strong flavour of Havanas produced in the traditional style. Such adherents should therefore keep an eye open for the Saints Luis Rey.

Samaná

These are among the mildest cigars of their Dominican Republic homeland. Whether the brand was named after the Samaná peninsular or the province of the same name, or the province's capital which also shares this name, is not known.

But neither is it of importance, for regardless of the reason behind the brand's name, the Samanás, first produced in 1997, remain not only very mild, but also of excellent workmanship – thus promising an umitigatedly pleasurable smoke both for the novice and for the rather more experienced smoker who readily envelopes himself in a morning blue haze. As far as the Samaná peninsular is concerned, from December to March it is possible to observe humpback whales in the bay of Samaná which they frequent for mating purposes.

Sancho Panza

Until recently, the Sancho Panza could mainly be bought in Spain, perhaps because the name refers to one of the figures of one of the world's great literary works, written by the Spanish bard Miguel de Cervantes Saavedra. The brand is named after the clever squire and faithful companion of Don Quixote, that tragic knight who courageously faced all possible and impossible adventures on his trusty steed Rocinante, not even shying from battling windmills. Today, these thoroughly medium-strong Havanas are also available in other European countries.

San Cristóbal de La Habana

Officially launched in 1999, this brand is also a reference to the Cuban capital of the same name. Although the city is usually called La Habana, the brand is often known by the short form, Cristóbals (or Cristóbales).

At first, many smokers had trouble warming to the San Cristóbal although, even at the launch, a certain potential was obvious. That potential has been well realised in the meantime, and anyone who chooses one of the four Cristóbal formats has by no means made a bad choice.

The *vitolas de salida* are derived from four defensive forts – the 16th century El Morro stands at the entrance to the bay of Santiago de Cuba, the former Cuban capital, while the three others, built between the 16th and 18th centuries, flank the entrance to the harbour of the present capital.

Santa Clara 1830

There are two unusual points about this cigar brand, which – together with the Te-Amo – is the best known and most popular from Mexico. This is not an allusion to the *puro* annotation of all its formats, since Mexico is well-known as the region in which the most cigars are made from home-grown tobaccos.

What is unusual are two *vitolas*. The first is the Bolero, for which two wrappers leaves are used, one in *Claro* and one in *Maduro* – giving the bunch the appearance of being wrapped alternately with both leaves. The other, The Magnum, presents the longest cigar available for purchase in the world, with its stately length of 19 inches or 482.6 millimetres and a ring gauge of 60 (23.8 mm). It only remains to mention that all the long filler are hand rolled and release lightly tangy aromas. This is also the case with the Magnum whose *torcedores* really must have big hands.

Santa Damiana

Although the Santa Damiana was only created in 1992, it has already become a favourite of those *aficionados* who prefer a relatively mild body without forgoing a certain breadth of aromas.

The growing popularity of the Damianas, which are made in La Romana to the west of the capital of Santo Domingo, is at least partly due to the excellent workmanship they display – a sign of the high quality requirements to which the *torcedores* there subject their work. The brand name appears to be a commitment for them – for it refers to a formerly famous Cuban Vega, and a no less formerly famous Havana.

S. T. Dupont

It took more than a century for a cigar brand bearing the name of S. T. Dupont to be presented to the public. Simon Tissot Dupont was hardly thinking about cigars when he set up a freight business. But this was only a

prelude, for, when the building hous-
ing the young business fell victim to a
fire, he bought a leather goods manufacturer with 30 employees – thereby
laying the cornerstone for a luxury
article business that today enjoys a
worldwide reputation.

Although Dupont focussed on producing first-class lighters after the Second
World War, writing utensils were
added at the beginning of the 1970s,
then leather goods, to be followed by
timepieces in the 1980s, and finally
cigar cutters and cases, ashtrays and
humidors.

Those responsible considered that the
next logical step for the business – producing luxury articles that one doesn't

necessarily need to live one's life, but nevertheless make life more beautiful – was to bring a cigar brand onto the market bearing their famous label. Since cigars have little to do with either metal or Chinese lacquer or even leather, experts were sought who understood something about cigar making. These were found on the Canary Islands, resulting in the appearance in 1998 of a good quality cigar bearing the name S. T. Dupont.

The quality is still more than satisfactory, the cigars, however, now come from the Dominican Republic. The hand-made long filler with a body that is now a little lighter commend themselves for those who value a balanced mixture with fine aromas.

Brand/Series	Origin	Filler	Binder	Wrapper	Strength
Saint Luis Rey (Lf)	Cuba	Puros: all tobaccos grown in Cuba			4–5
Samaná (Lf)	Dominican Republic	Dom. Rep. (DoOlor + PiCu)	Dom. Rep.	CoSh	1–2
Sancho Panza (Lf)	Cuba	Puros: all tobaccos grown in Cuba			3–4
San Cristóbal de La Habana (Lf)	Cuba	Puros: all tobaccos grown in Cuba			2–3
San Fernando (Lf)	Honduras	Honduras	Honduras	Connecticut	2–3
San Gonzalo (Sf)	Switzerland	Brazil (Ba) + Cuba + Dom. Rep.	Indonesia (Java)	Brazil (Ba)	4
San Martín (Lf)	Honduras	Honduras (CoSe)	Indonesia	Honduras (NiSe)	3–4
Santa Clara 1830	Mexico	Puros: all tobaccos grown in the Mexican San Andrés valley			2–3
Santa Damiana (Lf)	Dominican Republic	Dom. Rep. + Mexico	Mexico	CoSh	2–3
Savinelli					
• Classic Line (Lf)	Dominican Republic	Dom. Rep.	Dom. Rep.	CoSh	2–3
• Oro (Lf)	Dominican Republic	Dom. Rep. (CuSe)	Dom. Rep.	Indonesia	3
Sillem's (Lf)	Dominican Republic	Dom. Rep. (PiCu)	Dom. Rep.	Ecuador (CoSe)	2–3
Star Clippers (Sf)	Dominican Republic	Dom. Rep. + Cuba	Dom. Rep.	Indonesia	1–2
S. T. Dupont (Lf)	Dominican Republic	Dom. Rep. (PiCu + DoOlor + Ha2000)	Cameroon	Nicaragua (Ha2000)	2–4

Tabacalera

These are premium cigars are from the Philippines. Many may not have guessed that the cigars have their origin in that country. But these origins are to be welcomed, for the Tabacaleros offer cigars which are difficult to compare with other premium cigars, from the Caribbean for instance, thanks to their idiosyncratic style.

Quite mild, and yet finely aromatic cigars are hand made in a factory of the Compania General Tabacos de Filipinas under the direction of a Cuban expert in the art of cigar production, from a bunch comprising of home-grown tobaccos from the Isabela region, as well as a Java-Besuki wrapper. The result need hardly shy from public gaze. It promises an interestingly pleasing smoke at a relatively economic price.

Te-Amo

The formats of both the Te-Amo and the Santa Clara brands – the best-known and most popular Mexican cigar brands, whose origins date back to 1830 – are all *puros* (how could they be anything else?!). Whether or not one actually loves these cigars as their name demands, depends on the strength one prefers.

The Te-Amos are all mild to medium-strong, and the strength is affected by the various wrapper leaves, for many formats are offered in *Colorado Claro* as well as in *Colorado Maduro* and *Maduro*. Since these Mexican cigars can only be compared with other (non-)Caribbeans, the smoker simply has to find out for himself whether or not they are to his taste.

The Griffin's

It was the owner of a club in Geneva who created this brand more than 20 years ago. The name of the club – Griffin's. The name of its owner and operator – Bernard Grobet. The name of the production plant that produced the first Griffin's is also certain – Tabadom in the Dominican Republic (which has now become a daughter-house the Oettinger Davidoff Group). They are still produced there today, under the direction of Hendrik Kelner, who can, as always, rely on the specialist support of his master blender, Eladio Díaz. As these names are synonymous with quality, the *aficionado* can indeed do little wrong when deciding to take a closer look at these excellently made cigars. Those interested can currently choose from three series – the Classic Line, the Maduro and finally, the most recent creation, the Griffin's Fuerte – but irrespective of whichever cigar the *aficionado* chooses from this

Hendrik Kelner

wide range, all justifiably carry the appellation premium.

Toscano

The *connoisseur* first cuts this *sigaro* in two halves before fully enjoying its pleasures. That may sound unusual, but the Toscani are unusual in almost every respect. First there is the tobacco, or more precisely the tobacco seed. It comes from abroad – not from the Caribbean, but from the United States, which is where the next peculiarity arises. It is not the renowned Connecticut seed (for the bunch is made exclusively from tobaccos grown in Italy – in Tuscany to be precise – hence the name) but Kentucky seed. The wrapper too is of Kentucky leaves – although these are directly imported from that American state.

Both the filler tobaccos and the wrapper leaves undergo an intensive fermentation process, followed by a storage and drying period of up to nine months. This results in quite strong cigars that are hard and dry, and possess an incomparable tangy flavour. Furthermore, the Toscani are long filler made 100 percent from tobacco – by machine. An exception is the Toscano Originale, which is made completely by hand.

In contrast, no exception is made in the format – all Toscani are the same. With a length of about 155 millimetres, both the burning end and the head have a diameter of about 10 millimetres which widens to roughly 15 millimetres in the middle, forming a belly which is recognisable as such immediately. The cigar ring slides loosely over the cigar – another distinction from other brands – to ease removal, which should certainly be done, since the *connoisseur* must first cut the cigar in half before devoting himself to its pleasures.

This is only unnecessary with the Toscanellis, which have already been halved. There is quite a demand in Europe for this speciality which – unfortunately – is not available in all stores. But there always remains the mail order option.

Trinidad

On 10th May, 1999, the Trinidad was at last officially launched in Europe; more than a year after its presentation had taken place in Cuba's capital in February 1998. Roughly 500 *aficiona-*

dos were present to try out the legendary Havana that had until recently been reserved for state guests of the *Máximo Líder.*

The now living – or more accurately smoking – legend lived up to all that many had expected of it. Produced in the El Laguito factory, the home of the Cohibas, this very good Havana presented itself in only one format, the Fundadores. Whether the three further *vitolas* brought onto the market in 2004 will live up to the reputation of the first, remains to be seen, for considerable flavour fluctuations within each individual format could be remarked at the beginning. "Wait and see" is the order of the day since they certainly have the potential to reach the same level as the Fundadores.

Troya

The cigars of this 1932-created Havana brand are seldom to be found. The Troyas are available in only two formats, both of which are made by machine. Anyone who is not put off by this, and who loves a relatively mild-bodied Havana, should also not be put off giving them a try.

Brand/Series	Origin	Filler	Binder	Wrapper	Strength
Tabacalera (Lf)	*Philippines*	*Philippines*	*Philippines*	*Indonesia (JaBe)*	*2–3*
Te-Amo					
• *Clásico (Lf)*	*Mexico*	*Puros: all tobaccos grown in the Mexican San Andrés valley*			*2–4*
• *Maduro (Lf)*	*Mexico*	*Puros: all tobaccos grown in the Mexican San Andrés valley*			*2–3*
Temple Hall *(Lf)*	*Dominican Republic*	*Jamaica + Dom. Rep. + Mexico*	*Mexico*	*CoSh*	*1–2*
Tesoros de Copán *(Lf)*	*Honduras*	*Honduras*	*Honduras*	*Connecticut*	*2–3*
The Cigar *(Lf)*	*Nicaragua*	*Puros: all tobaccos grown in Nicaragua from Cuban seed*			*3–4*
The Griffin's					
• *Classic Line (Lf)*	*Dominican Republic*	*Dom. Rep. (SaVi + DoOlor)*	*Dom. Rep. (SaVi)*	*Ecuador (CoSe)*	*2–3*
• *Fuerte (Lf)*	*Dominican Republic*	*Dom. Rep. (SaVi + DoOlor)*	*Dom. Rep. (SaVi)*	*CoBr*	*4–5*
• *Maduro (Lf)*	*Dominican Republic*	*Dom. Rep. (SaVi + DoOlor) + CoBr*	*Dom. Rep. (SaVi)*	*CoBr*	*3*
Thomas Hinds *(Lf)*	*Honduras*	*Honduras*	*Honduras*	*Ecuador*	*3–4*
Tobajara					
• *Importados (Sf)*	*Brazil*	*Puros: all tobaccos grown in Brazil*			*2*
• *Panetela Brasil (Sf)*	*Germany*	*Cuba + Brazil (50:50)*	*Indonesia (JaBe)*	*Mexico (Ma)*	*3*
• *Panetela Sumatra (Sf)*	*Germany*	*Cuba + Brazil (50:50)*	*Indonesia (JaBe)*	*Indonesia (Sumatra)*	*3*
• *Premium No. 1 (Sf)*	*Brazil*	*Puros: all tobaccos grown in Brazil*			*2*
• *Presidente Brasil (Sf)*	*Switzerland*	*Cuba + Brazil (50:50)*	*Indonesia (JaBe)*	*Brazil*	*3*
• *Presidente Sumatra (Sf)*	*Switzerland*	*Cuba + Brazil (50:50)*	*Indonesia (JaBe)*	*Indonesia (Sumatra)*	*3*
Toscano *(Lf)*	*Italy*	*wet fermented US-Kentucky-tobaccos (W) + grown in Italy (no binder)*			*5–6*
Trinidad *(Lf)*	*Cuba*	*Puros: all tobaccos grown in Cuba*			*3–4*
Troya (Sf)	*Cuba*	*Puros: all tobaccos grown in Cuba*			*2–3*

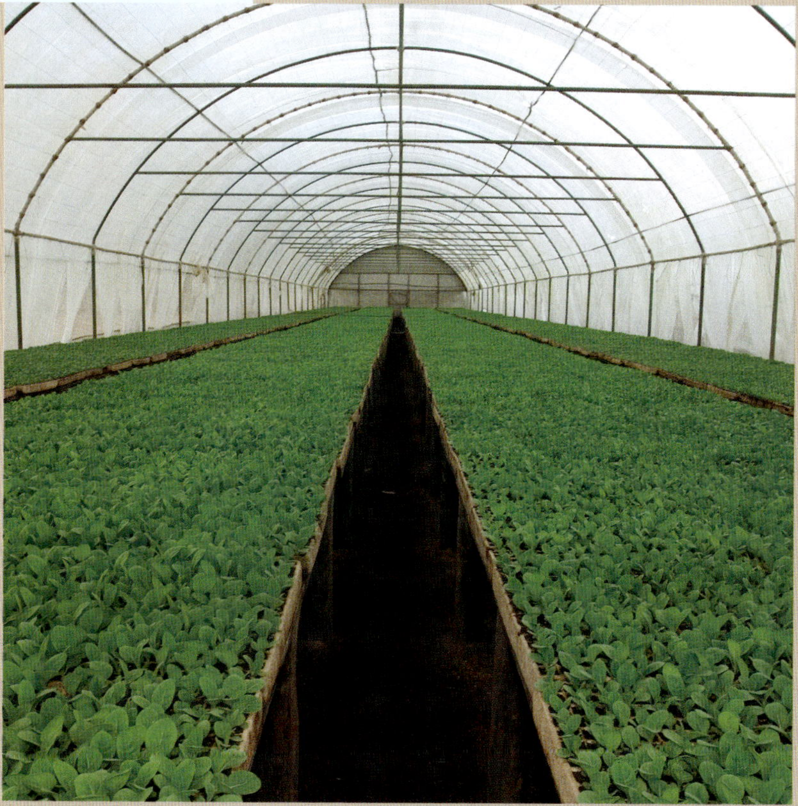

Vegas Robaina

Officially presented in June of the Cohiba anniversary year of 1977, it was at first obtainable in France and Spain but is now available in many other countries. The Vegas Robaina is one of the more recent creations of Cuban cigar makers.

The name refers to one of the last privately-owned *vegas* still in existence in Cuba. The plantation, which provides one of the best wrapper leaves harvested in the Vuelta Abajo, can boast a tradition of cultivating tobacco stretching back more than 150 years, as borne witness to by the date 1845 to be seen on the cigar ring around every Vegas Robaina.

The *vitola de salida* of the Prominente format is a reference to this tobacco-growing family with a long tradition. It carries the name of the current patriarch – Don Alejandro – who, at over 85, is still to be found daily in the tobacco fields of his *vega*.

Alejandro Robaina

Incidentally, the numbers added to the individual format designations give information about the ring gauge of the respective cigar.

The Vegas Robaina cigars are Havanas that are bound in the traditional style and characterised mainly by a powerful body. However, the individual formats develop a rich and often creamy flavour, excelling with their fine overall balance.

Vegueros

The Vegueros created in 1996 were actually intended to serve the home market as machine-produced long filler. But, since the cigar world is greedy for almost anything produced in Cuban *fabricas* where *tabacaleros* work, the people running Habanos S. A. decided to give in to the increasingly strong demands of the importers and market the Vegueros worldwide.

Available in European countries for quite some time now, the Vegueros have proved to be really well-made long filler that satisfy with a powerful strength reminiscent of the traditional Havana style – and they are not made by machine, as originally intended, but bear the *Totalmente a mano – Tripa Larga* quality seal.

Villiger

One of today's great names in the European cigar world, Villiger Söhne A. G. Cigarrenfabriken, has its headquarters in the Wynental, in the north of the Swiss canton of Lucerne, where the company was also founded more than 100 years ago. The company's importance is underlined by a few facts and figures. Every year, approximately 300 million cigars and cigarillos leave the gates of the works in Pfeffikon, in the Baden town of Waldshut-Tiengen, in Westphalian Bünde, as well as in the Irish town of Ballaghaderreen in the county of Roscommon, and in Indonesian Ngoro in the east of the tobacco island of Java.

They can then be found on sale in numerous countries around the world. To this must be added Villiger Polska, a joint venture with Polish producer of tobacco products, Polski Tyton in Krakow.

Jean Villiger could not have even imagined these developments when he set up his business in 1888. Setting up a cigar factory during that period of industrialisation was no extraordinary act. The general economic upsurge that gripped northern Europe at the time led to factories springing up like mushrooms. Almost every region was characterised by one industry or another. It was the cigar industry in the north of the canton of Lucerne.

The situation was so simple then – and so very difficult later. The period during and after the First World War, and towards the end of the 1920s, was anything but rosy for business.

Difficult times for the still young Villiger business began significantly earlier with the death of Jean Villiger in 1902. The business would have gone the way of many others that were forced to close their gates for ever, had not his young widow, Louise, bravely taken the reins of the company and made some far-seeing decisions.

It was not only farsighted, but also extremely courageous of Louise Villiger to set up in 1910 a subsidiary enterprise in Waldshut-Tiengen in Baden as an explicit signal for the future.

The future envisaged back then has become a well-established present. The business, currently managed in the fourth generation by Heinrich Villiger, owes its position at least in part to trend-setting product innovation.

For instance, the Villiger-Kiel, a cigar with a goose quill mouthpiece, was introduced at the turn of this century. Then the Rio 6 (the *Havana* for the ordinary man) appeared on the market, a cigar that is still the most frequently smoked cigar in Switzerland.

Apropos Havanas: it was Heinrich Villiger, who set up the world's first joint venture with Cuban partners for the import and marketing of Havanas in 1989. Today, 5th Avenue Products imports and markets around six million Havanas to Europe.

Brand/Series	Origin	Filler	Binder	Wrapper	Strength
5 Vegas (Lf)	Nicaragua	Nicaragua + Dom. Rep.	Nicaragua	Indonesia	5
Val Condega (Lf)	Nicaragua	Puros: all tobaccos grown in Honduras from Cuban seed			2–4
Vargas (Lf)	Canaries	Canaries	Canaries	CoSb	2–4
Vasco da Gama					
• Fina Corona Brasil (Sf)	Germany	Cuba + Dom. Rep.	Indonesia (JaBe)	Brazil	2
• Fina Corona Capa de Cuba (Sf)	Germany	Cuba + Dom. Rep.	Indonesia (JaBe)	Cuba	2
• Fina Corona Sumatra (Sf)	Germany	Cuba + Dom. Rep.	Indonesia (JaBe)	Indonesia (SuSa)	2
Vega Dominicana (Lf)	Dominican Republic	Dom. Rep. (PiCu)	Dom. Rep. (DoOlor)	Ecuador (CoSe)	2–3
Vegafina (Lf)	Dominican Republic	Dom. Rep. (DoOlor + PiCu)	Ecuador	Ecuador (CoSe)	2–3
Vegas Robaina (Lf)	Cuba	Puros: all tobaccos grown in Cuba			4–5
Vegueros (Lf)	Cuba	Puros: all tobaccos grown in Cuba			4–5
Villa Dominicana (Lf)	Dominican Republic	Dom. Rep. (PiCu)	Indonesia	Ecuador (CoSe)	3–4
Villiger					
• Long (Sf)	Germany	Cuba	Ecuador	Cuba	4
• Noblesse (Sf)	Switzerland	Cuba	Indonesia (Vola)	Cuba	4
• Perfecto (Sf)	Switzerland	Cuba	Indonesia (JaBe)	Cuba	4
• Premium A (Sf)	Ireland	various origins	Indonesia (JaBe)	Indonesia (Sumatra)	3
• President (Sf)	Switzerland	various origins	Indonesia (JaBe)	Cuba	3
• Tubos (Sf)	Germany	various origins	Indonesia (JaBe)	Indonesia (Sumatra)	3

Woermann Cigars

The Woermann Cigars family concern has been continuously on the up since 1963. In that year Heinz-Dieter Woermann joined the H. Woermann business and realised that it was a difficult task to make a profit in Germany from small numbers of hand-made cigars.

He acquired machines with which he considerably raised the numbers of cigars produced. Whereas a mere 10,000 cigars had been produced in the early 1960s, by the early 1990s around 300,000 left the factory in the East Westphalian town of Bünde. However, the H in the company's name does not stand for Heinz-Dieter, but for Heinrich. For it was Heinrich Woermann who set up the business in this "cigar town" in 1890, a time when cigar production in Germany was enjoying rates of growth in double digits.

Such rates are of course no longer common, although this traditional business, managed by Peter Woermann since April 1997 (and later by Thomas Strickrock), has grown continually in the past few years, both in economic terms and in the numbers of cigars produced annually: in 1998 almost nine million cigars came out of the factory in Rödinghausen-Ostkilver.

The move to this location near Bünde was necessary because the headquarters had become simply too small. The new works is designed to meet all the requirements of a modern cigar factory. The raw tobacco storage, bunch production and wrapper rolling section and despatch are arranged to ensure a compact line of production.

The top product of this more than 100-year-old company is the La Grandeza, a panatela which tapers towards the burning end. These cigars, like all the products of Woermann Cigars (as this traditional concern now calls itself) are made 100 percent from tobacco.

This is also true of the imported brands, in which the business has tended to focus on those produced in the Canary Islands.

Wuhrmann Cigars

At the close of the 19th century, there were the five factories producing cigars in the small Swiss town of Rheinfelden on the banks of the Upper Rhine in the canton of Aargau. This was a considerable number when one considers the town had a population of only 10,000. Today, only one remains – Wuhrmann Cigars AG, the last Swiss family-owned cigar factory.

The business, now managed by the fifth generation, places great emphasis on tradition, for only by filling the niches left by the large concerns is its future survival assured. For example, the Habana is available in a form that was once common but is now a rarity in Switzerland – a Bündli, a pack of ten cheroots wrapped in tissue paper.

The Krumme Hunde – Havana, a speciality reminiscent of times long gone, can also be found, among others, in the Rheinfeldener range. Both products are made 100 percent from tobacco (as are all the other products) – in itself a homage to the times before machine rolls of band tobacco.

Dr. Ernst Schneider

Zino

When Zino Davidoff and Dr. Ernst Schneider in the mid–1970s set to work on a solution to gaining access to the United States market, they turned their attention to Honduras (see also Davidoff). This country could point to a long tradition of cigar making. In addition, the soil and climate of this Central American country corresponded most closely to the conditions prevalent in the Vuelta Abajo region.

Perhaps this was not quite true, for there was also Nicaragua – seen by many as the "cigar country" of the future – but the political situation in that land was not conducive to establishing anything permanent. That assessment has been borne out.

In 1977, when the Zino brand (a long filler made in Honduras with home-grown tobaccos for the bunch and a *Connecticut Shade* wrapper in *Colorado Claro*) came onto the market it was met at first by an outcry from Havana enthusiasts who had previously considered Davidoff cigars synonymous with cigars from Cuba. They saw the Zinos as a sacrilege against the Davidoff tradition.

However, Zino Davidoff and Dr. Ernst Schneider had done everything right – the Honduran Zinos with their mild body and full aromas were soon in great demand from American *aficionados*. Today, only one series is still produced in Honduras. When the Zino Mouton Cadet series, created by Davidoff for the Baroness Philippine de Rothschild, was first made available in 1983, it was also crowned with success. The Mouton Cadets with their medium-strong body are still in great demand from numerous *aficionados,* for they are premium cigars of the highest quality.

Since the end of 2003 the *aficionado* has been able to add further Zinos to his humidor in the form of a Zino Platinum Crown or a Zino Platinum Scepter – two full-bodied cigar series which release a fine aromatic flavour as a result of their harmonious balance. New products need a new home. Or so thought those in charge of Davidoff, when they decided to develop these series together with Hendrik Kelner and his master blender, Eladio Díaz.

In addition to the proven tobaccos from Ecuador (wrapper) and Connecticut (binder), as well as the equally proven *San Vicente* und *Piloto Cubano* (filler) tobaccos, another tobacco is also used that until now has been effectively insignificant in cigar manufacturing – tobacco from Peru (which contributes considerably to the harmony of the bunch). Other leading manufacturers have also found Peruvian tobaccos to their taste thanks to

Davidoff's pioneering role, which yet again displayed the concern's innovative skill.

For a long time, Zino advertising used a slogan that differed from the Latin original of the Roman Empire's heyday in only one letter: *...in Zino veritas.*

There is, to all intents and purposes, nothing left to add. However, as this is the last entry in this book, something general should be said about cigars. As cultivation of both wine and tobacco are very similar in many respects, it could well be said that truth also lies in cigars – if only one understands how to gain pleasure from them and is willing to take the time to come to grips with them.

Brand/Series	Origin	Filler	Binder	Wrapper	Strength
Wallstreet					
• Broker (Lf)	Canaries	Nicaragua (ViSe)	Nicaragua	Connecticut	3
• Classic Coronas (Sf)	Austria	Cuba + Indonesia (Java) + Brazil	No details	Indonesia (Sumatra)	2
• Double Coronas (Lf)	Canaries	Dom. Rep. + Brazil (MaFi)	Dom. Rep.	CoSh	2
• Especiales (Lf)	Canaries	Nicaragua	Nicaragua	Connecticut	3
• Panetelas (Sf)	Austria	Cuba + Indonesia (Java) + Brazil	No details	Indonesia (Sumatra)	2
• Pyramides (Lf)	Canaries	Dom. Rep. + Brazil (MaFi)	Dom. Rep.	CoSh	2
• Robustos (Lf)	Canaries	Dom. Rep. + Brazil (MaFi)	Dom. Rep.	CoSh	2
Zino					
• Mouton Cadet (Lf)	Honduras	Honduras	Honduras	Ecuador (CoCuSe)	3–4
• Platinum Crown Serie (Lf)	Dominican Republic	Dom. Rep. (SaVi + PiCu) + Peru	CoSh	Ecuador (CoSe)	5
• Platinum Scepter Serie (Lf)	Dominican Republic	Dom. Rep. (SaVi + PiCu) + Peru	CoSh	Ecuador (CoSe)	4–5